NEW ASPECTS OF HISTORY AND CULTURE OF SOUTH KOSALA

NEW ASPECTS OF HISTORY AND CULTURE OF SOUTH KOSALA

Edited by
P.K. Nayak

POST GRADUATE DEPARTMENT OF HISTORY
SAMBALPUR UNIVERSITY
Sambalpur

ARYAN BOOKS INTERNATIONAL
New Delhi

NEW ASPECTS OF HISTORY AND CULTURE OF SOUTH KOSALA

ISBN: 978-81-7305-350-4

This monograph has been published with the financial assistance of UGC under Departmental Research Support made available to the PG Department of History, Sambalpur University.

First Published in **2010** by:
ARYAN BOOKS INTERNATIONAL
Pooja Apartments, 4B, Ansari Road, New Delhi-110 002 (India)
Tel.: 23287589, 23255799; Fax: 91-11-23270385;
E-mail: aryanbooks@vsnl.com, aryanbooks@gmail.com

Computer Typeset and Printed in India at
ABI Prints & Publishing Co., New Delhi.

Preface

It was a long cherished dream of the Department to hold a seminar on 'South Kosala', of which Western Orissa was a major constituent territory. Though there was continued and sustained effort, it could not be materialized due to unavoidable circumstances. In the long run our ceaseless endeavour resulted in successful organization of a national seminar on 'History and Culture of South Kosala' in 2003. We are thankful to the authorities of P.G. Council and University Office who rendered their help wherever and whenever required.

The seminar was conducted on 3rd and 4th of November 2003. Besides the Orissan delegates, distinguished scholars from outside the State having significant contribution to the history and culture of South Kosala had also joined the conference and presented papers on various aspects. To make the conference a memorable one, we planned to publish the papers in the shape of a book entitled *New Aspects of History and Culture of South Kosala* utilizing the funds available in the Department through DRS Programme.

The papers are arranged into four groups according to their contents. Also, we have incorporated some articles having relevance to the themes of celebrated historians of Orissa like Profs. N.K. Sahu, K.N. Mohapatra, S.C. Behera and S.C. De for the benefit of scholars of Orissan history. Major change is not noticed in the present-day Orissan history of what have been told in those articles. The journal in which these articles were published is now out of print and there is little chance of its reprint. Hence, as per the decision of the Editorial Board, these articles have been placed in the book. Other papers on the political history of Orissa throw new light on the placement of Satrubhanja in the genealogy of Bhanja dynasty as a son of Ranabhanja, role of a small village Panimora of Bargarh district in the Quit India Movement, Maratha rule in Western Orissa and war strategy of Surendra Sai with fresh interpretation.

South Kosala is famous for its art and culture. Prof. S.C. Panda in his paper highlighted the sculptural art of Western Orissa from the early times to the medieval period and has analysed them critically. The stellate plan of the temples is typical of South Kosala. The temple of Budhikomna has been dealt with reference to other such temples. The representation of *Saptamatrikas* in South Kosalan art speaks of the popularity and wide distribution of the cult in Western Orissa.

The book is enriched very much by the paper in the field of epigraphy and numismatics. Sadananda Agrawal has discussed thoroughly the newly-found *Ranipur-Jharial Plates, Terasingha Plates* of Bhanudeva with seal of Dhakkarisvara and the seal with the legend *Saivaramesvarasya*. The last one is unique – so far as Western Orissa is concerned – because it is the only seal which belongs to a *Shaiva* monastery of the region. S.B. Majumdar's paper on the coinage of ancient South Kosala includes the coins of early dynasties. The revised reading of *Apilaka* as *Saliluka* and fresh interpretation on some of the coins are really illuminating.

The religious history is represented by a good number of papers among which the paper on 'Western Orissa, the Homeland of Jagannath' attracts attention of everyone. It is a soul-stirring theme in which Dr. J.K. Sahu has tried to establish Western Orissa as the homeland of Lord Jagannath on convincing grounds.

A host of scholars have contributed their papers on the socio-economic aspect of South Kosala. Economy strengthens the state and society reforms and refines the state. The contributors have discussed about the urban centres, the port-town Suvarnapur, the crafts and commerce in land and reverine trade of South Kosala with their keen observation. The society and culture of the Chauhan period is also highlighted.

We are immensely grateful to Prof. M.C. Dash, Vice-Chancellor and Chairman of Reception Committee of the Seminar, for his thought-provoking speech in the form of inaugural address to the delegates which is incorporated in the book. We also express our gratitude to Prof. R.K. Sharma, Retd. Professor of Ancient Indian History, Culture and Archaeology, R.D. University, Jabalpur for delivering the Presidential Address with the history and culture of South Kosala as the theme, which also occupies a prominent place in the book.

The book contains the research papers of researchers and eminent scholars from various fields of specialization. This book, thus, covers various aspects like politico-religious, socio-economic, art, architecture, epigraphy and numismatics of South Kosala. We hope, the present collection of research write-ups can help the society to understand the past and the scholars for further research.

P.K. Nayak

Contents

Abbreviations

ASI	*Archaeological Survey of India*
ASIR	*Archaeological Survey of India, Annual Reports*
B. Samhita	*Bṛhatsaṁhitā*
c.	circa
Ch.	Chapter
CII	*Corpus Inscriptionum Indicarum*
cm	centimetre/s
EI/Ep. Ind.	*Epigraphica Indica*
IA	*Indian Antiquary*
IC	*Indian Culture*
IHQ	*Indian Historical Quarterly*
IIRNS	Indian Institute of Research and Numismatic Studies
IO	*Inscription of Orissa*
JASB	*Journal of the Asiatic Society of Bengal*
JBBRAS	*Journal of the Bombay Branch of the Royal Asiatic Society*
JBORS	*Journal of the Bihar and Orissa Research Society*
JESI	*Journal of the Epigraphical Society of India*
JNSI	*Journal of the Numismatic Society of India*
JRAS	*Journal of the Royal Asiatic Society*
JRASB	*Journal of the Royal Asiatic Society of Bengal*
MASI	*Memoirs of the Archaeological Survey of India*
MBH	*Mahābhārata*
OHRJ	*Orissa Historical Research Journal*

Inaugural Address

M.C. Dash

All the distinguished persons on the dais, Head of the Department, eminent historians, eminent citizens, ladies and gentlemen and dear students!

It is indeed a great pleasure to be associated with the Silver Jubilee Session of the History Congress of Orissa to be followed by a National Seminar on the Cultural History of this region in particular. I am indeed very glad that so many distinguished historians of Orissa have gathered here and that distinguished Professor of History, Prof. H. Kulke of Germany is also participating in the deliberation. I extend a hearty welcome to all of you to this beautiful campus, Jyoti Vihar and wish that your stay will be comfortable and the deliberations in the Congress will be academically rewarding.

I am a non-historian and do not like to venture to make comments on historical matters or History in general. However, why is History referred in popular discussions? In any intellectual forum on any discipline we often refer to the history of that discipline. In view of this human involvement and curiosity to know the past, thinking about the trend that would come in future has become inevitable. Therefore, History cannot be all nonsense. But often in a light-hearted way non-historians comment that History is nonsense. Is it because that historical analysis made by some historians are based on sectarian view instead of taking a holistic approach involving all aspects like economic, socio-religious conditions of the past? Is it because often mythology has been integrated into History to make it appear real? Is it because many historical analyses are not based on scientific analysis? These are some of the points that come to mind of the non-historians and general public. But the fact remains that everybody has a historical curiosity. Everybody is trying to find out his identity and root. It is perhaps human nature to look to the identity and to be curious. Studying History is also important from practical reasons when we take the contemporary politics and government policies into account. These are perhaps some of the aspects educated persons dwell upon, and therefore refer to History in popular discussions.

India boasts of the world's largest, richest and rewarding history and is considered a cradle of civilization. She has witnessed diversity of civilizations full with outstanding regional and cultural entities and boasts of magnificent monuments, temples, architecture, rock-edicts, rock art, palaces, tombs, etc. These are associated with very rich and rewarding history.

History becomes very pleasant reading, educative and a narrative delight when the historical writings are combined with socio-economic cultural analysis. The Harappan world, the Vedic values, the glorious Mauryas, the golden period of Guptas, the period of *Dharma* and defiance, the victories of the Sultans and Mogul empire followed by British conquest are unparallel histories in the world and when we join the epic of *Ramayana* and *Mahabharata*, the teachings of Buddha and Shankara, Guru Nanak and Sufi saints and services of Mahatma Gandhi, the historical accounts of India become unique.

However, these exciting aspects of Indian history should be analyzed rationally with scientific tools and temperament. No historical writings can claim authenticity unless the data are supported by good analysis. In the past we have experienced that history in some cases was written in a biased manner. In 1957, when we celebrated the centenary of 1857, it took intellectual courage and sound reasoning to question the biased Anglophile historical branding of the 1857 freedom struggle (First War of Independence) as mutiny. History can be authentic, monolithic or pluralistic depending upon the presentation by historians. In view of this, I am sure, the learned historians will deliberate on different aspects of the History and Orissan history in particular, and bring new things for educating the present generation and make the discipline exciting.

Recently we observed some sort of movement called 'Kosala Ratha'. This is again based on regional identity. Region-specific cultural trend is perhaps recent concern not only of historians but elites. This region of Orissa formed part of Dakshina Kosala. The civilization in Dakshina Kosala has evolved on the banks of Mahanadi, Sheonath, Tel and Indravati and the people were predominantly tribal. The area includes the modern districts of Bilaspur, Raipur, Durg and Raigarh under Chhattisgarh State and Sambalpur, Bolangir and Kalahandi under Orissa State. Although some excavations have been done in Malhar (Bilaspur district) and Asurgarh (Kalahandi district), extensive excavation has not been done and it is believed that extensive excavation will bring many a new things and will provide valuable information on the civilization that prevailed in this area. This region is very rich with Shiva temples, Buddhist *chaityas* and *viharas*. The root of 'Kosala Ratha' lies with regional imbalance in development and there is threat of regional identity. At the time of formation of Orissa State, taking all Oriya-speaking regions under one administration in 1936, signal contributions of many eminent people of Sambalpur and this region cannot be forgotten. Broadly, the culture of Oriya people are same at macro level, whether they live in Kosala, Kalinga or Utkala combinedly known as Orissa. Yet at micro level regional identities are there and these are to be nourished to make the Orissan culture much richer. Regional imbalance issues are to be addressed on priority basis on a time scale in a planned manner. If we look to this problem on another plain the question that arises is – If unity among diversity is possible? Science tells us that in any system diversity brings stability and continuance of the system. If we look at the natural ecosystems we find that diverse elements constitute ecosystem but unite them both structurally and functionally and each component – whether the production unit, consumer unit, decomposer unit and resource movement process or energy flow – is vital for the survival of the system. In nature diversity is a rule in any system and this diversity brings unity. But each component of that unit is as important as the other unit. So keeping the scientific finding and the Indian nation involving diverse regional cultures, races of people, etc. in view and looking at the unit, we can safely conclude that unity among diversity is not only the rule of nature but also applicable to nations.

In view of this, the importance of each regional culture and region should not be ignored and should form an equal part of the developmental process. Since this region has played a vital leading role in the formation of unified Orissa and generation of Orissan culture, it is high time that the regional imbalance be looked into on priority basis. I hope this National Seminar will at length discuss about the history and culture of Dakshina Kosala (Western Orissa) and its contribution to Indian culture in general and the Orissan culture in particular and new light will be thrown on past events.

I wish to thank the faculty and staff of the Department of History, which is doing excellent work, and for organising this Congress.

Keynote Address
History and Culture of South Kosala

R.K. Sharma

I am grateful to the authorities and members of the P.G. Department of History, Sambalpur University for inviting me to this national seminar on the history and culture of South Kosala. I am sure the papers presented and conclusions drawn in the seminar will go a long way in filling up the gaps that still exist in the political and cultural history of the region.

The scope of the subject is undoubtedly large. I do not know what to speak on the subject of this dimension within 15-20 minutes which are generally spared for a speaker in an inaugural function like the present one. Keeping this in mind, I will try to limit my views on some specific unsolved problems of the history and culture of South Kosala. I therefore will keep myself limited to the ancient period only.

The broad and variegated canvas of the ancient history of South Kosala is very tempting. The area comprising modern Chhattisgarh and Western Orissa has hoary antiquity. It was a passage of Aryan migration to the south and the cradle where highly interesting experiments in art and culture have taken place. It is but natural that for its rich cultural remains, scholars have been attracted to its heritage and I am glad to record that the present seminar is one in the series. During recent past, archaeological excavations were conducted at various sites in Chhattisgarh and Western Orissa. Explorations carried at hundreds of sites in the Mahanadi and its tributaries, along with rock-painting sites have thrown welcome light on the pre- and proto-history of South Kosala. Chance discoveries of inscriptions, coins, seals, sealings and manuscripts have helped in reconstruction of the political and cultural history of the region. Also, researches undertaken by various agencies to study the art of South Kosala have highlighted its contribution to this region.

These and other attempts have proved that tremendous scope of research exists towards reconstruction of the political and cultural history of this area, which once had an identity of its own.

The prehistoric and protohistoric explorations and excavations done in the Mahanadi Valley and its tributaries, mainly comprising the districts of Raipur, Bilaspur, Durg, Raigarh and Bastar of Chhattisgarh and Sambalpur and its adjoining districts in Orissa, in which geomorphology, palaeontology and quarternary stratigraphy of the region has been critically examined, have proved that there is an evolution of tools from Lower Palaeolithic to Mesolithic cultures in this region. As for the evidence of Neolithic culture in South Kosala, the evidence is limited both in Chhattisgarh as well as Western Orissa in spite of evidences provided by explorations and excavations of the Neolithic sites conducted by Thapar (1964) and Dash (1987). Similar is the case with Chalcolithic cultures, only very limited evidences of which have been found in a few excavations done within the region. In Chhattisgarh, Chalcolithic culture is known by the presence of a few sites only, viz., Malhar, Kharod and Rajim. Orissa provides a better picture as it comes from the excavations conducted at Sankerjang, Golabai, Bhejidihi, Kurmigudi, Khambeswaripalli and Nuagarh. However, the excavations of Megalithic remains at Dhanora and Karkabhat and discovery of about 3 to 4 thousand Megalithic burials at Karhibhadar, Kanyawada, Majagahar, Sorar, Chirchari, Tengna and Bhanwarmara in Chhattisgarh, and datable roughly to first-half of the first millennium BC, is an outstanding discovery which has opened up possibilities for further researches in this specific area.

The study of rock paintings datable to pre and protohistoric times has engaged much attention during the past fifty years or so. Discovery of several rock painting sites in the Raigarh district of Chhattisgarh is an old phenomenon, but location of new sites in the same district along with the districts of Durg, Sarguja, Raipur and Bastar has contributed much to the widening horizons of rock-art research in Chhattisgarh. Orissa found its place in rock-art map of India in 1933 when K.P. Jayaswal reported one of the earliest evidences of rock engravings in India from the rock-shelter of Vikramkhol in the Jharsuguda district. Since then much addition has been done by researches of different scholars to the subject of rock-art research in Orissa. Results of Sadasiba Pradhan's field-work conducted in the hills of Western Orissa (including South Kosala), during the last one decade, now published in a book form entitled *Rock-Art in Orissa* (New Delhi, 2001), has added new dimensions to the subject, particularly in bringing to limelight a distinct regional style in the rock-art heritage of India. One notices in the region a happy blending of engravings (petroglyphs) with paintings (pictographs), both being complimentary to each other, drawn in non-thematic and non-figurative pictorial codes. This is a rare phenomenon not encountered so far anywhere in India.

It is the literary tradition which connects the history of South Kosala with pre and protohistory. According to the *Puranic* account, Vinitapura, the celebrated capital of Dakshina Kosala, and the surrounding territory was inherited by Vinitasva, a son of Sadumnya, who was himself one of the ten sons of Vaivasvata Manu. As per another account, the region was ruled by Kusa, one of the two sons of Rama. He made Kusasthalipura his capital. It may be stated here that Rama's route for reaching Dandaka forest and finally to Lanka, passed through South Kosala and this is evidenced by finds of a large number of sculptures related to *Ramayana* in the districts of Raigarh, Sarguja, Bilaspur and Raipur, which in those days lay on this route. The route of Rama was later on followed by Samudragupta in 4th century AD in his South Indian campaign. It is needless to remind that Rama's mother Kausalya belonged to this region. To distinguish it from the Northern Kosala of the Ikshvakus, with Ayodhya as its capital, the southern region was called Dakshina Kosala. As regards Lanka, controversy still persists regarding its precise location. That Lanka cannot be identified with present Sri Lanka is now a historically proved theory. Whether its remains lie in one of the deltas created by Mahanadi in Orissa before it touches the sea, as suggested by Pt. D.P. Mishra in his famous book *The Search for Lanka* (Delhi, 1985) or somewhere else is yet to be researched.

In the historic period South Kosala was ruled by different dynasties, viz., the Nandas, the Mauryas, the Mahameghavahanas, the Sungas, the Satavahanas, the Pandavas of Mekala, the Meghas, the Guptas, the Vakatakas, the Nalas, the Rajarsitulyakulas, the Sarabhapuriyas, the Panduvamsis, the Telugu Chodas, the Kalachuris of Ratanpur, Raipur and Khalari, the Somavamsis of Kosala and Utkala, the Nagas, the Somavamsis of Kanker, and the Gangas. Regarding none of the above-mentioned dynasties it can be claimed that its political history as revealed on the basis of epigraphy, numismatic literature as well as archaeology, is well established. Every year welcome light is being thrown by new discoveries in respective fields to make a step forward in the advancement of the existing stock of knowledge regarding the political and cultural contributions of each dynasty. New *Corpuses of Inscriptions* have been published in the recent past to throw welcome light on the political history of the dynasties ruling over this area. Numismatic researches and publications in the form of books, monographs and research papers, publication of old manuscripts like *Kosalananda Kavyam* have added new dimensions to the study of political and cultural history of South Kosala. It is time for young researchers to lend their valuable contributions in revealing the glorious past of the region.

History is not simply the history of royal dynasties and administrative organizations. History must allot a very large canvas to social, economic, cultural and religious aspects of a particular age which form a distinct phase of a composite culture. No region should claim more attention in this regard than South Kosala for the reason that it was the gateway between the North and South India, and more so because the area was the homeland of several ancient Indian tribes whose successors even now live in the area. Their contacts with the Aryans and other urbanized populations migrating to the area led to interactions in several ways. Consequently, new experiments were performed in the fields of society and economy, art and architecture, religion and philosophy, literature and all other aspects of what constitutes culture. Epigraphic, numismatic, art and architectural, literary and other evidences are full of instances to prove that South Kosala was a land of experimentations wherein Aryan and non-Aryan thoughts collided, affecting both their mutual benefits. Many-sided developments took place leading to original contributions. I may quote here a few instances. The Kosali style of temple architecture is a new phenomenon in Indian architecture. Recently, it has attracted international attention. The so-called *Rudrasiva* sculpture of *Tala*, on which an independent book entitled *Riddle of Indian Iconography* (Delhi, 2000) has been published by L.S. Nigam, is a specimen of *hinduisation* of tribal deity, a phenomenon so attractive in Orissa. The Natyashala of Ramgarh, the mud-rampart forts of Chhattisgarh, the Buddhist monuments of Bastar and Sirpur, the brick-temple architecture of Chhattisgarh, the bronzes of Sirpur, Fusera and Salkhan, the repousse coins, the box-headed and nail-headed Kutila, and shell-charactered inscriptions are some of the typical and original contributions of South Kosala to the history and culture of India. Towards portrayal of complete pictures about each of these aspects, lot of research need to be done. It is here that our young archaeologists and historians are required to pay attention. It is towards partial fulfilment of this goal that arrangements of seminars like the present one is a desideratum wherein young researchers are expected to learn from their seniors.

The Postgraduate Department of History, Sambalpur University, since its inception, has done its best to reconstruct the political and cultural history of Orissa in general and that of South Kosala in particular. This has been accepted even by such august bodies like the University Grants Commission, which has recognized it as a centre fit for receiving special financial assistance. The present seminar is the latest instance. I am sure the Department will publish its proceedings to the benefit of all concerned.

Once again I thank the organizers for giving me the honour to speak on this occasion and share my views with the learned historians who have assembled here from all parts of the country. Thanks are also due to the learned gathering who has given me a patient hearing.

List of Contributors

M.C. Dash
Vice Chancellor, Sambalpur University, Sambalpur, Orissa.

R.K. Sharma
Retd. Professor, Ambrapali Duplex, 1591, Napier Town, Jabalpur, MP.

N.K. Sahu
(Late) Professor, Sambalpur University, Sambalpur, Orissa.

S.C. Behera
(Late) Professor, Sambalpur University, Sambalpur, Orissa.

Sushil Chandra De
State Archives, Bhubaneswar.

Kedarnath Mohapatra
State Museum, Bhubaneswar.

Sadhu Charan Panda
Sr. Professor & Co-ordinator, DRS, P.G. Department of History, Sambalpur University, Sambalpur, Orissa.

J.K. Sahu
Isavashyam, Near Dak Banglow, Barpali, Dist. Bargarh, Orissa.

Sadananda Agrawal
At/Po. Menda, Dist. Subarnapur, Orissa.

Baba Mishra
Sr. Lecturer in History, Govt. College, Bhawanipatna,
Dist. Kalahandi, Orissa.

Biswajit Pradhan
P.G. Department of History, Sambalpur University, Sambalpur, Orissa.

Debabandya Kabi
P.G. Department of History, Sambalpur University, Sambalpur, Orissa.

S.P. Nanda
Lecturer in History, Dept. of History, Rajendra College,
Bolangir, Dist. Bolangir, Orissa.

Patit Paban Mishra
P.G. Department of History, Sambalpur University, Sambalpur, Orissa.

Jeeban Kumar Pattnaik
Asst. Suptd. Archaeologist, Konark Branch, ASI, Konark,
At/Po. Konark, Dist. Puri, Orissa.

Jagdish Mishra
Lecturer in History, T.F. College, Bargarh, Dist. Bargarh, Orissa.

Jadumani Mohaptra
Sr. Lecturer in History, Dept. of History, J.L. College, Patnagarh, Dist. Bolangir, Orissa.

Rama Manjari Sahu
Sr. Lecturer in History, Angul College, Angul, Dist. Angul, Orissa.

Bhaktapuran Sahoo
Lecturer in History, Ghens College, Ghens, Dist. Bargarh, Orissa.

Prabhas Kumar Singh
Asst. Curator, Orissa State Museum, Bhubaneswar, Orissa.

Brajakishore Padhi
At/Po. Buguda, Dist. Ganjam, Orissa.

Samikshya Satpathy
C/o. P.K. Nayak, DRS Co-ordinator, Phase II, P.G. Dept. of History, Sambalpur University, Sambalpur, Orissa.

Jitamitra Prasad Singh Deo
Khariar Palace, Khariar, Dist. Nuapada, Orissa.

D. Chopdar
P.G. Department of History, Sambalpur University, Sambalpur, Orissa.

Susmita Basu Majumdar
Dept. of AIHCA, Kolkata University, Reformatory Street, Kolkata.

Jayanti Dora
P.G. Department of History, Sambalpur University, Sambalpur, Orissa.

Kedarnath Mishra
Lecturer in History, Sonepur College, Sonepur, Dist. Subarnapur, Orissa.

I

A Survey of the History of South Kosala

N.K. Sahu

ORIGIN OF SOUTH KOSALA

The tradition regarding the origin of South Kosala may be traced in the *Purāṇic* and epic literature. According to the *Purāṇic* accounts Sudyumna, one of the ten sons of Vaivaswata Manu, had three sons named Utkala, Vinitāsva and Gaya.[1] When Manu divided his extensive kingdom among his sons, Sudyumna received a portion out of which Utkala got the territory that was named after him, Vinitāsva received the region to the west of Utkala, and Gaya got Gayāpuri with some eastern region.[2] Vinitapura, the celebrated capital of South Kosala, was very likely named after Vinitāsva and as such, the western territory received by him was no other than South Kosala.

The *Purāṇas*, however, refer to a branch of the Ikshvākus as the earliest known ruling dynasty of South Kosala. According to the *Vāyu Purāṇa*,[3] forty-eight sons of the race of Ikshvāku ruled over the Dakshina region. This finds corroboration in the *Brahmāṇḍa*,[4] *Vishnu*[5] and *Brahma*[6] *Purāṇas*. The *Padma Purāṇa*,[7] following the tradition recorded in the *Ramachandra*,[8] states that after Sri Ramachandra Northern Kosala was ruled by Lava from Srāvasti, while Kusa, who married a Nāga princess, ruled over South Kosala and made Kusasthalipura, which was named after him, his capital. The last known Ikshvāku king of South Kosala, representing the line of Kusa, was Brihadvala who was killed in the famous Kurukshetra battle.

According to the *Mahābhārata*,[9] large mass of people inhabiting the eastern part of Kosala migrated to the South being terrified by the incursions of Jarāsandha. Pargiter[10] is inclined to believe that those people settled in the Chhattisgarh region and that the territory of South Kosala developed out of that exodus. The *Rāmāyaṇa* and the *Purāṇas*, however, make us believe that South Kosala came into origin as a result of the migration of the Ikshvāku tribe from the north of India to the Vindhya region.

TERRITORIAL EXTENT

The *Purāṇa*s represent the people of Kosala as inhabitants of the Vindhya region (विन्ध्यपृष्ठनिबासिन:) and we further know from the *Rāmāyaṇa*[11] that Kusasthalipura, the capital of South Kosala, was located in that region. The '*Vanaparva*' of the *Mahābhārata*[12] locates South Kosala in the north of Dakshiṇapatha and clearly distinguishes that territory from the kingdom of Vidarbha. The same *Vanaparva*[13] refers to the sacred places of Kosala, such as Rishabha Tirtha, Kala Tirtha and Badarikā Tirtha which can be traced in the Chhattisgarh region of Madhya Pradesh.[14]

In the *Allahabad Pillar Inscription*[15] (c. AD 350) Kosala has been included among the territories of Dakshiṇapatha in association with the kingdoms of Korala[16] and Mahakantara,[17] and according to historians it comprised the modern districts of Bilaspur, Raipur and Sambalpur.[18] During the Post-Gupta period (6th-7th century AD), the Sarabhapuriya kings ruled over Kosala with Sarabhapura (modern Sarabhgarh in Sundargarh district of Orissa) as their headquarters, which later on shifted to Sripura (modern Sirpur in Raipur district of Madhya Pradesh). The Chinese pilgrim Yuan Chawang[19] who visited Kosala in AD 639, described the kingdom as 6000 li in circuit and about 1800 li away from Kaliṅga to the north-west. On the basis of this account, Cunningham[20] presents the boundary of Kosala comprising the whole of the upper valley of the Mahanadi from the Amarkantak hills down to the middle valley of that river up to Sambalpur and Sonepur, and Hiralal[21] is inclined to include the ex-States of Patna, Bamra, Sonepur and Rairakhol in the ancient South Kosala.

EARLY HISTORY

As pointed out above, the *Purāṇa*s regard the Ikshvākus as the earliest ruling dynasty of South Kosala which was ruled by 48 kings of that dynasty till the time of the famous Kurukshetra battle. The Jaina tradition, however, represents the Chedis as the earliest rulers of South Kosala. According to the *Harivaṃśa Purāṇa*,[22] written by Jinasenachārya, the Chedi prince Abhichandra founded the Chedirashtra in the Vindhya region with Śūktimatipurī as the capital. Śūktimatipurī was the same as Sothivatinagar of the *Chetiya Jātaka*[23] and Śūktisahvaya of the *Mahābhārata*.[24] The *Harivaṃśa Purāṇa*, as well as the *Ādiparva* of the *Mahābhārata*,[25] locate this capital town on the bank of the river Suktimati which has been identified by scholars with the river Suktel in modern Bolangir district.[26] The Chedirashtra, founded by Abhichandra in the Vindhya region, may be said to be the same as South Kosala. The rule of the Chedis over Kosala in ancient time is suggested by various evidences. The *Vessantara Jataka*[27] reveals that the Chedis were ruling over the Vindhya region close to Kaliṅga and that the capital of the Chedi kingdom was at a distance of only ten *Yojanas* from Durnivishta (Dunnivittha), a Brahmin village of Kaliṅga. Khāravela, the famous king of Kaliṅga in the 1st century BC, belonged to the Chedi dynasty and in his *Hāthiguṃśa Inscription*, he declares himself as a descendant of the Chedi King Vasu who according to the *Harivaṃśa Purāṇa* was the son of Abhichandra, the founder of the Chedirashtra. The tradition regarding Abhichandra and Vasu seems to have been popular during the time when Khāravela ruled over Kaliṅga. The rule of the Chedis in South Kosala may tentatively be placed after the end of the rule of the Ikshvāku line of kings.

The *Hāthigumpha Inscription* as well as the *Manchapuri Cave Inscription* of Kudepasiri state that both Khāravela and Kudepasiri belonged to the Mahāmeghavāhana-Chedi family. In other words, both these rulers belonged to the family of Mahāmeghavāhana who was a Chedi king of Kaliṅga. Mahāmeghavāhana appears to be the first Chedi ruler to acquire sovereignty over Kaliṅga and he was very likely a scion of the Chedi ruling family of Chedirashtra (South Kosala). Khāravela being the third ruler of Kaliṅga in the family of Mahāmeghavāhana, the latter may be ascribed to the early part of the 1st century BC. It has been suggested that the rise of the Andhra-Satavahanas under Simuka in Maharashtra region and that of the Chedis under Mahāmeghavāhana in Kaliṅga were synchronous events in history and may be ascribed to the time when the Sunga-Kanva power declined in Magadha.[28]

The Chedi-Mahāmeghavāhanas continued to rule over Kaliṅga about a century after Khāravela and were subsequently ousted from power by the Satavahanas early in the 2nd century AD. The *Nasik Cave Inscription*[29] of Vasishthiputra Pulumāvi reveals that the fortune of the Satavahanas was revived by Gautamiputra Satakarni who started his reign in AD 106[30] and subjugated the neighbouring territories in the Deccan. In AD 124 he defeated and killed the Khaharata Satrap Nahapana and established his suzerainty over the Malwa-Maharashtra region. He is also known to have acquired the territories of Kaliṅga and Kosala by conquest. The Chinese pilgrim Yuan Chwang[31] describes the Po-lo-mo-lo-ki-li where Gautamiputra Satakarni constructed a magnificent *vihāra* for his philosopher friend Nagarjuna. The Po-lo-mo-lo-ki-li or Parimalagiri has been identified with the modern Gandhagiri (Gandhamadanagiri) located on the border of Sambalpur and Bolangir districts of Orissa.[32] This region formed a part of the ancient South Kosala.

Gautamiputra Satakarni ruled up to AD 130 and was succeeded by his son Vasishthiputra Pulumavi who extended the Satavahana power up to the territory between the mouths of the Godavari and the Krishna. But soon after his death, which took place sometime after AD 154,[33] the Satavahana power declined and the territories of Kosala and Kaliṅga no longer continued to be under their rule.

THE MEGHAS

The decline of the Satavahanas brought about remarkable change in the history of eastern India. Kaliṅga came under the occupation of a foreign power known as the Murundas, while an indigenous power named the Meghas, who were very likely the descendants of the Mahāmeghavāhanas, raised their heads in Kosala. The *Purāṇas*[34] describe the rule of nine generations of Megha kings over Kosala during the period before the rise of the Guptas. These kings who were noted for their valour and wisdom had a prosperous rule from the middle of the 2nd century AD to the first quarter of the 4th century AD. Details about them are, however, not known from the *Purāṇas* and reliable records are yet to be found out to properly construct the history of this period.

THE GUPTAS

The *Allahabad Pillar Inscription* of Samudragupta throws some light on the history of South Kosala about the middle of the 4th century AD. It is known from this record that Samudragupta in course of his campaign against the rulers of Dakshiṇapatha first encountered King Mahendra of Kosala who was defeated by him. The other rulers in the neighbourhood of Kosala were Mantaraja of Korala and Vyaghraraja of Mahākāntara, both of whom sustained defeat at the hands of the Gupta invader.

As pointed out above, Kosala by that time comprised the modern districts of Raipur and Bilaspur in Madhya Pradesh and the district of Sambalpur in Orissa[35] while the kingdom of Korala has been identified by scholars with the Sonepur region of Bolangir district.[36] The Mahākāntara territory according to the *Mahābhārata*[37] extended from the east of Kosala up to the banks of the river Veṇā, a tributary of the Godavāri.

This has also been referred to in two of the *Amaravati Stupa Inscriptions*[38] as Mahavana and has been identified with the districts of Kalahandi and Koraput of Orissa and Bastar of Madhya Pradesh. Thus, the three kingdoms Kosala, Korala and Mahākāntara comprised mainly the western and south-western parts of Orissa and after subduing these territories Samudragupta could easily proceed towards the eastern coast through the ancient trade route that linked Kosala with Kaliṅga.

The kingdoms in South India claimed to have been conquered by Samudragupta did not form parts of the Gupta empire. Mahendra, Mantaraja and Vyaghraraja, along with other kings were reinstated in their respective kingdoms. According to some scholars the claim of Samudragupta regarding his suzerainty over the territories south of the Vindhyas, as recorded in the *Allahabad Pillar Inscription*, is an exaggerated one. No other Gupta emperor made military campaigns towards the south and the extent of the Gupta empire over Kosala and Kaliṅga has remained a subject of controversy.

THE VAKATAKAS

About the middle of the 5th century AD, Kosala was occupied by the Vakataka king Narendrasena who ruled from c. AD 440 to AD 460. The Balghat plates[39] of his son Prithvisena II reveal that Kosala along with Malava and Mekala formed parts of the Vakataka empire during his rule. Both Narendrasena and Prithvisena were engaged in deadly wars with the Nalas of Bastar-Koraput region. The Nala king Bhavadattavarman defeated Narendrasena and marched as far as his capital Nandivardhana near Nagpur. But his son Arthapati is known to have received serious reverses at the hands of Prithvisena II. Arthapati was probably killed in about AD 475 and his brother Skandavarman who succeeded him continued the war. The Nala king Skandavarman and the Traikutaka king Vyaghrasena were the formidable enemies of Prithvisena II and the Nalas appear to have taken possession of South Kosala during the chaotic period of his rule. After Prithvisena the leadership of the Vakatakas passed to Harisena, the king of the Basim branch, who, as known from the *Ajanta Inscription*,[40] successfully defeated the Nalas and the Traikutakas and conquered Kuntala, Avanti, Lata, Kosala, Kaliṅga, and Andhra countries. The success of Harisena was short-lived and after his death in c. AD 510, South Kosala threw away the yoke of the Vakataka rule.

THE RAJARSHITULYA KULA

The *Arang Plates*[41] of King Bhimasena dated in the Gupta year 282, i.e., AD 602 throw important light on the history of South Kosala during the post-Harisena period. The record discloses the rule of six generations of kings belonging to the dynasty named 'Rajarshitulya Kula'. Maharaja Sura, the earliest king of this line, can well be assigned to c. AD 510 – the year of death of Harisena. He seems to have made South Kosala independent of the Vakataka rule. He was succeeded by Dayita I and the latter by Bibhīshaṇa. The next king was Bhimasena I and after him Dayitavarman II ruled over Kosala. Bhimasena II, the son and successor of Dayitavarman II, issued the *Arang Plates* mentioned above. The silver coins of Bhimasena II bearing the peacock device have been brought to light.[42] He was without doubt a very important ruler of South Kosala at the beginning of the 7th century AD. The *Arang Grant* was issued from Suvarṇanadi, which according to Sri S.N. Rajguru[43] was a mistake for Suvarṇapura. In that case the donated village Batapallika may be identified with modern Barpali in Sambalpur district. We do not know of the fate of this 'dynasty after Bhimasena II'.

THE PARVATADVARAKAS

The rulers of this dynasty were the worshippers of the goddess Stambheswari installed at a place called Parvatadvara and the dynastic name is suggested after this sacred seat of the tutelary deity. The *Terasinga Copper-plates*[44] furnish the accounts of two kings of this line who ruled in the Tel River Valley during the first-half of the 6th century AD. The first grant was issued probably by King Sobhanaraja at the time his mother Kaustubheswari was bed-ridden with high fever (*Daha Jvara*). It records the grant of Debhogaka *kshetra*, modern Debhog in Madhya Pradesh in the Tel Valley, to Brahmana Dronaswami of *Kasyapa gotra*. The second grant was made by Sri Maharaja Tushtikara from his headquarters Tarabhramaraka identified with modern Talbhamara on the Tel River in Kalahandi district. The same Dronaswami was the donee and the donated village was Prastaravataka identified with Patharla in Kalahandi district.

The Tel Valley came under the possession of the Sarabhapuriya kings in the 7th century AD.

THE SARABHAPURIYAS

A chieftain named Sarabha started the rule of a new dynasty in eastern part of South Kosala towards the close of the 5th century AD. He is referred to by the *Eran Pillar Inscription*[45] of the time of Bhanugupta, dated in Gupta year 191, i.e., AD 511. The headquarters Sarabhapura named after him has been identified with Sarabhgarh in modern Sundargarh district of Orissa. His son and successor was Maharaja Narendra who issued the *Pipardula Grant.*[46] Both Sarabha and Narendra were very likely the feudatories of the Vakataka Emperor Harisena who conquered Kosala along with other territories. The dynasty became independent during the time of Maharaja Prasannamatra whose relation with Maharaja Narendra is not yet clearly known. Prasannamatra issued both gold and silver coins and founded a town named after him as Prasannapura. He was succeeded by his son Jayaraja who issued the *Arang Charter,*[47] donating the village Pamva in the *Purvarāshtra* of Kosala.

Jayaraja had a premature death and was probably succeeded by his brother Manamtra popularly known as Durggaraja. The two sons of Maharaja Jayaraja – named Pravararaja I and Vyaghraraja – are known from the *Malhar Grant.*[48] This grant was issued by Vyaghraraja from Prasannapura. Both Pravararaja I and Vyaghraraja ruled one after the other and died without any male issue. So, after Vyaghraraja the succession passed to the collateral branch represented by the two sons of Manamatra. They were Sudevaraja and Pravararaja II. The rule of Sudevaraja or Mahasudevaraja is known to us from a number of copper-plate grants issued by him. Those are the *Khariar Grant*[49] issued in his 2nd regnal year, the *Arang Grant*[50] and the *Kauvatala Grants*[51] issued in the 7th regnal year and some other undated grants like the Sarangarh[52] and Raipur[53] charters. The copper-plate grants indicate that the territory under Mahasudevaraja comprised the modern districts of Raipur and Bilaspur in Madhya Pradesh and the districts of Sundargarh, Sambalpur and Kalahandi in Orissa.

Pravararaja II was the last ruler of Sarabhapuriya family and he is known to us from his *Thakurdiya Grant*[54] issued in his 3rd regnal year. He seems to have made Sripura his headquarters. Pravararaja II probably died issueless and after him the kingdom of Kosala passed to the hands of Tivaradeva, son of Nannadeva who was a high official and venerable person in Kosala. The succession was very probably a peaceful one and Tivaradeva founded the rule of a new dynasty called Panduvamsi or Somavamsi in Kosala.

THE SOMAVAMSIS

In the first half of the 6th century AD, a chief named Udayana began the rule of the Somavamsis in the Mekala region. One of the *Gandhesvara Temple Inscriptions*[55] at Śirpur presents the genealogy of the family starting with Udayana. In this inscription Cunningham[56] wrongly read the name of the family of Udayana as Savara. But the correct reading of it as pointed out by Hiralal[57] is Sasadhara, meaning the moon. The son and successor of Udayana was Indravala who, besides being the ruler of his principality, was holding the posts of *Sarvadhikaradhikrita* and *Dutaka* under the Sarabhapuriya king Mahasudevaraja.[58] Indravala's successor Nannadeva was also working as a high official under the Sarabhapuriyas and the *Kauvatala Grant*[59] refers to him with great veneration. Thus, the early Somavamsi chiefs were working as high dignitaries under the Sarabhapuria kings of South Kosala and were commanding great respect in that territory. When Pravararaja II died issueless, Tivaradeva, the son of Nannadeva, obtained the throne of Kosala. Judging from the close relationship between the Somavamsi and the

Sarabhapuriya families extending over several generations, it is presumed that the succession of Tivaradeva was a peaceful one.

The rule of Tivaradeva over South Kosala is known from three of his copper-plate grants – the *Boṇḍā Grant*[60] issued in the 5th regnal year, the *Rajim Grant*[61] issued in the 7th regnal year, and the *Balda Grant*[62] in the 9th regnal year. Tivaradeva as known from the *Adhabhara Grant*[63] of his son Mahanannaraja, was also the master of *Utkala maṇḍala*. He interfered in the civil war that took place in Kongoda between the two Sailodbhava princes, Dharmaraja and Madhava, but was defeated by Dharmaraja. In consequence of this defeat Tivaradeva withdrew from Utkala. His son and successor Nannaraja II ruled for a short time and after his premature death Chandragupta, the brother of Tivaradeva, came to occupy the throne. The next ruler was Harshagupta, the son of Chandragupta. His queen Vasata was the daughter of Suryavarman, a king of Magadha.[64] Harshagupta was succeeded by his son Bālārjuna and since Bālārjuna was a young boy at the time of his succession, the queen-mother Vasata acted as regent for some time. She caused to be built a magnificent temple for Hari at Śripura, the capital of Kosala. Mahāśivagupta Bālārjuna is known from a large number of copper-plates and stone inscriptions. He had a long rule and the *Lodhia Copper-plate Inscription*,[65] his last known record, was issued in his 57th regnal year. The Somavamsi kings from Tivaradeva to Harshagupta were all devout Vaishnavas. But the religious ideology of the family changed with Bālārjuna who constructed a number of Shiva temples and called himself Paramamāheśvara. Bālārjuna was, however, a patron of Buddhism and two of the inscriptions of his time found at Śirpur[66] and Mallar[67] indicate that Buddhism flourished with great vigour in his kingdom alongside Śaivism.

The Somavamsis appear to have been ousted from the Śirpur region by the rising Kalachuris about the middle of the 9th century AD. None of the records of Janamejaya I, who was very likely the son and successor of Bālārjuna, was issued from Śirpura. Janamejaya I Mahābhavagupta found a new territory – the Sonepur-Bolangir region – and he does not seem to have established any permanent capital during his whole career. He, however, assumed the title of *Kosalendra* and *Trikalingādhipati* and declared himself *Mahārājādhirāja Parameśwara*. In his 3rd regnal year[68] we find him issuing charters at Suvarṇapura, modern Sonepur. But by his 6th regnal year[69] he shifted to Murasima identified with modern Mursing, 13 miles south of Bolangir, and there he placed his headquarters at least till his 11th regnal year.[70] In his 17th regnal year[71] Janamejaya is found issuing grants from a new headquarters called Arama, indentified with Rāmapura about 25 miles west of Sonepur.[72] He continued there at least up to his 31st regnal year.[73] Suvarṇapura again became his capital wherefrom he issued his last known record – the *Kālibhana Grant* – in his 34th regnal year.

Janamejaya I seems to have a continuous career of wars. He fought with the Kalachuris in the west and with the Bhanjas of Khinjali (Odra) in the east. His wars with the Bhanjas ended in success. We know from the *Brahmeswara Temple Inscription*[74] that Janamejaya killed with his *Kunta* the king of Odra. The king of Odra can be no other than Ranabhanjadeva, the ruler of Ubhaya Khinjali maṇḍala which is invariably called Odradesa in the records of the Somavamsis. Janamejaya was thus able to extend his territory towards the Baudh regions in the later part of his career. His war with the Kalachuri king Sankargaṇa was not so successful and it continued even after his death, which took place about AD 885 corresponding to his 35th regnal year.

The son and successor of Mahābhavagupta Janamejaya I was Mahāśivagupta Yayāti I, who continued the war with the Kalachuri king Sankargaṇa (c. AD 878-910) with varying results. The conflict was a long drawn one and the ultimate victory went in favour of the Kalachuris. Yayāti I refers to this war in the records of his 8th regnal year[75] when his headquarters was at Vinitapura (modern Binka) on the Mahanadi. In his 9th regnal year,[76] Yayāti visited Toshali which was then under the rule of his sister Prithvimahādevī. It may be pointed out that Prithvimahādevī was given in marriage by her father Janamejaya I to the then Bhauma king Kusumahara, alias Subhakaradeva IV, and after the death of her husband she eventually became the ruler of the Bhauma dominion by AD 894 when she issued two of her Baudh Charters (in *Bhauma* year 158).[77] This year corresponds to the 9th regnal year of Jayati I Mahāśivagupta. Yayāti I and Prithvimahādevī both being loyal to the interest of the Somavamsis probably made a secret manoeuvre to extend the Somavamsi empire to east at the cost of the Bhauma-Karas. This gave rise to a rebellion in the Bhauma court and Siddha Gauri Tribhuvana Mahādevī, who issued the *Dhenkanal Grant* in AD 896 (*Bhauma* year 160),[78] usurped the Bhauma throne setting aside Prithvimahādevī with the help of her courtiers and feudatories. Yayāti I who was then busy with the wars against the Kalachuris failed to render effective help to his sister at the time of the crisis.

Under Yayāti I, Mahāśivagupta Vinitapura continued to be the capital town of the Somavamsis at least up to his 15th regnal year.[79] Later on he founded a new township on the Mahanadi, close to the town of Gandhatapati, and named it after him as Yayatinagar, which can be identified with the modern village Jagati on the Mahanadi, seven miles to the west of Baudh. The capital was shifted to Yayatinagar sometime after his 15th regnal year and this town continued to be the capital till the end of the Somavamsi rule in AD 1110.

Yayāti I Mahāśivagupta was succeeded by his son Bhīmaratha Mahābhavagupta who had a peaceful and prosperous rule. After him his son Dharmaratha Mahāśivagupta came to the throne. His *Khandapara Plates*[80] issued in his 11th regnal year reveal that by that time the territory of the Somavamsis had extended over the coastal region of Orissa and that the Bhauma rule had come to an end in that region. This charter refers to the Antarudra Vishaya, now in Puri district, as a part of the Somavamsi territory. This Vishaya formed a part of the Bhauma-Kara kingdom in the *Bhauma* year 73 (AD 810) as known from the *Chaurasi Grant* of Śivakaradeva.[81]

Dharmaratha had a step-brother named Indraratha born of Durgā, the second queen of King Bhīmaratha and when Dharmaratha died childless, Indraratha who was his favourite, obtained the Somavamsi throne.[82] His succession was challenged by Abhimanyu, son of Vichitravira and grandson of Janamejaya I Mahābhavagupta, but subsequently Abhimanyu was defeated and was expelled with his family and relations from the Somavamsi kingdom. Indraratha is also known by his second name Naghusha or Nahusha. He was defeated and killed by the general of Rajendra Chola who invaded Yayatinagar in AD 1022-23.[83] Afer this tragic end of Indraratha, Chandihara, the son of Abhimanyu, returned from his exile and ascended the throne of Yayatinagar assuming the royal name Yayāti II Mahāśivagupta. He constructed the temple of Lingaraja at Bhubaneswar where his wife Kolavati constructed the Brahmeswara temple. The son and successor of Jayati Mahāśivagupta was Udyotakesari Mahābhavagupta who probably added the *Jagamohana* to the *Vimana* of the Lingaraja and it was in his 18th regnal year that the Brahmeswara temple constructed by Kolavati was consecrated.[84] The same year was also consecrated the Navamuni *gumpha* at Khandagiri by the Jaina Acharya Subhachandra, the disciple of the illustrious Acharya Kulachandra.[85]

Udyotakesari Mahābhavagupta consolidated the Somavamsi dominion and divided it into two main units – one comprising the Kosala portion and the other the Utkala region. The old chief Abhimanyu, who was the grandfather of Udyotakesari, was made a ruler of the Kosala division which was sometimes called Paschima Lanka[86] and sometimes as Paschima Kaliṅga.[87] Suvarṇapura, modern Sonepur, at the confluence of the Tel and Mahanadi, was the capital of Kosala division. After the death of Abhimanyu, the succession in Kosala passed to Kumara Someswaradeva who was either a brother or a son of Chandihara Yayāti II. The last known Somavamsi ruler of Kosala was Yuvaraja Dharmaratha whose unpublished *Nuāpātna Grant* was issued in the 5th regnal year of Janamejaya II, the son and successor of Udyotakesari. He was probably defeated by Yasoraja, the Telugu Choda general of the Chhindaka Naga king Somesvara, as a result of which Kosala came under the rule of the Telugu-Chodas in c. AD 1070.[88]

In the Utkala portion the Somavamsis continued to rule for sometime more. After Udyotakesari, his son Janamejaya II occupied the throne of Yayatinagar and during his time the Somavamsi kingdom began to be disintegrated.[89] He was succeeded by his brother Puranjaya whose rule was probably short-lived. The last Somavamsi king of Utkala was Karnadeva, the son of Janamejaya II. He was defeated by Chodagangadeva who occupied Utkala about AD 1110.[90]

THE TELUGU CHODAS

As suggested above Yasoraja I, the Telugu Choda lieutenant of the Chhindaka Naga king Somesvara conquered Kosala about AD 1070 and founded the rule of a new dynasty in that territory. Yasoraja probably acted as a Governor of his Chhindaka Naga over-lord in Kosala. But his son Somesvara I assumed the status of a subordinate ruler. The capital of the Telugu Chodas was at Suvarṇapura. Three copper-plate grants of this family issued from Suvarṇapura are available to us. These are the *Mahada Grant*, issued by Somesvara II in the 23rd regnal year of his Chhindaka Naga over-lord Somesvara, and the *Kumarisingha* and *Patna Grants*[91] issued by Somesvara III in the 11th and 17th years of his reign, respectively. The date of the *Mahada Grant* is about AD 1090 and the dates of the other two grants can also be found out as similar – the *Kumarisingha* was issued on the full moon day of *Magha*. In the 1st decade of the 12th century AD such an eclipse took place twice[92] – on 21st January 1106 and 10th January 1107. So the *Kumarisingha Grant* was issued either on 1106 or 1107 and the *Patna Grant* either in 1112 or 1113.

Somesvara I, the son of Yasoraja I, was succeeded by his son Yasoraja II alias Dharalladeva and the latter was succeeded by Somesvara II, the issuer of the *Mahada Grant* in AD 1090. Somesvara II probably died issueless and after him Yasoraja III, the son of Yasoraja I (and the brother of Somesvara), became the ruler of Kosala. He must have been advanced in age and ruled for a short period. He was succeeded by his son Somesvara III in AD 1095-96.

The Kalachuris of Dāhala were a rival power of the Telugu Chodas and were making attempts to take possesion of the Sonepur region. But the Chhindaka Nagas were a formidable power to be reckoned with and the Telugu Chodas were getting all possible support from them. In AD 1114 the Kalachuri king Jajalladeva[93] crushingly defeated and captured

Somesvaradeva who has been identified with the great Chhindaka Naga king Somesvara.[94] He is also known to have imprisoned Bhujavala of Suvarṇapura who was none other than the Telugu Choda king Somesvaradeva III.[95] Thus, the Telugu Choda rule suddenly collapsed and Kosala passed to the hands of the Kalachuris.

THE KALACHURIS

The Kalachuri Chief Kokkala ascended the throne of Dāhala about the middle of the 9th century AD. He successfully drove away the Somavamsis from the Śirpur region and Janamejaya I had to build a new kingdom in Sonepur-Bolangir tract. Janamejaya fought against the Kalachuris to restore the paternal territory, but to no effect. He was defeated by the Kalachuri king Sankargaṇa who succeeded Kokkala about AD 878. The victory of Sankargaṇa alias Mugdhatunga has been described in the *Bilhari Stone Inscription*[96] as well as in the *Benaras Grant,*[97] where he is called Prasiddha Dhavala. Yayāti I Mahāśivagupta, the son of Janamejaya I Mahābhavagupta, continued the war with great vigour, but failed to regain the territory occupied by the Kalachuris.

By the time the Telugu Chodas became the rulers of Kosala, the Kalachuris consolidated their power in Dāhala with Tummāṇa as their capital. The leader of the Kalachuris was Kalingaraja whose great grandson Prithvideva claimed in his *Āmod Grant*[98] dated AD 1079, as the lord of the entire Kosala. The *Āmod Grant* has also referred to the victory of Gangeyadeva (AD 1030-1041) whose brother Kamalaraja 'having churned the king of Utkala with emaciated war made over the goddess of victory to his over-lord Gangeyadeva'.

In AD 1114 the Kalachuri king Jajalladeva obtained a decisive victory over the Chhindaka Naga king Somesvaradeva and got possession of Kosala with the capital Suvarṇapura.

It was the time when the Ganga king Chodaganga after his occupation of Utkala (AD 1110) was preparing for the conquest of Kosala. The *Kharod Stone Inscription*[99] reveals that Ratnadeva II, the grandson of Jajalladeva, defeated Chodaganga and foiled his ambition for further aggression. Kāṃrṇavadeva, the son of Chodaganga, is also known to have been defeated by the Kalachuris who thus became the undisputed masters of the Kosala territory.

THE GANGAS

The conflict between the Kalachuris and the Gangas seems to have taken place first for the possession of the Trikalinga territory and later on for

Kosala. The Gangas from the time of Indravarman I (AD 537) declared themselves as the lords of Trikalinga. When the Kalachuri king Gangeyadeva alias Vikramaditya (1030-41) conquered Utkala, he assumed the title of *Trikalingadhipati* and this title was used by all the succeeding kings of this dynasty till the time of Vijayasimha who ruled from AD 1180 to 1195. The Ganga king Vajrahasta V (AD 1038-1070) attempted reconciliation by marrying Vijayamahadevi, a Kalachuri princess. But Rajarajadeva, the son of Vajrahasta V, entered into conflict with the Kalachuris when his general Vanapati invaded Oḍra and Kosala.[100] The defeat of Chodaganga, the son of Rajaraja, at the hands of the Kalachuri king Ratnadeva II has been noted above. Chodagangadeva's son Kamamava also fought against the Kalachuris and was defeated by Prithvideva II, the son of Ratnadeva II. The Ganga-Kalachuri conflict continued for a long time and the issue between them remained unsettled till the time of accession of Anangabhimadeva in AD 1211. The *Chatesvara Inscription*[101] reveals that Vishnu, the general of Anangabhimadeva, crushingly defeated the Kalachuri king of Tummāṇa while fighting on the banks of the Bhima, on the outskirt of the Vindhyas and also on the seashore. As a result of this victory the Gangas could occupy the Sonepur-Bolangir region by driving out the Kalachuris. The occupation of Sonepur by the Gangas is known from the *Khamveswari Temple Inscription*, which reveals the rule of a Ganga governor of that region during the time of Bhānudeva (AD 1264-1279). The Kalachuris seem to be continuing their hold in Sambalpur region for sometime till Vatsarājadeva, the 3rd Chauhan Rājā of Patna, conquered that territory in AD 1400.

Ramāideva, a Chief of the Chauhan dynasty, founded the rule of his family at Patna, modern Patnagarh in Bolangir district, about AD 1360 which ushered in a new chapter in the history of Kosala. The Ganga rule in Kosala was supplanted by that of the Chauhans who gave rise to a new spirit of culture and tradition and moulded the political life of Western Orissa till the advent of the British rule.

NOTES AND REFERENCES

1. Pargiter, *Anc. Ind. Hist. Tradition*, pp. 253-54.
2. *Vayu*-XXCV, *Matsya*-XI, *Brahma*-VII.
   सुद्युम्नस्य तु दायादस्त्रयः परमधार्मिकाः। उत्कलष्ठच गयश्चैव विनीताश्वश्च भारत।।
   उत्कलस्योत्कलं राष्ट्रं विनीताश्वस्य पश्चिमं। दिक् पूर्बा तस्य राजर्षेर्गयस्य तु गयापुरी।।
3. *Vayu*-XXCI, XXCVIII.
4. *Brahmanda*, ID, LXIII, 8-11, 21-25.
5. *Vishnu*-IV, 2-3.

6. *Brahma*-V; I, 45-48, 51.
7. *Padma* (*Anandasrama series*)- VI. CCLXXI. 54-55. (8); *Ram*-VII, CXX. 7; CXXI, 5.
9. *Sabhā Parva*-XIII, 591-92; XXX, 1117.
10. *Anc. Ind. Hist. Tradition*, p. 78, Note I, also *JRAS* 1908, p. 32.
11. *Ibid.*
12. *Vana*-LVIII, 22.
13. *Ibid.* LXXXIII, 10-13.
14. *The Gunji Rock Inscription* (*JKHRS,* Vol. ll, No. 1, p. 2) refers to *Rishabha Tirtha* 15. *CII,* Vol. III, pp. 6 ff.
16. Sonepur region.
17. Comprised parts of Bastar, Koraput and Kalahandi districts.
18. *Pol. Hist. Anc. Ind.* (1950), p. 538.
19. Watters, Vol. II, p. 200.
20. *ASR,* XVII (1881-82), pp. 68-69.
21. *IA,* LXII, p. 162.

    बिन्ध्यपृष्ठेऽभिचन्द्रेण चेदिराष्ट्रमधिष्ठितं।
    शुक्तिमत्यास्तटेऽधायि नाम्ना शुक्तिमतीपुरी।।
23. *Jataka,* III, pp. 454-61.
24. *Vana Parva*-XX, 50; *Asvamedha Parva*-XXXIII, 2.
25. *Adiparva,* LIII, 35.
26. Sircar, D.C., *Geog. of Anc. and Med. India,* p. 55. Pargiter identifies the river Suktimati with the Ken River and locates the Chedirashtra to the north of the Plateau of Malwa and the hills of Bundelkhand.
27. *Jataka,* VI, pp. 514-21.
28. Vide U.U., *Hist. of Orissa,* Vol. I, p. 333.
29. *Ep. Ind.,* Vol. VIII, pp. 65 ff.
30. The *Junar Cave Inscription* of Nahapana is dated in *Saka* year AD 46 or 124. This is taken to be his last date and the 18th regnal year of Gautamiputra Satakarni.
31. Watters, Vol. II, p. 201.
32. Sahu, *Buddhism in Orissa,* pp. 99-100.
33. His *Nasik Cave Inscription* is dated in his 24th regnal year.

    कोशलानां तु राजानी भविष्यन्ति महावला:।
    मेघा इति समाख्याता बुद्धिमन्तो नवैव तु।।
35. Raichadhuri, *Pol. Hist. of Anc. India* (1950), pp. 51, 538.
36. Dandekar, R.N., *Hist. of the Guptas,* p. 51.
37. *Sabha Parva*-XXXI.
38. Burgess, notes on *Amaravati Stupa Inscriptions,* Nos. 8 and 231.
39. *Ep. Ind.,* Vol. IX, p. 271.
40. *Ep. Ind.,* Vol. XXVI, pp. 137 ff.
41. *Ep. Ind.,* Vol. IX, pp. 342 ff.
42. Cunningham, *Arch. Surv. Reports,* IX, p. 26.
43. *Inscriptions of Orissa,* Vol. IV, p. 281.

44. *Ep. Ind.*, Vol. XXX, pp. 274-78.
45. *CII*, Vol. III, pp. 91 ff.
46. *IHQ*, Vol. XIX, p. 239.
47. *Insc. of C.P. and Berar*, p. 105.
48. *Ep. Ind.*, Vol. XXXIV, pp. 45 ff.
49. *Ep. Ind.*, Vol. IX, pp. 170 ff.
50. *MKSP*, pp. 39-40.
51. *Ep. Ind.*, Vol. XXXI, pp. 314-16.
52. *IHQ*, Vol. XXI, pp. 294-95.
53. *CII*, Vol. III, pp. 196-200.
54. *MKSP*, pp. 44-45.
55. *IA*, Vol. XVIII, pp. 179-81.
56. *Arch. Surv. Reports*, XVII, pp. 25, 57. *Insc. in C.P. and Berar*, p. 98.
58. See the *Sarangarh Grant*, *Ep. Ind.*, Vol. IX, pp. 283 ff.
59. *Ep. Ind.*, Vol. XXXI, pp. 314-16.
60. *Ep. Ind.*, Vol. XXXIV, pp. III-16.
61. *CII*, Vol. III, pp. 291-99.
62. *Ep. Ind.*, Vol. VIII, pp. 102-107.
63. *Ep. Ind.*, Vol. XXXI, pp. 219-22.
64. *Ep. Ind.*, Vol. XI, pp. 184-201.
65. *Ep. Ind.*, Vol. XXVII, pp. 319-25.
66. *Ep. Ind.*, Vol. XXXI, pp. 197-98.
67. *Ep. Ind.*, Vol. XXIII, pp. 113 ff.
68. *Ep. Ind.*, Vol. XI, pp. 93-95.
69. *IHQ*, Vol. XX, pp. 238-50.
70. *Ep. Ind.*, Vol. XXII, pp. 135-38.
71. *Ep. Ind.*, Vol. XXIII, pp. 248-55.
72. *Ep. Ind.*, Vol. III, pp. 345-51.
73. *IHQ*, Vol. XX, pp. 245-50.
74. *JASB*, Vol. VII (1837), pp. 557-62.
75. *JASB*, Vol. I (New Series-I905), pp. 14-16.
76. *Ep. Ind.*, Vol. III, pp. 351-55.
77. *Ep. Ind.*, Vol. XXIX, pp. 210-20.
78. *JBORS*, Vol. II, pp. 419-27.
79. *Ep. Ind.*, Vol. XI, pp. 95-98.
80. *Insc. of Orissa*, Vol. IV, pp. 280A-280 ff.
81. *JBORS*, Vol. XIV, pp. 292-306.
82. *JASB*, Vol. VIII, pp. 271-76.
83. *SII*, Vol. II, pp. 108-09.
84. *JASB*, Vol. VII, pp. 557-62.
85. *Ep. Ind.*, Vol. XIII, pp. 166 ff.
86. *Kelga Plates-Ep. Ind.*, Vol. XXVIII, pp. 322-26.
87. *Nuapatna Plates.* Not yet published.
88. The earliest known date of King Somesvara is *Saka* 991 or AD 1069. *Ep. Ind.*, Vol. X, pp. 31 ff.

89. *Ep. Ind.*, Vol. XXVIII, pp. 283 ff.
90. *JKHRS*, Vol. I, No. 3, pp. 29 ff.
91. *Ep. Ind.*, Vol. XIX, pp. 97 ff.
92. Vide Sewell, *Eclipse of the moon in India.*
93. *Ep. Ind.*, Vol. I, pp. 32 ff.
94. Hiralal, *Insc. of C.P. and Berar*, p. 117.
95. *MKSP*, II, p. 61.
96. *Ep. Ind.*, Vol. I, pp. 251 ff.
97. *Ep. Ind.*, Vol. II, pp. 306 ff. Hiralal, *Insc. of C.P. and Berar*, pp. 23-25.
98. *Ep. Ind.*, Vol. XIX, pp. 75 ff. Hiralal, *Insc. of C.P. and Berar*, pp. 118-19.
99. *Ep. Ind.*, Vol. XXI, pp. 161 ff.
100. *Ep. Ind.*, IV, pp. 314-15.
101. *JASB* (old series, 1898), Vol. LXVII, pp. 322-26.

Note: Recent researches reveal that Mahābhavagupta, the grandfather of Janamejaya I, had conquered Sonepur area along with Trikalinga. Janamejaya was coronated at Suvarṇapura, present Sonepur (vide Gopalpur Charter of Janamejaya I, 1st set). Nahusa and Indraratha are not identified but they were brothers and Indraratha, the usurper of the Somavamsi throne, was killed by Rajendra Chola. Karnadeva, the last king of Somavamsa, was defeated and Utkala was conquered by Chodagangadeva in or before AD 1108 (vide Mukhalingam Inscription of AD 1030) (Editor).

2

Historical Geography of South Kosala

S.C. Behera

In the currents of Indian history, empires rose and fell. But the ancient kingdoms like Magadha, Gauḍa, Vaṅga, Avanti, Lāta, Saurāṣṭra, Kosala and Utkala in the north and Kaliṅga, Āndhra, Mahārāśṭra, Karṇāṭa and Chola in the south seem to possess eternal quality of life. These regions under different names and ruling families survived for centuries throughout the course of Indian history.

Of these states Kosala is well known in Indian tradition and literature as the country of Rāma and its rise in the sixth century BC is attested by Anguttara Nikaya. According to *Rāmāyaṇa*,[1] the kingdom of Kosala after Rāma's death was divided between his two sons, Lava and Kuśa, the former getting the northern half and the latter the southern half. Scholars like Pargiter[2] believe that Rāma's long stay in Dakshina Kosala gave rise to the name of Kosala in the south. Whatever it might be, in addition to Kosala or North Kosala with its capital Ayodhya, we have another Kosala or South Kosala comprising roughly the present Raipur and Bilaspur districts of Madhya Pradesh and Sambalpur, Sundargarh, Bolangir, Kalahandi, Baud-Phulbani and Koraput districts of Orissa. D.C. Sircar* thinks that it was colonised by the princes of Ikshvaku dynasty of Ayodhya at the dim dawn of civilisation.

In literature and inscription this extant region has been named Kosala although in recent times some scholars have wrongly referred to it as Mahakosala.[3] To distinguish it from North Kosala, whose capital was Ayodhya, we have to designate the region as South Kosala. B.C. Law[4] thinks that the river Sarayu served as the wedge between the kingdoms of the North and South Kosala. But this suggestion does not appear to be correct because the northern boundary of Dakshina Kosala is never known to have reached up to the river Sarayu. It is perhaps only once that under Bhavattavarman[5] the northern boundary of Dakshina Kosala was extended as far as Allahabad. Probably the northern boundary of South Kosala reached as far as the river Son** in the palmy days of her history.

K.D. Bajpai[6] while writing a paper on 'Mahakosala in Ancient Literature' observes that the people of Mahakosala are conspicuous by their absence in the *Mahābhārata* while the Vaṅgas, the Kaliṅgas, the Tamraliptas and the Pundras are named as four peoples of neighbouring kingdoms. Although the author of *Mahābhārata* does not refer to the Kosalas in this context, he refers to the fact that Sahadeva in course of his *Digvijaya* in the south conquered and annexed the territory of South Kosala (*Sabhā* XXXI, vrs. 12-13). The *Purāṇa*s refer to Vindhyan range as part of Dakshina Kosala and connect the same with Mekala and Utkala.

Padma Purāṇa[7] says:

मेकलान् उत्कलाँश्चेदीन् दशाण्र्णान् कुकरानपि।

Matsya Purāṇa[8] says:

मालवाश्च कुरुषाश्च मेकलाश्चोत्कलैः सह।
उत्तमर्ण्ण दशाण्णश्चि भोजाः किष्कन्दकैः सह।।
तोसला-कोसलाश्चैव त्रैपुरा चैदिकास्तथा।
तुमुरा स्तुम्बुराश्चैव षट्सूरनिषधैः सह।।

Vāyu Purāṇa[9] too presents the same topography and refers to Kosala as a country situated in the Vindhyan base.

Varaha Mihira,[10] who flourished in the sixth century AD, locates (south) Kosala in the Āgneya Koṇa along with the countries like Kaliṅga, Aṅga, Vaṅga, Vidarbha, Vatsa, Āndhra. The grouping of countries indicates that here the author refers to Dakshina Kosala and not Uttara Kosala. It further proves that in the sixth century AD, Vidarbha and Dakshina Kosala were two separate states although they were contiguous. However, it is presumed by some scholars[11] that at a time when Dakshina Kosala had not assumed its name as such, it was generally designated by the term Vidarbha, which in that case must have comprised a much bigger area than the present Berar. Whatever it might be, by the third century AD, if not earlier, South Kosala as a country was distinct from Vidarbha, for while the Vakatakas ruled over Vidarbha, the Maghas ruled over South Kosala.[12] The mention of Mahendra as the king of Kosala in the *Allahabad Pillar Inscription*[13] clearly shows it was not a part of Vidarbha which was then under the Vakatakas.

Mekala, which according to the *Purāṇa*s was contiguous to South Kosala, is indentified with Maikal.[14] It is also the name of the mountain range in which the Narmada rises. Narmada has been called Mekala Kanyā or the daughter of Mekala. Thus, it is evident that on the north-western boundary of Dakshina Kosala was the country of Mekala, round the modern Amarkaṅṭaka hills where according to the *Bahmani Copper-Plate Grant*[15] the Panduvamsis of the line of Jayabala ruled for some time. *Vāyu Purāṇa*[16] says that while the kings of the Mekalas would be seven, those of which with the title Megha would be nine. *Matsya Purāṇa* and *Kurma Purāṇa* inform that Amarkaṅṭaka was the western boundary of Kaliṅga. In that case South Kosala might have been a part of Kaliṅga at that time.

Vatsayana[17] in his *Kāmasutra* refers to Kosala as a territory bordering on Strīrājya. Dr. Hiralal[18] has indentified the Strīrājya with the western part of modern Chanda district as it was located to the west of Vajradanta, identified with modern Wairagarh in the same Chanda district of Madhya Pradesh. On the eastern and south-eastern frontier of Kosala was situated the country of Kaliṅga whose boundary varied from time to time. As cited above, Varaha Mihira has treated Kosala and Kaliṅga as adjoining territories. Pulakesin in course of his northward military campaign is known to have defeated the Kaliṅgas along with the Kosalas (vide *Aihole Cave Inscription*).[19] Samudragupta in course of his South Indian campaign had proceeded from Kosala towards Mahendragiri which was a hill fort of ancient Kaliṅga.[20] Hiuen Tsang[21] is also known to have proceeded from Kaliṅga in the north-western direction for above 1800 *li*, i.e., 300 miles to Kosala.

In the post-Gupta period on the eastern frontier of South Kosala there emerged the two states of Kongoda[22] and Utkala[23] with definite territorial dimension under the Sailodbhavas and the Bhaumas successively.

The aforesaid account reveals that although the boundaries of Dakshina Kosala varied under different ruling dynasties, it stretched from the river Son[24] in the north to the river Vamsadhara in Kaliṅga in the south, and from the coastal tract of Orissa comprising Utkala, Kongoda and Kaliṅga in the east up to Vindhyapāda[25] in the west.

The historical geography of South Kosala is known to us from one authority in clear and definite terms – the Chinese testimony left by Hiuen Tsang that enables us to get a clear picture of the country. The pilgrim[25] observes:

> This country (Kiao-sa-lo, i.e., Kosala) is about 5000 *li* in circuit; the frontiers consist of encircling mountain crags; forests and jungle are found together in succession. The Capital is about 40 *li* (=about 7 miles) round; the soil is rich and fertile and yields abundant crops. The towns and villages are close together. The population is very dense. The men are tall and black complexioned. The disposition of the people is hard and

> violent; they are brave and impetous. There are both heretics and believers here. They are earnest in study and of high intelligence. The king is of the Kshattriya race; he greatly honours the law of Buddha and his virtue and love are far renowned. There are about one hundred Saṅghārāmas and somewhat less than 10,000 priests; they all alike study the teaching of the Great Vehicle. There are about seventy Deva temples, frequented by heretics of different persuations.

We learn from the *Life of Hiuen Tsang* written by Hui Li[27] that although the pilgrim had decided to go to Ceylon from Tāmpralipti by sea-route, on being advised by a South Indian priest he changed his mind so that he could visit every part of Orissa extensively and witness the Buddhist sites. Thus, the pilgrim visited U-cha (Utkala), Kong-U-To (Kongoda), Kie-ling-kia (Kaliṅga) and then journeying for about 1800 *li* or 300 miles in the north-western direction, reached the country Kiao-sa-lo (Kosala).[28] Hence, the condition of Kosala narrated by the pilgrim is accurate to a remarkable degree.

The capital of the country varied from time to time. Puskari seems to be the earliest known capital of South Kosala under the Nalas. It is located in the modern Umarkot taluq of Koraput district.[29] Under the Sarabhapuriyas the capital was shifted to the city of Sarabhapura, indentified by L.P. Pandeya[30] with Śarabhagarh in the Sundargarh district. Subsequently, under the same rule the capital was transferred from Sarabhapura to Sirpura, identified with Sirpur. Sirpur[31] is a small village on the right bank of the Mahanadi, situated at a distance of 40 miles from Raipur. Here extensive ruins cover the ground for about two miles. But the most noticeable among them are the temples of Gandhesvara and Lakshamanesvara bearing some inscriptions of the time of Bālārjuna. It was during the time of Mahābhavagupta Janamejaya that the capital was again shifted from Sirpura to Suvarṇapura,[32] rightly identified with Sonepur. From Suvarṇapura or Sonepur, Mahāśivagupta Yayāti shifted the capital to Vinitapura,[33] identified with modern Binka near Sonepur. Subsequently, the same ruler in course of his military campaign having conquered the Baudh region selected there the site of his new capital, which was named Yayatinagara.[34] Yayatinagara is probably the same as Jagati, seven miles to the west of Baudh on the bank of Mahanadi. The twin temples of Gaṅdharaḍi near Jagati reveal the popularity of Hari-Hara cult under the patronage of the Somavamsis.

The natural geography of South Kosala may broadly be divided into two divisions: 1. River valleys and 2. Hill tracts. A close study of the history of South Kosala reveals that civilization in this region flourished chiefly on the bank of the river Mahanadi. The river Mahanadi has been repeatedly mentioned in the Somavamsi copper-plates. Sirpur, capital of the Sarabhapuriyas[35] and Panduvamsis,[36] is situated on the right bank of Mahanadi. Yayatinagara, identified with modern Jagati, seven miles to the west of Baudh, was also situated on the right bank of Mahanadi. Thus, while describing the location of Yayatinagara, the royal panegyrist in the Somavamsi copper-plates[37] says:

महानदी तुङ्ग तरङ्ग भङ्ग
स्फारोच्छल च्छीकरवद्भिरारात्
यस्मिन् रतासिक्त मदाङ्गनानां
श्रमापनोद: क्रियते मरुद्भि:
तस्मात् श्रोययाति नगरात्।

(Where the fatigue of the women enjoying conjugal caresses with ardent attachment is removed by the breezes surcharged with the particles of water sent up by the breaking and swelling of the high waves of the Mahanadi.)

Suvarṇapura, another headquarter of the Somavamsis, rightly identified with Sonepur, is also situated on the confluence of the two rivers, Mahanadi and Tel. The present river Tel has been mentioned repeatedly in the *Somavamsi Charters*.[38] Such was its importance that a district called Telatata visaya was formed on the valley of the river Tel. River Aung, another tributary of the river Mahanadi, has also been mentioned in the *Patna Plates* of Janamejaya Mahābhavagupta[39] as Onga and the district that was formed on its valley was known as Oṅga-taṭa visaya.

Of the mountains of South Kosala the most well known is 'Po-lo-molo-ki-li' (Parimalagiri) described by Hiuen Tsang.[40] The pilgrim observes:

> To the south-west of this country above 300 *li* from the capital was a mountain called Po-lo-mo-lo-ki-li which rose lofty and compact like a single rock.

Here King Yin-cneng (Sadvaha) had quarried for Nāgārjuna a monastery in the mountain and had cut in the rock a path, communicating with the monastery for above 10 *li*. The monastery had cloisters and lofty halls; these halls were in five tiers, each with four courts with temples, containing golden life-size images of the Buddha of perfect artistic beauty.

Polomolokili or Parimalagiri has been identified with Gandhagiri, which is the same as present Narsinganath-Harisankar[41] mountain on the border of Sambalpur and Bolangir districts. It is situated at a distance of 20 miles south-west of Padampur.

Other hills of significance are the prehistoric cave of Vikramkhol and the Buddhist cave at Titilagarh. However, these names are not known to have been mentioned in the inscriptions of South Kosala.

South Kosala under the Somavamsis is known to have been divided into the following districts[42]: Piharajabhukti, Penthamabhukti, Aṣṭadvāra visaya, Kośira Nandapur visaya, Redamśakabhoga, Layoddaka visaya, Oṇibhoga visaya, Lupattarā Khaṅḍa, Pota visaya, Oṅgataṭa visaya, Kasaloda, Nimuna visaya, Pons visaya, Sammani visaya, Tokkarā visaya, Sunulā visaya, Gandaṭapati maṇḍala, Tela-taṭa visaya, Kosala Sakhanga-dyanha visaya, Prithura Bhukti, Bhranda visaya, Paschima Laṅkā, Lāvḍā-bhukti and Devībhoga. All these districts have not been satisfactorily identified. However, most of the *visayas* mentioned from the time of Mahābhavagupta I Janamejaya have been identified by scholars. 'Lupattarā khaṇḍa' or 'Lipa tuṅgā' of the *Vakra-tentali Grant* has been suggested to be the same as Upalā of *Āthmalik*.[43] But such identification is hypothetical. It is probably identical with Lepta, six miles from Bolangir. Potā visaya mentioned in the *Kalibhana Copper-plate Grant* is probably the same as[44] Poa in Bolangir district. Murasima, the place of issue of the said charter, is undoubtedly the same as present Murasimha near Jarasimha in Bolangir district. Ongatata visaya mentioned in the *Patna Plate* is the same as the Aung Valley. The district of Kasloḍa,[45] mentioned in the *Nagpur Museum Plates*, has been identified with Kusarḍa, fifteen miles south-west of Bargarh and the village Satallama of the said district is identified with Satalma in the Sambalpur district. Prithurabhukti of the *Mahakosala Society Plates* is probably the same as Pithoḍa near Padmapur. Lavda district[46] mentioned in the *Patna Plates* has been identified with Lebḍa, forty-eight miles south-west of Bolangir. Gandatapati maṇḍala of the *Nivinna Plate* is identical with Gaṅdharaḍā, close to Jagati in the Baudh region. The district of Devibhoga, mentioned in the *Cuttack Plates* of Mahābhavagupta Bhimaratha, appears to be identical with De-bhogaka *kshetra* of the *Terasinga Plates* of Tustikara[47] and it may be identified with Degam near Terasinga.

A survey of the historical geography of South Kosala reveals that covering a landscape of about 800 miles in circuit the country, which attained celebrity for the best diamonds, stretched from the northern border of Kaliṅga in the south to the vicinity of the Son in the north, and from the northern border of Ganjam in the east up to the country of Mekala in the west. It is the river valley of Mahanadi that was the cradle of Somavamsi power and it was here that the civilization of South Kosala was manifested at its best.

NOTES AND REFERENCES

* *The Vakataka Gupta Age*, p. 84.

** *MBH-Vana Parva*, 01. 84.

1. *Rāmāyaṇa*, VII, XX 7, CXX 5.
2. *AIHT*, p. 278; *JRAS* (1894), p. 231.
3. *IC*, Vol. III, p. 57. R.D. Banerji, *History of Orissa*, Vol. I, p. 142. Cunningham, *ASIR*, Vol. I, XVII, p. 68. *JKHRS*, Vol. I, pp. 201-202.
4. *Geography of Early Buddhism*, p. 6.
5. Rajaguru, *Inscriptions of Orissa*, Vol. I, Part II, p. 110.
6. *JKHRS*, Vol. 2, p. 203.
   Mahābhārataki Nāmānukramanikā (Gita Press), p. 90.
7. *Padma Purāṇa*, *Adikhanda VI*, p. 36.
8. *Matsya Purāṇa*, 133, Vrs. 52-53.
9. एते जनपदाः सर्बे बिन्ध्यपृष्ठनिबासिनः।
10. आग्नेयो दिशिकोसलकलिङ्ग बङ्गोपबङ्गापराङ्गाः।
11. *JKHRS*, Vol. I, p. 204.
12. *Journal of Ganganath*, The Research Institute, Feb. 1944.
13. *CI*, Vol. III, p. l.
14. Pandey, R.B. and B.N. Sharma, *Jabalpur (Tripuri) Past and Present*, p. 1.
15. *EI*, XXVIII, p. 132.
16. *Vayu Purāṇa*, *Adhyaya* 9, Vr. 347.
    vide Pargiter, *Dynasties of Kali Age*, p. 51.
17. *Kama Sutta* II, 5, 27.
18. *JKHRS*, Vol. I, p. 204.
20. Rajaguru, *op. cit.*, Vol. I, Part I, p. 104.
21. Watters, *On Yuan Chwang's Travels*, 1961, p. 200.
22. Dharmaraja of Koṅgoda had inflicted a crushing defeat on Tivaradeva of Kosala (vide *Nivina plates*), *EI*, XXI, p. 134.
23. Tivaradeva of Kosala had occupied for some time a portion of Utkala (vide *Adabhara plates*), *EI*, XXX, p. 219.
24. It formed the boundary line between the Uttara Rāṣṭra and Dakshina Rāṣṭra of the adjoining state of Mekala. *Inscriptions of Orissa*, Vol. IV, p. 313.
25. Mādhava, the younger brother of Dharmarāja of Kongla, who took shelter under Tivaradeva of South Kosala spent his last days at Vindhya Pada (*EI*, XXI, 34. N.L. Dey, *Geographical Dictionary*).
26. Beal, S., *Travels of Hiuen-Tsang*, Vol. IV, Susil Gupta Publication, 1958, pp. 414-415.
27. *Life of Hiuen Tsang*, pp. 133-134.
28. Watters, *op. cit.*, pp. 193-200.
29. *Inscriptions of Orissa*, Vol. I, Part II, p. 107.
30. Proceedings of the Fifth Oriental Conference, p. 461.
31. Cunningham, *op. cit.*, Vol. VII, p. 168.
32. *Inscriptions of Orissa*, Vol. IV, No. 16, p. 95.

33. *OHRJ*, Vol. III, p. 132.
34. *Ibid*.
35. *EI*, XXII, p. 15.
36. Vide *Rajim plate* (*CII*, III, 291-299).
37. See lines 11-16 of the *Patna plates* (*JASB*, Vol. I, pp. 8-12).
38. *Inscriptions of Orissa*, Vol. IV, pp. 190, 192, 195, 196, 198, 207.
39. *Ibid*., pp. 105, 110.
40. Watters, *op. cit*., p. 201.
41. *ASIR* (1882); *Bihar and Orissa District Gazetteer*, Sambalpur (1931), pp. 248-257; G.R. Bhandarkar, *Report of the Archaeological Survey of India* (1904-05).
42. Vide *Inscriptions of Orissa*, Vol. IV.
43. Das, S.P., *Sambalpur Itihas* (In Oriya), 1962, p. 68.
44. *Ibid*.
45. *EI*, XI, p. 201.
46. *Ibid*., LXI, p. 261.
47. *Inscriptions of Orissa*, Vol. I, Part I, p. 84.

3

Study of Some Muafi Grants and Interesting Facts Gleaned from Them

Sushil Chandra De

The word *Muafi* is an Arabic word derived from the root 'Muaaf', meaning 'pardon'. It is used to denote lands exempted from payment of revenue. In the Sambalpur district *Muafi* grants are, in most cases, charitable grants made to Brahmins for their maintenance, or to persons in charge of temples for expenses of the worship of the deities installed therein. These grants are mostly made in perpetuity. The grantee is termed *Muafidar*. When an entire village is granted for charitable purposes, the village is called a *Muafi* village.

The Deputy Commissioner, Sambalpur in his letter No. 3717 Dt. 2-10-87 to Commissioner, Chhattisgarh, stated that *Muafi* plots in the *Muafi* villages in the Sambalpur district were of two kinds, viz., (i) the plots granted by the Raja previous to confirment of villages on *Muafidar*s and (ii) plots granted by *Muafidar*s, from his *bhogra* or by *gaontia*s preceding the *Muafidar*s and kept up by the latter. Plots of the first kind granted to Brahmins in charity were to be held in perpetuity, while the second kind could not be considered as *Muafi* plots as they were granted by *Muafidar*s and could be resumed with their lapse.

So a *Muafi* village may contain some plots previously granted by the Rajas in charity in perpetuity. The *Muafidar* of a village is to own the village excepting the plots already granted. *Muafi* grants are not only granted for charitable purposes, but also for other purposes.

A study of about one hundred and fifty *Muafi* grants[1] reveals that *Muafi* grants are not only made to Brahmins on religious occasions, or to *marfatdar*s of temples for expenses of worship of the deities installed therein, but also to relatives of the Rajas as presents or as dowry to the bridegroom. In some cases *Muafi* villages have been granted to persons in appreciation of the services rendered by them to the ruler. Rani Mohan Kumari granted a number of villages to Banamali Rai Brahman Khansama for his services against the Marathas. Raja Narayan Singh similarly granted a number of villages to Narayan Das and Krushna Das in appreciation of services rendered by their father who was killed in action. One grant was made by Raja Jaita Singh (Jayanta Singh) to Padmanabh Misra to cleanse himself from the sin of causing the death of a Brahmin.[2]

GENEALOGY AND CHRONOLOGY OF THE CHAUHAN DYNASTY OF SAMBALPUR

There is a detailed genealogical table of the Chauhan dynasty of Sambalpur in the office of the Depty Commissioner, Sambalpur.[3] Extract from it giving the list of rulers from Raja Balabhadra Deo to Raja Narayan Singh is given below:

1. Raja Balaram Deo
2. Raja Hridnarayan Singh
3. Raja Balabhadra Sai
4. Raja Madhukeswar Sai
5. Raja Baliar Singh
6. Raja Ratan Singh
7. Raja Chhatra Sai
8. Raja Ajit Singh
9. Raja Abhay Singh
10. Raja Jay Singh (Jayanta Singh) VS 1833-55 (AD 1775-97)
11. Rani Ratna Kumari (VS 1855-61) (AD 1797-1803)
12. Raja Jayanta Singh (VS 1874-75) (AD 1817-18)
13. Raja Maharaja Sai (VS 1879-84) (AD 1821-26)
14. Rani Mahan Kumari (VS 1884-90) (AD 1826-32)
15. Raja Narayan Singh (VS 1890-1906) (AD 1832-49)

Mr. Netherstole, Settlement Officer, Sambalpur compiled the following genealogy of the royal family of Sambalpur.[4]

Raja Balabhadra Sai

Raja Madhukar Sai — Gajaraj Singh
Raja Baliar Singh — Raghunath Singh
Raja Ratna Singh — Kanak Singh
Raja Chattar Sai — Hari Singh
Raja Ajit Singh

Raja Jait Singh — Raja Abhay Singh | Joti Singh — Ran Singh
Maharaja Sai | Sadasiv Singh — Bhawani Singh
Ananta Singh

Note: Mr. Dyer, E.A.C. to Capt. Fostel in his letter No. 60, Dt. 29-11-1859 stated that he was indebted to Bhawani Singh for aid in suppressing disturbances in Gadloisingh Basipara, Bahmal, Jhankarpali, Borloi and Bir Singh.[5]

NAME AND DATES OF THE RULERS OF CHAUHAN DYNASTY OF SAMBALPUR AS GLEANED FROM THE MUAFI GRANTS

1. Raja Balaram Deo: No date is recorded in any of the six grants studied. Five of the grants are made for support of the temple of Bimaleswar Mahadeo in village Huma in Sadr Tahsil and one for the temple of Samalai Devi of Sambalpur.

2. Raja Hridnarayan Singh: His name is not to be found among the donors of grants.

3. Raja Balabhadra Sai: As above.

4. Raja Madhukeswar Sai: He made one grant for his kinsman Raghunath Singh, a Chauhan Rajput and another for Kuleswar Mahadeo. No date is mentioned in the above two grants.

5. Raja Baliar Singh: From among the *Muafi* grants studied, he is the donor in case of 21 grants. Grants are made to Brahmins, and as endowments for the temples of Dadhibabanji in Brahmapura, Balaji Daninath, Mandhata Mahadeb, Jagannathji in Mudipara of Sambalpur, Jharidevi in village Dhama. Jhaleswar Mahadeb in Tampagarh, Bimaleswar on the bank of river Ele, Jambeswar Mahadeb in Kalapani, Burharajade in Papanga, etc. seven of the grants are dated. The dates are AD 1405, 1605 (in 2 cases), 1705, 1755, 1805, and 1824.

6. Raja Ratna Singh: His name is not among the list of donors of the grants under study.

7. Raja Chattar Sai: He is mentioned in case of six grants. Of the grantees, two are Brahmins, one is the *marfatdar* of the temple, Gopalji near Hatpara and two Rajputs for their services in the temple of Samlai. Only in one case the date, AD 1955, is mentioned.

8. Raja Ajit Singh: He is the donor of 17 grants under study. Of these, five are endowments for the temples of Balunkeswar Mahadeo in Brahmapura Bariha in Sambalpur, Gopinathji in Bisalkhand and Mahadeo in Suplapara. Three grants are made for persons of Rajput caste and the rest for Brahmins.

Eleven of the grants are dated: The dates are AD 1743, 1755 (in 2 cases), and 1805 (in 7 cases).

9. Raja Abhay Singh: He made 13 grants, three to Brahmins and ten as endowment for the temples of Somanath Mahadeo in Gulgunda, Jagannathji

in Arda, Paschimeswar Mahadeo in Arhapara (2 grants), Jagannathji in Somasingha, Anantji in Labhanga, Bateswar Mahadeo in Chakli, Balunkeswar Mahadeo in Tulsirgida, and Jagannathji in the same village. Seven of the grants are dated. They are AD 1684, 1689, and 1705 (in 5 cases).

10. Raja Jayanta Singh: He is the most prolific donor among the Rajas of Sambalpur, the total number of grants made by him being 36. Of his grants fourteen are for Brahmins, two for Brahmachar Gosain and one for Sitaram Gosain in trust for the temple of Jagannath, Puri, one for Chauhan Ananta Singh as dowry on the occasion of marriage of Raja's sister and the rest as endowments for the temples of Balunkeswar Mahadeo, Lankeswar Mahadeo, Bhubaneswar Mahadeo in Sambalpur, Jaleswar Mahadeo in Baham, Dadhibaban Jagannath, Chandidevi in Lapanga, Baldevji, Burharaja Mahadeo in Barapahar, Kedarnath Mahadeo and Jagannathji at Ambabhora, etc. 21 of the grants are dated. The dates are AD 1655, 1705 (2), 1755, 1765, 1783, 1803, 1805 (6), 1815 (3), 1825 (4), and 1845.

11. Rani Ratna Kumari: She is the donor of only one grant made in 1807 to one Brahmin on the occasion of Rani's bath in the Ganges at Allahabad on the occasion of solar eclipse.

12. Raja Maharaja Sai: He is known from only two grants, both of them being endowments, one for the temple of Raghunath in Bhatra, and the other for Radhakrishnaji in Tabla. The dates given in the above two grants are AD 1845 and 1835.

13. Rani Mohan Kumari: She is known from eight grants, five of which are endowments for the temple of Gopalji at Sambalpur, one for Baishnab Rai Brahman Khansama for his services against Marathas[6] and two for Chauhan Ranjit Singh, a near relative of the Rani. Of the above grants six are dated, the dates being AD 1829 (2), 1831, and 1833 (3).

15. Raja Narayan Singh: He is the donor in case of eleven grants. Of these grants six are endowments for the temples of Jagannathji and Madanmohan at Sambalpur, Ramlakshmanji at Cherupara, Raghunathji in Mangalpur and Dadhibaban Jagannath.

The most interesting thing in case of the grants made by Raja Narayan Singh is that two of his grants were made in favour of Surendra Sai, his deadliest enemy. The villages granted are Khinda, Kolabira and Talabira[7] in the year 1844. Evidently, Surendra Sai accepted those grants.

Narayan Singh made those grants obviously for placating Surendra Sai and desisting him from his activities directed against him. It is, however, curious to note that Surendra Sai accepted them from Narayan Singh.

One grant was made in favour of Narayan Das and Krishna Das in appreciation of the services of his father who was killed while trying to suppress Gond rebellion. Two illegitimate sons of Narayan Singh were also granted some land for their maintenance.

Nine of the grants are dated. The dates are AD 1818, 1827, 1835 (3), 1844 (2), 1845, and 1882.

The dates as given in the grants are quite fantastic, and so unreliable. It is very curious that quite impossible dates like AD 1405 in case of Raja Baliar Singh, AD 1653 in case of Raja Jayanta Singh or AD 1882 in case of Narayan Singh should be found in the grants made by those kings, and the range of dates, in some cases, should extend over more than a century. We seldom find wrong dates in grants. The dates as given in the copper-plate grants of Raja Jayanta Singh, Rani Ratna Kumari and Raja Narayan Singh (*O.H.R.J.*, Vol. II, No. I, pp. 47 ff and Nos. 3 and 4, pp. 25 ff), are quite correct.

So there can be no other explanation for wrong dates in the grants excepting that they are either due to clerical mistakes or wrong decipherments. The chronology of the last six rulers of Sambalpur is quite fixed being based on authentic materials. If we calculate upwards from the reign of Ajit Singh assigning him the period 1740-1766 and allowing a maximum rule of 20 years to each ruler, Balaram Deo, the first ruler of the dynasty, can be placed between AD 1640-60 at the earliest. I give below a tentative chronological table of the Sambalpur dynasty.

Balaram Deo	:	AD 1640-1660
Hridnarayan Singh	:	AD 1660-1680
Balabhadra Sai	:	AD 1680-1700
Madhukeswar Singh	:	AD 1700-1720
Chattar Sai	:	AD 1720-1740
Ajit Singh	:	AD 1740-1766
Abhay Singh	:	AD 1766-1777
Jayanta Singh	:	AD 1777-1797 AD 1817-1818 (In Nagpur jail from 1797-1817 during Maratha rule of Sambalpur).
Ratna Kumari	:	AD 1804-1807
Maharaja Sai	:	AD 1820-1827
Mohan Kumari	:	AD 1827-1833
Narayan Singh	:	AD 1833-1849

So, the beginning of Chauhan rule in Sambalpur cannot be assigned an earlier date than the beginning of the 17th century AD.

It is also interesting to note that there are two grants of which Raja Anangabhim Deo (AD 1211-38) is the donor. In one case he granted plots with a total area of 52.36 acres in village Deskumbhari in Bargarh Tahsil as an endowment for the temple of Dadhibaban.[8] In another case, he granted certain plots with a total area of 78 acres in village Tamparsara, in Bargarh Tahsil as endowment for the temple of Dadhibaban in that village.[9] The grants were made during the visit of Raja Anangabhim Deo to that part. The visit of Raja Anangabhim Deo might have been for inspection of frontier region for taking necessary steps against any surprise attack by Haihaya rulers of Ratnapura. However that may be, the temple of Dadhibaban in the village Tamparsara in Bargarh Tahsil is quite old.

The grants also bring to light many temples situated in different parts of the district for which endowments were made by the Rajas of Sambalpur.

NOTES AND REFERENCES

1. The *Muafi* grants of Sambalpur were compiled by Mr. M. Hamid, Settlement Officer, Sambalpur in 1925. They are recorded in *Muafi* Registers of different Tahsils of Sambalpur.
2. *Muafi Register*, Sambalpur Tahsil 51, No. 5, pp. 44-45.
3. *OHRJ*, Vol. II, Pts. 3 & 4, p. 33.
4. *Muafi* proceedings compiled by Mr. Netherstole, S.O. Sambalpur dated 6-2-188.
5. Rev. Deptt., File IX, Rev. 19, No. (V), pp. 4-5.
6. *Muafi Register*, Bargarh Tahsil, pp. 6-7.
7. *Register of Muafi Grants*, Sambalpur, pp. 66-67.
8. *Muafi Register*, Bargarh Tahsil, pp. 28-29.
9. *Ibid.*, pp. 46-47.

4

PO-LO-MO-LO-KI-LI of Hiuen Tsang's Account

Kedarnath Mohapatra

Hiuen Tsang's account, which gives a detailed description of various kings, kingdoms, religious places and sects of ancient India, is regarded as a treasure-house of historical facts and informations by the antiquarians. The late Mr. Cunningham, the pioneer historian and research scholar of the 19th century, in his book *The Ancient Geography of India* analysed and commented on the historical and geographical informations contained in this memorable work. But some of the views held and identifications of Buddhist holy places made by this great scholar are unacceptable in the light of modern research. It is now a proved fact that the identifications of the following Buddhist holy places and big towns, of ancient Orissa, e.g., Pu-se-po-ki-li of Utkala, Kongadanagar, Che-li-ta-lo port and capital of Kaliṅga made by late Mr. Cunningham are wrong. He identified Pu-se-po-ki-li with the Khandagiri near Bhubaneswar, the capital of Kongada with the town of Ganjam, the port Che-li-ta-lo with the town of Puri and the capital of Kaliṅga with Rajamahendri. But these places have been definitely identified with Ratnagiri and Lalitagiri hills of Cuttack, Banpur on the Salia near the lake Chilika, Konarka on the sea-shore and the town of Mukhalingam in the Paralakhimedi estate respectively, by the modern scholars. But no historian has yet tried to identify correctly the Po-lo-mo-lo-ki-li of Kosala, which was a famous centre of Buddhism in India in ancient times by refuting the wrong identification made by late Mr. Cunningham. This humble writer has attempted in his essay to make a correct identification of this great Buddhist centre of Utkala.

Leaving behind the capital of Kaliṅga, which was Mukhalingam in the Parlakhimedi Estate (and not Rajamahendri as ascertained by late Mr. Cunningham), Hiuen Tsang started towards the capital of Kosala. The account of the pilgrim runs thus:

> From this (Kaliṅga) going north-west through forests and mountains about 1800 *li*, we come to the country of Kaio-sa-lo (Kosala). The country was about 5000 *li* in circuit; the frontiers consist of encircling mountain crags, forests and jungles are found in succession. The capital is about 40 *li* round.
>
> Near the south of the city (capital) there was an old monastery with an Asokan tope, where Buddha had vanquished Tirthikas by the exhibition of supernatural powers and in which Nagarjuna Pusa had afterwards lodged. Contemporary with this Pusa as the king called So-to-pho-ho who treated Nagarjuna with ceremonious respect and kept a guard at his residence.
>
> To the south-west of this country about 300 *li* (50 miles), from the capital was a mountain called Po-lo-mo-lo-ki-li which rose lofty and compact like a single rock. Here Yin-ching had quarried for Nagarjuna, a monastery in the mountain and had cut in the rock, a path communicating with the monastery, for above 10 *li*. The monastery had cloisters and lofty halls. These halls were in five tiers each with four courts, with temples containing life-size images of Buddha, of perfect artistic beauty. It was well supplied with running water, and chambers were lighted with windows cut in the rock.

From the above description it is quite clear that the kingdom of Kosala was adjoining to Kaliṅga or the modern districts of Ganjam and Chicacole. The *Aihole Inscription* written in AD 634 of Chalukya king Pulakesin II, who was a contemporary of the pilgrim, also supports his statement.

गृहिणां स्वगुणैस्त्रिबर्गतुङ्गा बिहितान्य क्षितिपालमानभङ्गाः
अभबन्भु पजातभीतिलिङ्गाः यदनीकेन सकोष्ठालाः कलिङ्गाः

(*Aihole Inscription*, Sloka 26)

The *Nepal Inscription* of Jayadeva, dated AD 759 and the *Dasavatara Temple Inscription* of the Rastrakuta king Pantidurga, dated AD 755, mention Kaliṅga and Kosala as adjoining kingdoms.

माद्यद्दन्ति समूह-दन्त-मुसल-क्षुणरिभूभृश्रिरो
गौडोड्रादि कलिङ्कोशलपति श्रीहर्षदेबाम्तजा

(*Nepal Inscription* of Jayadeva)

दन्डै नैब जिगाय बल्लभबलं यः सिन्धुदेशाधिपं
काश्मीरं सकलिङ्ग कोशलपतीं श्रीशैलदेशैश्वरं।

But Mr. Cunningham wrongly identified Kosala with Berar and western part of C.P. which were far away from Kaliṅga and consequently placed its capital at Chanda, with Nagpur, Amaravati, or Ilichpur as alternatives. But the identification of Kosala and the location of its capital are unacceptable for the following reasons.

The Chinese pilgrim and the inscriptions quoted above clearly state that Kaliṅga and Kosala were adjoining kingdoms from very ancient times. But Berar, fixed as 'Kosala' by Cunningham, was far away from Kaliṅga and was never contiguous with it in any period of Indian history. Secondly, Berar or Gondawana has never been mentioned as Kosala in any ancient Indian inscription, or historical record. From very ancient times up to the time of Muslim rule in India, the Berar side of C.P. has never been called Vidarbha, Malava, or Avanti. Therefore, it will be a great travesty of truth to identify Kosala with Berar or Gondawana.

Thirdly, proofs adduced by Mr. Cunningham in corroboration of his statement are based on flimsy ground. He says:

> This (the identification of Kosala with Berar) agrees exactly with the position of Kosala described in the *Ratnavali* and the *Vāyupurāṇa*. In the former it is said, that the kingdom of Kosala is surrounded by the Vindhya mountains and in the latter, it is stated that Kusa, son of Rama, ruled over Kosola at his capital of Kusasthali or Kusavati on the Vindhyan precipices.

Mr. Cunningham's interpretation of the evidences produced from the *Ratnavali* and the *Vāyu Purāṇa* is very narrow. The Vindhya mountain is well defined by the modern geographers, but in ancient *Purāṇa*s and epigraphic records it is described in a general and vague way to have penetrated into the heart of Orissa. There are many female deities in the hilly and also in the plain parts of Orissa, which have the names like Vindhyesvari, Vindhyabasini, etc. So there is no mistake when the Sambalpur tract, which was called Kosala in the medieval age, is described by the author of *Ratnavali* to have been surrounded by the offshoots of the Vindhya range. Secondly, Kusasthali or Kusavati, mentioned as the capital of Kosala in the *Vāyu Purāṇa*, has been definitely identified with 'Kansil', a place on the Tel in the Patna State, is still adorned with venerable monuments of the past.

All the epigraphic records of the Vakatakas (contemporary of the Earlier Guptas), Saravapur kings and Soma kings of Sambalpur tract, prove beyond all doubt that the modern Raipur in M.P. and the Sambalpur district of Orissa, with the ex-feudatory states of Patna, Sonepur, and Bamra, formed the Kosala or Dakhina Kosala kingdom from the 3rd century BC up to the

15th century AD as all the villages and rivers mentioned in the grants of the kings of these dynasties are still existing in the Bolangir, Sambalpur and Raipur districts. Therefore, the Sambalpur tract which is just to the north-west of Kaliṅga was the Kosala kingdom in the 7th century AD.

The description by the Chinese pilgrim of the physical features of the southern portion of Kosala agrees well with the geography of the country, to the south of the Mahanadi. The high mountain, which he saw in the northern part of Kaliṅga, is the Mahendra Mala or the Eastern Ghat mountains which stretch up to Banapur in the Puri district. The pilgrim followed the route from Kaliṅga to Kosala which is still used for trade by the businessmen and to the south of which the present Vijayanagar-Raipur Rail line has been constructed. This road passed through the Agency tract of Ganjam by 'Baliguda', 'Mohangiri', 'Tusra', 'Dhanghara', 'Kansil', 'Sonepur' to Sambalpur and Raipur. The Chinese pilgrim followed this mountain route to go to the capital of Kosala and to Po-lo-mo-lo-ki-li, which undoubtedly existed in the Sambalpur area. Therefore, it is useless to locate the capital of Kosala in Chanda Nagpur, Amaravati or Ilichpur and Po-lo-mo-lo-ki-li in Ellora or Ajanta as the Kosala kingdom never extended beyond the Raipur district of M.P. Therefore, Po-lo-mo-lo-ki-li hill with its famous Buddhist monastery must have existed somewhere in the Sambalpur area. It is described as very lofty and without either spurs or valleys, so that it resembled a mere mass of stone. It was to the south-west of the country Kosala above 300 *li* (50 miles) from the capital. In this mountain King So-to-po-ho or Satabahana hewned a pavillion of five storeys, which was accessible by a rock-cut path, many miles in length. This dwelling was excavated for the holy Buddhist sage Nagarjuna. This monastery was well supplied with running water. This hill was also famous for its medicinal herbs. The description of the natural features of Po-lo-mo-lo-ki-li given by the pilgrim agrees well with the physical aspect of 'Gandha Mardan Hill' or Gandha-giri standing between the Bolangir and Sambalpur districts. This hill is described by L.E.B. Cobden Ramsay, the author of *Orissa Feudatory States' Gazetteer*, in the following manner:

> The north-western boundary of the Patna State is formed by the magnificent range of hills known as Gandhamardan which separates the Patna State from the Bora Sambar *Zamindari* of Sambalpur. On the northern crest of this range springs the famous spring which descends to the foot of the hill in fine water-falls and finally issues forth to the plains at Narasinghnath, a sacred place of pilgrimage in the Sambalpur district. On the southern slope a similar stream issues from the crest of the range and is known as Hari Sankar, in the Patna State. The crest of

> this range of hills is a fine plateau some ten miles long, with an average height of 3000 ft. and rising as high as 3234 ft. The principal rivers rising from this hill are the Tel, the Ang, the Suk Tel and the Sunder.

The Gandhamardan hill having a flat top running for miles, with perennial springs and water-falls on both sides, bearing the ruins of many historical and archaeological monuments and famous in the traditions of the country as a repository of medicinal herbs, is certainly identical with Po-lo-mo-lo-ki-li of Hiuen Tsang's account.

If we discuss the word 'Po-lo-mo-lo-ki-li', phonetically we arrive at the same conclusion. The Sanskrit equivalent of ki-li is giri (mountain), e.g., Pu-se-po-ki-li (Puspagiri), I think, Po-lo-mo-lo is the Chinese pronunciation of Pa-ri-ma-la. Po, lo, mo, and lo, are the Chinese pronunciations of the letters Pa, ri, ma, and la, respectively. Therefore, the Sanskrit name of this hill was certainly 'Parimala-giri' as it clearly represents every letter of the Chinese word. During the days of Hindu revival, this hill began to be called 'Gandha-giri' and the *Nrusimha Mahatmya* and other historical records and inscriptions describe the greatness and glory of this Gandha-giri. Parimala and Gandha (sweet-scent) being synonyms, it is quite natural that the all-assimilating Hindu reformers, in order to eclipse the glory and fame of the Buddhist Parimala-giri, named it 'Gandha-giri' when Hinduism re-established its supremacy in the Buddhist holy caves and monasteries. This Gandha-giri in course of centuries began to be called Gandhamardan hill, by which name it is still famous in the Sambalpur tract.

The Chinese pilgrim says that Po-lo-mo-lo-ki-li was famous for medicinal herbs, and the holy sage Nagarjuna who was a great physician gave a medicine to his patron, the Satavahana king which would have made him immortal. The Chinese pilgrim states this matter in the following manner:

> Nagarjuna Bodhisattva was well-practised in the art of compounding medicines; by taking a preparation (pill or cake) he nourished the years of life for many hundred of years so that neither the mind, nor appearance decayed. Sadvaha-raja had partaken of this mysterious medicine, and his years were already several hundred in number.

Strange to say, this Gandhamardan hill has been mentioned in the Oriya *Dāndi-Rāmāyaṇa* (AD 1510), and the *Sarala Mahābhārata* (AD 1460) and other *Purāṇas*, as a place which was famous for *Amar Ousadhi* or 'Immortalising medicine' since time immemorial, and Hanuman the monkey-leader brought this medicine for Lakshman, when he was made lifeless by the arrows of Indrajit. This shows that Gandhamardan hill is the Po-lo-mo-lo-ki-li of Hiuen Tsang's account.

The Satapoha, Sadbaha or Satavahana king very often mentioned by the pilgrim, must be Goutamiputra Sri Satakarni, a most powerful king of this dynasty whose mighty sway extended as far as Bengal and Bihar. It is known from his inscriptions and from other sources that he was a great patron of Buddhism like Asoka, and the Buddhist monuments at Amaravati, Joggaeyapeta and Nagarjunikonda and the caves at Ajanta clearly bear testimony to this fact. Nagarjuna in his book called *Suhridlekha* makes mention of a Satavahana king who has been identified with Goutamiputra Sri Satakarni. Therefore, this devout Buddhist king might have excavated a five-storeyed *vihāra* in the Kosala kingdom, which was under his subjugation, for the residence of his preceptor Nagarjuna.

It is very difficult under the present circumstances to trace the existence of this *vihāra* in the Gandhamardan hill as proper survey and exploration work have not yet been done either by the Archaeological Survey of India or by the State Department of Archaeology. But many Buddhist caves are still seen at different parts of this mountain. Tradition says that Bhima during the days of exile of the Pandavas built an impenetrable stone-house near this mountain. This is now called *Pathar-ghar* or 'Stone house' which may be an old Buddhist monument. The caves called 'Durgi khol', 'Bhim dambar', and 'Bharab khol' are still famous in this locality. The rock-cut path, communicating with the Buddhist monastery excavated in the Po-lo-mo-lo-ki-li, was discovered by the engineer of the ex-Patna State. This is like a tunnel and is hidden under dense vegetation. Many beautiful Buddha images, seated on lotuses and artistically carved are still found in the niches of the side-walls of this tunnel. This is undoubtedly the rock-cut path mentioned by the Chinese pilgrim. The discovery of this path in the Bolangir district to the south of the Gandhamardhan hill, indicates clearly that the rock-cut monastery of the Po-lo-mo-lo-ki-li was in the southern side of the Gandhamardan hill. Tradition says that Gandha-giri was called Vindhya hill before the sage Kapil began to reside here.

The hermitage of sage Kapil still exists in the southern foot of this hill. Perhaps the story of this sage Kapil was fabricated in the later period, to push the story of Nagarjuna to the background. Near this place 'Bana Durga Devi', called 'Bhairabi Devi' (perhaps *Mahayana* goddesses), are still found. Besides, a fort called 'Bhojgarh' which had a stone wall running for 9 miles on the top of the Gandhamardan hill is really a wonderful place of great antiquarian interest. All these clearly show that the Gandhamardan hill, which is full of ruins of ancient times, was surely a place of great historic importance in the past. There are also Buddhist caves at Titilagarh on the Kumdahills at a distance of 22 miles from Ranipur-Jharial in the western part of the district. The word Titilagarh is derived from the Sanskrit *Tritalagarh* (three-storeyed building). Titilagarh was a famous Buddhist centre in the past and is not far away from the Gandhamardan hill. Many Buddhist images have also been found in Kansil, the ancient capital of Kosala and in many other places of this region. All these Buddhist monuments indicate that the *Mahayana* form of Buddhism was once predominant in Patna area or Kosala.

The capital of Kosala was not at Chanda, Nagpur or Ilichpur, as ascertained by Mr. Cunningham but it was surely somewhere in the Sambalpur tract. The villages Ranipur-Jharial and Kansil of the Bolangir district, which are adjacent to one another, perhaps formed the capital city of Kosala in the time of Hiuen Tsang.

It is a general feature of ancient Indian history, that the centres of Jainism and Buddhism were transformed into Hindu holy places during the age of Hindu revival and renaissance. Similarly, the Gandhamardan hill with the temple of Hari Sankar on the south and Nrusinghanatha on the north, now attracts thousands of Hindu pilgrims of M.P. and Sambalpur tract and has become a famous place of pilgrimage in the north-western part of Orissa. The glory and magnificence of the Buddhist monastery of Po-lo-mo-lo-ki-li, which was a centre of Buddhist religion and culture for centuries, are now lost in deep oblivion. With the disappearance of the universal religion of Gautama Buddha, from the land of its birth, Po-lo-mo-lo-ki-li along with other Buddhist centres of ancient Orissa stood neglected and isolated in the grim solitude of the jungles and mountains, beyond the eyes of the research-scholars. It is the fond hope of the Oriyas that its own government, which must be the proudest in India for its glorious legacy of hoary-headed antiquities and venerable monuments, will render necessary financial assistance to the newly started Sambalpur University to take up a scheme for the archaeological exploration and survey of the Gandhamardan region in order to bring to light the once-famous Buddhist *vihāra* of the Parimala-giri or Po-lo-mo-lo-ki-li.

5

Art Heritage of South Kosala

A Study of the Extant Sculptures in Western Orissa

Sadhu Charan Panda

Art is not only a finer realization of the spiritual possibilities of human civilization, but also an authentic yardstick for measuring the socio-cultural life of the people of a locality through centuries of their existence. On this conceptual framework, the artistic achievements of the people of South Kosala strike one as being indicative of a superb and vibrant lifestyle in the background of an energized, tranquil world of hills and rivers, and informed by a rich cultural experience of long centuries dating back to prehistoric times. It is no wonder that, like Kaliṅga, which had the unique distinction of inducing Chandasoka to assume the personality of a Dharmasoka, the impact of the civilization of Dakshina Kosala transformed Samudragupta's passion for *Asurika Vijaya* into an impulse for *Dharma Vijaya*.

The earliest artistic activities of the region are found in the cave paintings of Gudahandi, Jogimath, Ghat Ghumar (Kalahandi district), Manikmuda and Ushakothi (Sundargarh district). The pictographic writing of Vikramakhol (Sambalpur district) is still considered to be the earliest in India, and the gigantic cave at Manikmuda (length 89.5 m, height 7.32 m, living space 11.50 m) is believed to be one of the largest in Asia. This area, like most parts of india, furnished artistic creations on perishable materials like mud, brick, reed and timber in the centuries preceding the Christian era. This is probably the main reason, apart from the vagaries of nature, wanton human vandalism and iconoclastic ill temper, why we find few antiquities of much earlier times in Western Orissa barring the artefacts excavated from certain sites of Kalahandi and Phulbani districts.[1]

Even though we come to know from the accounts of Hiuen Tsang of the existence of a renowned Buddhist *vihāra* at Po-lo-mo-lo-ki-li (identified with Parimalagiri in the Gandhamardan hill range located at the boundary of Sambalpur and Bolangir districts), there is no image available today except for a block of stone without shape and size conveying no iconic form. Maraguda Valley,[2] which abounds in archaeological remains dating from early times down to the nineteenth century, may, therefore, be taken to be the place yielding the earliest *Pratima* in Western Orissa in the form of a *Sakta* goddess seated on a lion in *Alidha* attitude. The image is awfully weather-beaten, and does not facilitate proper identification. But the *Sakta* shrine of the *Trishul* mound with various structural remains help us to confirm the image as a *Sakta* goddess, chiselled in the early part of the fifth century AD during the reign of the Nala king Bhavadutta Varman.[3]

The geographical location of Kosala has brought the four quarters of India to a pleasant meet in the fellowship of art and culture. In the domain of art and sculpture, the Kosalan artists displayed their close affinity with religious modes and sastric injunctions and exhibited their skill and finesse by introducing marginal features relating to local tradition. Though archaic art is rare, classicism and mannerism have found a lively expression throughout the length and breadth of South Kosala between 4th and 10th centuries AD. Boque, or the trend of profuse ornamentation and voluptuous physiognomy, does not appear to have become an obsession with the artists of this region in the early medieval period. The Central Indian art-tradition assumed a new significance and expression under the Kalachuris and their feudatories,[4] and the tradition of Dakshina Kosala with its classical idiom, transplanted itself in Utkal and eventually played a decisive role in the making of the art of Bhubaneswar and Mukhalingam.[5]

Sculptures are ornamental adjuncts which add charm and grandeur to the architectural structures and exhibit the conceptual manifestation of man's interaction with his surroundings. They may be constructive, decorative or representative. Constructive sculptures consist of pillars, pilasters, cornices, ceilings, podium moulding, etc. usually found in the temples; decorative sculptures include symbolic motifs like *Kirthimukhas* (*Baidynath, Chardā* and *Bāud*), *Kichakas* or *Bharavahakas*, *Gạnas*, *Vyālas*, *Gajasardulas*, *Naga* and *Nagis* (*Gandharadi*), *Gajakranta* (*Saintala*), beautiful floral designs, meandering scrolls, climbing creepers, leafy vines, nice lotuses, auspicious *Ghatapallavas*, and so on. Animals and birds form a group of decorative motifs. *Gajapithas*, *Arapithas* and *Narapithas* are the prominent decorations in the podium mouldings of the temples. Propitious birds and playful parrots, very naturalistically carved, also enrich the ornamentation in almost everywhere in Kosala. With wings raised a little, indicating attempted flights, they are depicted in pleasing postures. Parrots often figure as companions of indolent maidens called *Sukavilasa* or *Sukasarikā* as found in the temples of Baidyanath and Patnagarh. Besides, inorganic decorative motifs such as *Kumbha, Khura,* pedants, trellies and geometrical patterns also adorn the panels and sections of the temples in South Kosala.

Representative sculptures are found either in naturalistic manifestation, symbolically portraying hills, forests, rivers and villages, or in conventional ways through secular and religious forms. The secular figures meant primarily for ornamentation serve to indicate the levels of aesthetic perception and meaningful community existence. While the *Alasakanyās* exhibit a sense of fine delicacy in portraying and modelling the supple human frame, scenes presenting glimpses of the daily life of the common folk not only indicate the concern of the artists for their fellow beings but also portray the social acceptance of the means in everyday life by the royalty and the nobility.

SECULAR

A delightful lot of indolent maidens, *Nartakīs*, lovely dryads, and sylvan nymphs contemplated in several graceful postures and enchanting moods, with attractive coiffures, elegantly posed trunks and legs, fine drapery and shapely ornaments adorning the body are found in the different sections of the monuments. In the temple of Baidyanath and Chardā, there is a rich treasure of sculpture. Unfortunately, most of them have continued to lie in a bad state of preservation. The figures in the temple of Baidyanath have demi-medallions as canopies overhead, like those found in the Kharod temple. All the figures in these temples exhibit balanced proportions, careful carving and delicate modelling. Two of sculptures depicting *Sukasarikā* are found in the Kosalesvara temples of Baidyanath and Patnagarh. The image in the *mandapa* of the temple is in a *bhanga* pose with the body slightly filled swaying to the right side. The left hand, even though missing from the upper portion of elbow, and the figures in situ indicate the posture of being in akimbo. She is engaged in the act of removing the lower apparel as suggested by the raised right hand, holding one end of the drapery in a bunch. Her downward look is probably fixed on the parrot sitting on a wooden stand. The deliberate attempt of the lady to exhibit her vital parts and the rayed halo behind her head make the figure an unusual and curious composition of *Sukasarikā*. Almost an identical treatment is observed in the *Sukasarikā* figure in the temple of Patnagarh. Another figure in the said temple is the image of a *Nāyikā*, who, too, is shown as shedding her last garment. This sculptural piece, with its accentuated sensuous effect, remains one of the finest of its kind.[6] The *Sālabhanjikā*, in the *mandapa* of the temple of Baidyanath, is a fine specimen of sculpture portrayed in a supine pose against the tree, keeping negotiated steps with its flexibility. The attitude is stationary but the treatment reveals a potential dynamism. A very pleasing and attractive masterpiece of classical art is the *darpana*, carved in deep relief, on a pillar in the north balcony of the temple of Baidyanath. With an elegantly diminutive height, gracefully posed, fixed legs, and bent right-foot, a charming slender waist, plastic prominent abdomen, well-developed and resilient breasts, beautiful supple limbs, a round, haloed, contented face with a sweet smile embedded between sensuous lips, the figure holds a *darpana* (now broken) in the left hand while the right hand is arched naturalistically in the act of putting vermillion at the parting of the hair, on the head. The pose depicted is one of ease and relaxation and the treatment is tender and elegant with graceful flowing outline of the body and sloping shoulders. In another depiction on the south balcony of the Baidyanath temple, a female is carved standing at ease on the right leg below the tree, the left leg resting on the stem of the tree. The left hand holds one of the hanging leafy branches of the tree. Another female holding a baby on the waist by the right arm, standing beneath the tree laden with fruits, is drawing a branch by her left hand. By the help of the right forearm she is engaged in raising the right hand of the baby towards the fruit, perhaps to help the baby pluck the same. Behind her is a small figure of a female attendant. Such an image in *Tribhanga* is also noticed among the heap of sculptures at Belkhandi.

Numerous dancing damsels in a rich variety of dance poses are found embellishing the temples of Kosala. A dancing panel discovered at Maraguda Valley clearly demonstrates the artistic skill and musical taste of the people. The panel depicts two scenes. One of these scenes captures a lively moment just before a dance performance. The scene portrays in a telling manner the silent communication between the lady dancer and the male drummer. The lady, who is getting ready to dance, finally checks herself and firmly ties the jingling ornament – 'nupura' – on her ankle. The bearded drummer, who has stretched his hands to start beating the drum, takes note of the dancer's discomfiture and indicates her with a meaningful smile to be quick on the job. The dancer, obviously embarrassed, tilts her head to the right in such an angle as to cast a quick glance at the drummer imploring him to wait just for a while. The second scene shows a dancer dancing to the tune of a flute being played by a male.

*Mithuna*s (amorous/erotic couples) are an indispensable adjunct of the decorative scheme. In the earlier period amorous couples were much more in vogue than erotic couples. Sometimes the amorous couples present a harmonious blending of *Mithuna*s and *Sālabhanjikā*. A number of *Mithuna*s can be observed standing under shady trees where the girl is depicted pulling down a branch of the tree overhead and the male with amorous emotions writ large on his face, drawing the girl towards himself. The standing lovers in the *mandapa* of the temple of Baidyanath is a classic example of plasticity mended on stone. The girl with a luscious feminine body, delineated in the creeper-climbing pose, clinging to the torso of the male, encircles the neck of the male by her supple hands so that her left breast naturally appears to be peeping through her left arm-pit. The male delicately holds in his right hand the tender foot of the girl's raised left leg and by the palm of his left hand gives a soft support to the girl's hindhead from which flows down, on the back, a pretty plaited braid. The pair wear fine and transparent drapery, as indicated by the loin cloth of the girl in perfect position. The overall presentation convincingly portrays intimate embracing, caressing and kissing, but not the sex-act proper. 'Indeed,' comments Charles Fabri, "it would be false to call this an erotic image: this is not eroticism, this is loving tenderness, love in its full sense."[7] Such an image is also found at Belkhandi, but the portrayal is stoic and the treatment is rather crude and dishevelled.

Erotic sculptures depicting the primal instinct are not lacking in the earlier period. In small niches on the top of the shaft of the two pillars, nearest to the sanctum entrance, in the *mandapa* of the temple of Nrusinghanath, small male and female figures are found interlocked in the act of love. The riser of the sill of the door-frame, belonging to an old temple, but fixed at present to the varanda of the modern Chandi temple of Saintala, has its two extreme corners occupied by identical erotic couples depicted in the commonest pose of coitus. However, the erotic couples in quite obscene and with unabashed and naked realism as depicted in the Jain temple of Arang and the Bhoramdeo temple (South Kosalan territory at present in Madhya Pradesh), do not appear on any significant monument of this part of South Kosala.[8] The erotic motifs with such banal representations, like the woman's superior pose are as voluptuous and passionately sensual as their counterparts found in the Khajuraho temple and the Konark temple.

Other secular sculptures of Western Orissa beautifully depict contemporary life and reveal the versatility and acumen of the artists. Sculptures depicting both the nobility and the common folk not only highlight the available physical aspects during a specific period but also indicate the level of civilizing trends. Sculptures in the door-jambs of the temple of Saintala, among the loose sculptures at Belkhandi and in the railings of the balconies of the *mandapa* in the temple of Baidyanath specifically present before us the lifestyle of the tribals. In the upper portion of the railing in the north balcony of the *mandapa* there is the depiction of a robust man in loin-cloth, with broad chest and muscular hands. He holds a bow and arrows and is accompanied by his pet dog. This scene obviously indicates the common tribal activity of hunting. On the right side, there is a panel depicting one of the commonest activities of females in the rural areas. A female figure of well-built stature but only with a loin-cloth around her waist-line is holding a typical tribal winnowing fan in her left hand. A child is found standing on the right side. This depiction of domestic life is highly impressive, and if considered from the angle of the social set-up, it certainly suggests the importance of tribals in the then society. In another panel, a man is shown stretching out his legs to form a lap for his child to sit on. This panel indicates a common, tender, rural family scene. Such sculptural depiction of the common folk is rare but singularly vital to know about the ordinary people in rural areas who do not usually feature either in the epigraphs or in the literature sponsored by the elite and patronised by royalty.

Among the secular sculptures presenting classical idiom and perfect workmanship, mention may be made of the head and waist portion of a lady found from the precincts of Nrusinghanath temple and the Naga figure in round of the Maraguda Valley, at present kept in the Khariar Museum. The head with plaited hair and breaded hairbands has a devotional countenance glowing with inner satisfaction. The treatment of eyes, eye-lashes, the oval chin and thin lips are delicate and pleasing. The features are so lovely and sophisticated that one is led to believe that it might be the figure of a royal lady, may be Queen Vasata or someone like her. The torso with the waist-line is so proportionate and shapely that it prompts one to associate it with the above head. The Naga figure full of youthful exuberance and manly vitality with a pleasing countenance, roundish cheek, open eyes (not showing the exaggerated long slit that becomes habitual in the 10th and 11th centuries), and narrow chin is adorned with least ornamented *kundalas*. In both the ears, there are two necklaces of beads, plain armlets and bracelets and a *Yagnopavita*. The right hand with *Vijapurika* or a citrus on the palm in a giving position is placed upon the right thigh and the left hand with a close fist very stylistically (may be a variation of *Katyavalambita* pose) rests on the thigh near the knee. He sits erect without any garment in the upper portion of the body, with the raised chest characterising masculine vigour and dignity. He wears a *dhoti* covering both the legs and a separate cloth is bound around the waist-line with a knot below the navel. The hair in the head is well-combed and closely fitted with a netted cap. The entire figure, which is marvellously carved with meticulous care and fine sense of proportion, exhibits on close examination a gracious yogic posture.

With the above-mentioned features of the Naga figure, we find an art style exhibiting implicitly some of the features of the Classical Age in Indian art, and explicitly some of the features of the period of mannerism in the art and also a few features of the Baroque style in nascent form which blossomed to its full glory after AD 850. From the general make and physiognomical treatment of the body including the face, head-dress, manner of wearing clothes, the beads of the necklaces and the impressive countenance surcharged with inner feelings, one finds it having all the characteristics of post-Gupta sculptures but it is conspicuous with the absence of profuse ornamentation and accessories around the head, the marked and most dominant features of medieval sculptures. Therefore, the image certainly belongs to an age of transition when the classical tradition[9] of Gupta period was gradually changing and acquiring new characteristics of refinement, form, delicacy and normal manners. A broken piece of sculpture in the Dr. N.K. Sahu Museum, Sambalpur University, christened as a 'lady peeping through the window' is a marvellous representation of post-Classicism in Indian art and romantic poetic parlance. It appears that the *Abhisarika*, after a long wait, with her expectation mounting high, looks outside through a half-closed window, pressing her right breast on the dosed panel and clasping her right hand on the top of the panel.

An analytical enquiry into the art of this tract of South Kosala relating to secular presentation clearly reveals a robust synthesis of the real and the ideal, an integrated and inclusive vision of life rejecting the exclusiveness of urbanized culture. When one refers to the Vedic and the tribal cultures – the two fundamental sources of Indian culture – one realizes how the art of South Kosala represents the authentic mainstream of Indian tradition. It is further revealed how the secular urge of the artists of this region protected them from being merely hieratic hirelings, and made them function as creative historians of the ethos of the entire community. While the Kalingan craftsmen engaged in depicting patterned acrobatic feats, pilgrimage camps, battles and procession, the artists of this region nurtured a richer sense of earthness, a more inclusive and closer feel of the live reality and a fascination for ordinary existence by depicting the day-to-day activities of the original inhabitants of the hilly tracts along with the life of the urban elite. As a result, their artistic creations stand as a class by themselves discovering beauty in commonplace reality and projecting a healthier outlook on life, harmonizing the real and the ideal, and nurturing a comprehensive vision.

RELIGIOUS

Sculptures of the cult icons, their consorts, sons and attendants, the composite forms of deities, minor gods and goddesses, *Navagrahas*, *Yakshas*, *Gandharvas*, *Dikpālas*, *Vidyādharas*, *Chauri*-bearers and traditional and legendary scenes belonging to Vaiṣṇavism, Śaivism, Śaktism, Buddhism and minor religious cults are found in both figures in round and those adorning the different components of the religious shrines. Basically, they are depicted in accordance with the norms of iconography as known from different *Purāṇas*, *Śilpasātras*, *dhyās* and *ślokas* of *Malikas* and the like. Sometimes, variations do occur but such variations do not distort the concept; they rather help periodisation and cataloguing, and signify the school and the locality.

A number of Viṣṇu images in various emanatory and incarnatory forms are found in different parts. Unfortunately, most of them are damaged or defaced. Yet, a few remarkable figures are available in tolerably good condition and they in their present state of preservation, can rank with the finest of their kind in the country. Images of Viṣṇu generally conform to the iconographical features prescribed in Sanskrit works like the *Agni Purāṇa*[10] and *Rupa Mandana*.[11] The images have been carved in alto relievo out of a panel and are provided with haloes. *Sthānaka* (standing) images are four-armed with the usual Viṣṇu emblems, i.e., *Sankha*, *Chakra*, *Gada* and *Padma*. They wear fine drapery extending up to the knees. Their scarfs are worn across the shoulders, tied loosely around the waist or flowing down from behind through the upper arms. The Nilamadhava image in the Nilamadhava temple of Gandharadi has the scarf put across the chest and tied to a knot on the left shoulder. The images are adorned with *kirita mukuta* necklaces, *kundalas*, armlets, bracelets, girdles, anklets, *upavita* and *vanamālā* but usually the coronet is of conical shape in this region whereas they are usually cylindrical in the Madhya Pradesh region of South Kosala. However, the headgear of the Viṣṇu image of Nrusinghanath is typical: while we find either Sri and Pushti or Sri and Bhudevi or Sri and Garuda in almost all the images of Viṣṇu as attendants, the damaged Viṣṇu images of Saintala have Lakshmi on the right side and Saraswati playing the *vina* on the left. Images of Viṣṇu depicted in the recumbent pose exist in the temples of Charda and Sambalpur in usual iconic representation. Images of Lakshmi Narayan are also found in Belkhandi and Nrusinghanath. While the images of Belkhandi are mutilated, that of Nrusinghanath are a rare specimen. The figures in the niche on the outer wall of the *mandapa* of Nrusinghanath temple are depicted as sitting in *Lalitasana*. Lakshmi is found seated on the thigh of her consort and her right hand is put gently on the right shoulder of her lord and the other hand holds a stalked lotus bud. Viṣṇu has the shell inverted and placed vertically, with the discus and the mace in the right lower, right-upper and left upper hands, respectively. The fourth one encircles the back of Lakshmi, emerging out of her left arm-pit and gives by the open palm a tender touch to the underside of her left breast. Seated (*asina*) images of Viṣṇu are not so common in this area as standing ones.

Of the various incarnatory forms of Viṣṇu, the first two, namely, *Matsya* and *Kurma*, have generally been represented in theriomorphic form and find place in the *Dasavatara* panels of the door-jambs. The *Varaha* (boar) incarnations are found at Ranipur-Jharial and Nrusinghanath with a little variation of the common iconic representation. These figures do not clasp their hands on the chest, though their bent left hands support Bhudevi on their elbows. Images of the fourth incarnation, namely, *Nrusingha*, are depicted in the lion-headed human form. Images of the man-lion form without the demon are very rare. One of the earliest of such images is to be found in a small shrine at the rear entrance of the Nrusinghanath temple. The icon is standing erect on a pedestal holding the wheel, conch and the club in the right upper hand, left upper and left lower hands, respectively. The right lower hand is in the *Varadā Mudrā*. With a lion's head and static human body, the figure is found wearing high boots, usually found in early images. The mane is falling into tassels on the shoulders. The sublime countenance and the vision of the half-closed eyes fixed on the tip of the nose make the figure assume a yogic posture. This treatment is certainly meant to present the icon in a benign aspect. The figure may be called a variant of *Kevala Nrusingha*, which is not found elsewhere in the Kosalan territory. Portrayal of the *Vamana* incarnation of Viṣṇu in both the dwarfish and *Trivikrama* forms are found at Nrusinghanath and Sauntpur. The other incarnations of Viṣṇu do not have independent images of their own and are generally depicted in the *Dasavatara* panel as in the image at Saintala. Episodes from the life of Krishna such as Krishna and Balaram killing a demon, Kaliyamardan, Krishna's amorous and erotic sportings, etc. are found in the temples of Saintala, Baidyanath, Gandharadi and Sambalpur.

Śiva icons, in the form of the *linga*, are most common. *Linga* obelisks of various sizes and shapes are fixed to a square or circular or rectangular *yoni pitha* attached with a spout. The most significant and artistic shape of the *linga*s are with square column rising in an octagonal number and ending with cylindrical tops conveying the Hindu Trinity, namely, Brahmā, Viṣṇu and Śiva or Skanda. Devi and Śiva are found in Baidyanath, Gandharadi, and Baud. Śiva images, in the anthropomorphic form, representing various aspects of God, are generally found for decorative purposes. Nataraja, the most popular iconographic form of Śiva, standing on a pilaster in the *mandapa* of the temple of Charda draws one's attention as a beautiful piece of sculpture with the usual iconic form and sparse decoration. Śiva is presented here dancing on a fully blossomed lotus. The enchanting flexed limbs, the eyes closed as if in intoxication, the vivacious attitude, and the rhythm and sprightliness of the dance portray the God in his eternal passionate *tandava*. The image found recently at Deuli (Phulbani district) is chiselled so finely that it looks almost alive. The cult image, enshrined in the *mandapa* at the middle of the circular sixty-four *yogini* temple of Ranipur-Jharial, has three faces and is depicted in dancing pose, performing *Anandatandava*. With a serene countenance, the God appears to be absorbed in the dance.

Another form of depicting Śiva, that of portraying Him along with Parvati, popularly called Umā-Maheśvara, is found at Belkhandi exhibiting balanced proportions and perfect symmetry. The composite hermaphrodite form of Śiva and *Sakti*, representing the unity of the primal parents, is portrayed as *Ardhanarisvara*. Outside the *mandapa* of the Kosalesvara temple of Baidyanath, an image of *Ardhanarisvara* lies prostrate on the open ground. The image is broken and weather-beaten, causing disfiguration to the still discernible delicacy of a superb carving, flowing plasticity and pleasing dignity. The image found at Patnagarh is equally damaged but traces of fine workmanship are clearly visible in the treatment of pose, head and general make of the body. The elaborate coiffure, the fine drapery in their folds, and the charming face make the image a creation of master-craftsmanship that has absorbed the treatment of art in the post-Gupta period.

Sakta deities (*Sakti*) popularly referred to as *Devi* not only find representation along with Śiva or their make counterpart but also are portrayed independently. In her benign aspect, as the mother and the saviour, she is portrayed as Parvati, Simhavāhini, Mahisasuramardini and Sasthi. In the temple of Baidyanath is found a standing two-handed image with the right hand in the gesture of *Varada* and the left placed gently on the left thigh. The attendant stands on the right at waist height. The image looks exquisitely beautiful with the ornate girdle and jewelled tiara and proportionate bodily features. In the corner, to the right of the entrance doorway of the Somesvara temple of Ranipur-Jharial, a beautiful four-handed image of Simhavāhini Durga, seated on a lotus, has been kept independently. With an elegant tall tiara, *ratna kundala*s in the ears and a slender waistline, the figure looks imposing and worshipful.

The commonest form of *Devi* representing one of her terrific aspects is her depiction as Mahisasuramardini. A six-handed image, collected from

Belkhandi and preserved in the Dr. N.K. Sahu Museum of the Sambalpur University, has a vigorous pose, displaying her superior strength over the vanquished demon who is in a pitiable condition and has horrified looks. The image of Bhagavati, enshrined in the modern Bhagavati temple of Sonepur, identified with Panchāmvaribhadrāmbika, the tutelary deity of Suvarṇapur (Sonepur), and the image found at Durgei Khol between Sumergarh and Hamirgarh on the Gandhamardan hill near Nrusinghanath considered to be the tutelary deity of the Chauhans before their establishment at Patnagarh, are fine specimens of sculptures with a distinct touch of sophistication and elegance. The twenty-armed Mahisasuramardini from Salebhata, now kept in the Dr. N.K. Sahu Museum, is a fine composition but appears to be a variation of Chandika Chamunda, the fiercest manifestation of the *Sakta* goddess, which is noticed very rarely, that too in as crude a form as that of Deuli. *Saptamatrika* figures, which came to limelight as a result of excavations at Belkhandi,[12] are some of the best of their kind. The sixty-four *yogini* which are the various forms of the Divine Mother, find full-scale representation in the *yogini* temple of Ranipur- Jharial. Images of *Sakta* tantric deities are found in the Titilagarh-Khariar region of Western Orissa at Ghodar, Udepur, Bheiua Sikuan, Bamhni, etc. Most of them exhibit regional treatment and convey a decadent art style.

Images of minor deities like Surya, Ganesh, Kartikeya, Brahma, and Sarasvati are found at Belkhandi, Baidyanath, Charda, and at Dr. N.K. Sahu Museum with the prescribed iconic features in usual manner. Some composite figures like Harihar, Biranchinarayan, etc. are also noticed at Baidyanath, Salebhata, and other places. The Biranchinarayan image of Salebhata now preserved in the Patna State Museum, even though damaged, has a polished, smooth texture and conveys excellent original workmanship.

Images of Buddha are not that common in this area though Buddhism had flourished here from the beginning of the Christian era.[13] With the introduction of tantrism, Sahajayana evolved around the Tel Valley not caring too much for iconic considerations in the sculptural representation. However, the two images of Buddha at Ganiapali and a few images including that of a larger than life-size Buddha at Baud present before us knowledgeable acquaintance of the artists of this area with Buddhist iconography and exhibit a fine sense of proportion and idiom in chiselling the Buddha image. Two life-size (figure in round) Buddha images – the Muchchalinda Buddha and the other depicting Buddha in the pose of delivering the first sermon at Sarnath – are found on a small *mandapa* at Ganiapali. In spite of the ravages of nature and human vandalism, they still appear imposing and magnificent and have retained their classical touch.[14] While both the Buddha images are considered to be the earliest representations of Buddha in the plastic art of Orissa,[15] the Muchchalinda Buddha is considered to be the only one of its kind in the region of Eastern-India,[16] and in the art of India proper, similar images of this kind are but few in number.[17] Both the images are now in an eroded state, almost beyond recognition. They have been mended by some local artisan who has smothered out a good deal of the images, with fanciful cement coatings. The gigantic figure of Buddha, by far the best preserved, is seated on a full-blown lotus and is absorbed in deep meditation with an equanimous countenance. The panel consists of five slabs, carved with the various parts of the figure which are dressed together with perfect symmetry.

Images made of metals and wood are found at Baud, Sonepur, Barpali and Kadobahal areas.[18] Many of the images made of metal cast and that of wood are either votive or folk-depictions of traditional and conventional themes.

Art activities in South Kosala clearly manifest two diametrically different but major styles. In chronological sequence, the initial stage during the reign of Sarabhapuriya and Panduvamsis was followed by the Gupta classicism with elegant simplicity and sophistication in rational proportion of charming ovodial faces, slender waistline and naturalistically flexed poses. The other style contemporary with the Kalachuri phase portrays a mannerism which may be termed as 'Provincial' with

> limbs progressively lengthened, faces swelled and broad plump chest suddenly constricted downwards into an almost triangular waist containing a central lump at the coeliac region, below which are attached a pair of feet like stiff appendages.[19]

The artistic conception of the first phase was carried by the Somavamsis to the lower valley of the river Mahanadi and this shaped the distinctive Orissan culture,[20] while the second one could not become popular in Western Orissa. With the withdrawal of royal patronage of the Somavamsis and the careless handling of this territorial division by the Kalachuris and their feudatories, art activities in this area got a jolt and a slow process of decline set in. A decadent style with stereotype and repetitive postures, as noticed in the *yogini* figures of Ranipur-Jharial, appears to have continued till the Chauhans made a feeble attempt to revive the central pattern in art and architecture of Western Orissa.

Art, architecture and sculptures of this area assume great significance as an indispensable and authentic source for a proper study of life and culture of this region, as the artisans and craftsmen here refused to be followers of any canonical text or *Śilpaśāstra*. Comments Charles Fabri:

> There has never been a copyist, in this country (Orissa), never a mere imitation of other master's work. I know of no artist of ancient Orissa who ever followed the Silpasastra.

The heritage of art, on the basis of which Fabri so strongly claimed a separate identity for the artists of Orissa, had developed on the valleys of upper Mahanadi and its tributary Tel, during the post-Gupta period and was carried to the coastal plains by the Somavamsis who had originated as Panduvamsis in the 6th-7th century AD in Dakshina Kosala. In due course of refinement and proliferation, art ideals and aesthetics became more pronounced than the immediacy of lived reality, the quality which had imparted to the art of this area of South Kosala a marvellous distinctiveness. The sculptures of Western Orissa stand as a unique, incomparable creation, a still articulate witness to the glories of robust culture that had learnt the art of harmonious living, encompassing physical, psychological, aesthetic and spiritual urges within one undifferentiable totality.

NOTES AND REFERENCES

1. Excavations conducted by the P.G. Department of History, Sambalpur University at Asurgarh located at about five kilometres to the West of Narla Railway Station in Kalahandi district and at another Asurgarh located on the confluence of the rivers Mahanadi and Tel near Sonepur in the Phulbani district have yielded some terracota figurines. (Interim Excavation Reports, Sambalpur University, 1982.) A human head found at Nehna near Khariar (Kalahandi district) preserved in Khariar Museum also deserves mention.
2. Maraguda Valley is situated in the Nuwapara sub-division of Kalahandi district. It abounds in structural remains and artefacts belonging to a number of dynasties that ruled from there in between 4th to 14th centuries.
3. Sahu, N.K., 'Preliminary Report on the Excavation of the Trishul Mound in Kalahandi district', *Satavarsiki Smaranika*, Khariar Sahitya Samiti, 1983.
4. Mishra, R.N., *Sculptures of Dahala and Dakhina Kosala, and their Background*, Agam Kala Prakashan, Delhi, 1987, p. 8.
5. Panigrahi, K.C., *Archaeological Remains at Bhubaneswar*, Calcutta, 1961, p. 251.
6. Das, N.K., *Life and Culture in Medieval South Kosala* (AD 700 to AD 1100), Ph.D. thesis (unpublished), Sambalpur University, 1980, p. 351.
7. Fabri, Charles, *History of the Art of Orissa*, Oxford University Press, Calcutta, 1974, p. 34.
8. Yadu, H., *Dakhina Kosala ki Kala* (Hindi), Ramananda Vidhya Bhavan, New Delhi, 1990, p. 36.
9. Saraswati, S.K., *A Survey of Indian Sculptures*, Munshiram Manoharlal Pvt. Ltd., New Delhi, 1975, p. 141.
10. *Adhyaya* 48, 1-12.

11. *Adhyaya* 5.
12. *JRASB, Letters XIII*, pp. 63-74.
13. Mohapatra, K.N., *NAHO*, 1971, p. 31.
14. Panda, S.C., *NAHO*, Vol. III, 1981, p. 48.
15. Sahu, N.K., *Smaranika*, Sambalpur District Writers Conference, 1976, p. 4.
16. *Ibid.*, p. 5.
17. Ojha, R.P., *Monuments*, Lucknow, 1979, p. 43.
18. Images of Buddha made of bronze are found at Syamsunderpur, Baud. There is a good collection of icons of Hindu gods and goddesses in the Gundicha temple of Sonepur and Gopalji temple of Sambalpur. One old wooden image is preserved in the Dr. N.K. Sahu Museum. A number of wooden images depicting folk themes have been procured from different parts of Sambalpur and preserved in the Dr. N.K. Sahu Museum.
19. Dikshit, M.G., *Madhya Pradesh ke Puratattva ki Ruparekha* (Hindi), Sagar, 1954, p. 32.
20. Panigrahi, K.C., *op. cit.*, p. 253.

6

Western Orissa
The Homeland of Lord Jagannath

J.K. Sahu

A significant reference to Jagannath cult and temple is found in the oft-quoted verse of *Dasgova Copper-Plate Charter* of Rajarajadeva III (AD 1198).[1] It reveals three important things, viz., (i) that Gangesvara Chodagangadeva rebuilt the temple of Purosottama at Purusottama *kshetra,* (ii) that the temple was very much there before Chodaganga and was apparently built by a Somavamsi king, and (iii) that the kings before Chodaganga, i.e., the Somavamsi kings neglected the temple (*Aai-Nrupaih Upekshitam-Ayam-Chakretha Gangesvarah*). It is interesting to note that the first temple of Jagannath was built by a Somavamsi king but was much neglected by his Somavamsi successors.

Who was the Somavansi king? The *Madala Panji*[2] gives credit to Yayāti Kesari who is, no doubt, the Somavamsi king Mahāśivagupta Yayāti I (c. 890-925) of Kosala. It is described in the *Panji* that in the past when Raktabahu invaded the kingdom of Sobhanadeva, Lord Jagannath was shifted to Gopali near Sunupura (Sonepur) where he was worshipped in an open *mandapa* for 45 years and after that the deities were kept buried underground in fear of further invasion. The names of the kingdom and the dynasty of Sobhanadeva are not given in the *Panji.* K.C. Panigrahi[3] identifies Raktabahu with Rastrakuta king Govinda III and Sobhanadeva with Bhauma king Subhakaradeva I of Kosala. The invasion of Govinda III on eastern India took place in the opening decade of 9th century AD (c. AD 805) and as there was no other significant invasion during that period, the identification of Dr. Panigrahi stands unchallenged. The Rastrakuta invasion has been described in the *Sanjan Copper-Plate* as follows:

> that Vikrama (Govinda III) conquered the countries like Malava, Kosala, Kaliṅga, Vengi (?), Dahala and Odraka and placed his own agents in charge of those countries.[4]

The name of Kosala is not mentioned here. Dr. Panigrahi thinks that Odraka was probably Kosala. At that time Kosala, under the Bhaumas, had grown as a prominent power in coastal Orissa extending from Vaitarani to Risikulya. If Govinda III had conquered it, the poet must have mentioned its name along with Kosala, Dahala, etc. Odra, on the other hand, denoted the highlands of Central Orissa, extending from Keonjhar to Phulvani. Dhenkanal, Angul, Sambalpur, Sonepur, Baud, etc. were included in it. It is unfortunate that the history and culture of this region during that period have been neglected by scholars. The Bhanja rulers had established their supremacy over this region for a long period. Towards the close of 8th century, i.e., sometime before the Rastrakuta invasion, the Bhanja power had disintegrated and Odra country was split into two divisions. A new power, the Sulkis, established a semi-sovereign kingdom, the Kodalaka Mandala, in the Brahmin Valley of Angul and Dhenkanal with the help of the Bhaumas of Kosala when they owed nominal allegiance. After this Bhanja power was confined to Mahanadi Valley in Sambalpur, Sonepur and Baud regions and this new territory was known as Khinjali Mandala. Thus, by AD 800, the larger Odra country was known as Khinjali and the smaller Odra as Kodalaka. In the *Sanjan Plates,* the Kodalaka-Odra has been recorded as Odraka. Kanchana Stambha, the founder king of Kodalaka or his son Kula Stambha alias Kalaha Stambha faced the invasion of Govinda III and was dethroned. But the Rastrakuta hegemony there did not last long. Kula Stambha drove away the Rastrakuta agent of Vikrama Govinda and assumed the title of *Vikramaditya* as revealed in one *Dhenkanal Copper-Plate.*[5] B. Mishra while editing the plates says that Kula Stambha drove out a Savara chief named Dhekata. But in fact it was the Rastrakuta agent whom he ousted and assumed the proud title.

So, the Raktabahu invasion was, in fact, the invasion of Govinda III on Odraka-Kodalaka and it was on this occasion that Lord Jagannath was shifted from this country to Sunupura in Odra-Khinjali. It may here be noted that in many tantric texts Odra-Pitha has been described as a great tantric centre where Jagannath was worshipped as Bhairava. Although these texts are ascribed to 10th-11th centuries, they certainly preserve an earlier tradition. In *Kalika Purāṇa,*[6] it is stated that Odresa Jagannath (Lord of Odra) is worshipped in the western part of Odra-Pitha with Odresvari Katyayani. This tantric centre in the western part of Odra was probably located at Sambala of Indrabhuti, which has been identified with Sambalpur in the

Mahanadi by Dr. N.K. Sahu.[7] Some other scholars, however, think that Sambalpur is a modern town with no antiquities and they identify the centre with Samal near Talcher in Brahmani Valley where rich antiquities have been discovered in nearby places like Jagati, Vajrakot, etc.[8] Siddha Indrabhuti has confessed in his *Jnana Siddhi* that he obtained his *Vajrayana Tattva* due to the grace of Jagannath and whatever he was preaching belonged to the Lord.[9] Anangavajra, the preceptor of Indrabhuti, also has paid his reverence to Jagannath in his famous works.[10]

So in the first decade of 9th century AD, Jagannath was shifted probably from Sambhala in western Odra to Sunupura in the eastern part where he was kept hidden underground near Gopali. During this time the Somavamsis of South Kosala established their power in Western Orissa where they defeated the Bhanja rulers of Khinjali and occupied the Band-Phulvani regions along with Sonepur, etc. When King Yayāti was reorganizing the newly conquered Odradesa, he got interested to know where the spiritual Lord of the Odra king was kept hidden. On getting information he recovered the deities and had them newly built by the Daitas. The *Madala Panji* states that after this Yayāti installed the deities at Purusottama *kshetra*.[11] Historians believe that it was Puri *kshetra* on the sea-shore. Puri is the modern name of the holy place which at the time of Yayāti was lying unrecognized. It was then in the country of Kosala under the Bhaumas. It does not appear probable that the people of Odra or the king Yayāti himself would have desired to shift the Lord to such an unimportant place in an alien country. On the other hand, there is a popular local tradition that Jagannath was installed by Yayāti in Kotsamalai at the foot of Trikutaka hill near Biramaharajpur in Sonepur state, and the deities were worshipped there for many years before they were taken to Purusottama *kshetra*.

Now the question arises when and how the deities were shifted from Kotsamalai to Purusottama *kshetra*? Before this we must find out when this holy place came to be known as Purusottama *kshetra*. In this connection, our attention is drawn to the old temple of Nrisimha near the Jagannath temple. This temple which seems to be earlier to that of Jagannath was also built by a king of the Somavamsian or the Bhauma dynasty. Many scholars are inclined to ascribe the building of the temple to the Somavamsi king Yayāti I and his sister Prithvi Mahadevi who was married to the Bhauma king Subhakaradeva IV of Kosala.[12] Prithvi Mahadevi was the ruling queen of Kosala from about AD 890 to 895. In her royal charters, she is described as *Parama Vaishnavi*.[13] Although the Somavamsi kings were devout Shiva, Nrisimha Vishnu was worshipped in their harem as family god probably from the time of Vasata, mother of Balarjuna. The *Sirpur Stone Inscription*[14] reveals that Vasata was worshipping Nrisimha as Purusottama. After her, the cult of Purusottama Nrisimha probably continued till the time of Janamejaya and Yayāti. Prithvi Mahadevi took the cult to Tosala and built the temple of Purusottama Nrisimha on the sea-shore with the help of her brother Yayāti. After this, the place developed into a holy pilgrimage and was known as Nrisimha *kshetra* or Purusottama *kshetra*.[15] Thus, in the 10th century AD for about a hundred years, there developed Jagannath *kshetra* at Kotsamalai in Western Orissa and Purusottama *kshetra* on the sea-shore of Eastern Orissa.

After Yayāti I, his son Bhimaratha became king. During his time, the Bhauma rule came to an end and Tosala was annexed to the Somavamsi empire. Bhimaratha had two sons, Dharmaratha and Naghusa, who succeeded him one after the other. He had also three sons, named Indraratha, Bankaratha and Sankararatha, from an illegal queen named Durga.[16] Indraratha was intelligent, resourceful and ambitious. He was appointed by his brother as the governor of southern region (Kaliṅga) where he soon rose to be powerful. He aspired to become the king of Somavamsi empire. As he knew that he had no legal claims for it, he looked for an opportunity to use force. When Dharmaratha died and Naghusa became king, he invaded Yayatinagara complaining misrule and anarchy. Naghusa and his close relation Abhimanyu died in fighting and Chandihara, the son of Abhimanyu, fled to save his life. After this, Indraratha became the king of the Somavamsi kingdom in about AD 1000.

King Indraratha patronised the tribal people and their[17] tantric rites. The *Banpur Charter*, which is the only available copper-plate issued by him, was donated in favour of Khadiravani, a tribal deity. Very likely, the tantric trinity Jagannath of the tribal people of Odra attracted Indraratha who might have desired to build a special temple for the deities. In this connection, we remember that Indraratha was the only Somavamsi king who had no legal claim for the throne and occupied it by force with much bloodshed. We will presently point out that he was, thereafter, condemned by his Somavamsi successors and his works and achievements were ignored and neglected. This exactly tallies the description of the *Dasgova Plates*, discussed above, and on this basis we can say that Indraratha built the first temple of Jagannath at Purusottama *kshetra*. He probably persuaded the Daitas and Sevakas that the worship of Jagannath should be wide open by installing the deities in a holy place like Purusottama *kshetra*. He promised them that the rites and rituals of the deities would remain unchanged and even invited them all permanently to settle in the *kshetra* at the royal expenses so that they should worship and serve the deities as before.

So at last, Lord Jagannath was ceremonially taken from Kotsamalai to Purusottama *kshetra* where the deities were enshrined in a beautiful *mandapa* near the Nrisimha temple. Indraratha did not construct any *sikhara* in order to respect the sentiments of the tribal people. He also built the temple at Vimala on the south-west of the main shrine. Probably at the request of his queen, Vimala became the tantric consort (Bhairavi) of Jagannath.

Indraratha ruled from about AD 1000 to AD 1023. He was defeated and killed in the battle by the Chola king Rajendra Chola.[18] After this, Chandihara, who was then probably the only surviving heir of the Somavamsis, ascended the throne in the name of Mahāśivagupta Yayāti II. It was this Chandihara who had fled from his country to save his life after his father Abhimanyu and the ruling king were killed by Indraratha. So after becoming king he, Yayāti II, condemned Indraratha, tried to obliterate his name from the annals of the Somvamsis and ignored all that he had done during his race including the building of the temple of Jagannath at Purusottama *kshetra*. Yayāti II also built the gigantic temple of Lingaraj Shiva to challenge and check the growing popularity of Jagannath temple.

Although denied of royal patronage, the popularity of Jagannath could not be checked and the glory of the God spread far and wide. The typical images of the deities, the tantric rites and rituals and the non-Brahmin Daitas and Sevakas had a special attraction for the pilgrims. Gradually, there developed an idea that it was Lord Jagannath, and not Lord Nrisimha in the nearby temple, who represented the Purusottama *kshetra*. The Brahmin priests and *pandit*s were unhappy with these developments.

Towards the end of the 11th century AD (about AD 1095), Ramanujacharya, a great Vaishnavite saint, visited Purusottama *kshetra* and condemned the peculiar forms of the deities and the tantric rites of the non-Brahmin priests. He was shocked to know that Jagannath in that form was regarded as Purusottama by the pilgrims and common people. He felt helpless and desired to reform the mode of worship in the light of *Pancharatra* cult. He found it difficult and sought the help of the Somavamsi king Karnadeva. The king was indifferent probably because being a devout *Shaiva*, he did not like to patronize directly a Vaishnavite saint. Being disappointed, Ramanuja went back to Andhradesa.[19]

Chodagangadeva, the Ganga king of Kaliṅga, occupied Utkala by defeating the Somavamsis about AD 1108. Ramanuja influenced Chodagangadeva through Virachoda, the father-in-law of the king, to reform the cult of Jagannath.

Thus, Chodaganga was the first king after the fall of Indraratha to take interest in the long-neglected Jagannath temple. He renovated the old *mandapa* and built on it a beautiful *sikhara*, higher than that of Lingaraj temple. The *sikhara* contained twenty-four types of images of the four-handed Vishnu at the lower *Jangha*, the images of ten incarnations at the upper *Jangha*, the three *Parsva Devatas*, viz., Varaha, Nrisimha, and Trivikrama, the four Garuda images at the upper *Raha-Paga*, and the images of child Krishna in different places. Chodaganga converted the temple at Jagannath to a beautiful shrine of Purusottama Vishnu. But here, he made a halt. He did not dare to change the deities which had been worshipped for centuries by the tribal and common people. He enshrined them on the *Ratna Simhasana* without any change. He also wanted to change the mode of worship gradually and not overnight. Because of this Chodagangadeva was criticized by Brahmin *pandits* as a tantric king. The *Madala Panji*[20] described him as a discipline of Nitai Dhovini and as Randipua Chodaganga. Subsequently, however, the system of worship was reformed and the Brahmin priests acquired the sole right to worship the deities in Hindu ways whereas the Daitas were relegated to the background.

From that time, the non-Brahmin Daitas have been given prominence only on two occasions, i.e., the *Anasara* period which occurred annually and the *Nava Kalevara* which occurred occasionally. Every year, on the full-moon day of *Jyestha* (June), the deities take annual bath and then they suffer from fever for a full fortnight. This period is known as *Anasara*.[21] During this period, the Daitas take utmost care of the deities with the belief that some bereaved members of their family are suffering. The Brahmin priests avoid the Lord in this difficult period. In the time of Navakalevara, it is the Daitas who build the main idols of the deities with utmost care following the traditional *Silpashastra*. With this, they get the satisfaction that the Lord belongs to them. The old idols which are considered as dead bodies are handed over to the Daitas who bury them and perform funeral rites for twelve days in Hindu way as if some member of their owner family were dead. Here also the Brahmin priests remain unaffected. We get here a clear evidence that Jagannath in fact belongs to the tribal Daitas whose ancestors in the past had brought the Lord to Purusottama *kshetra* from Kotsamalai.

Before concluding, we shall give here an interesting evidence from the Kalachuri record, the *Bilhari Stone Inscription*[22] of Yuvaraj II (c. AD 985).[23] Describing the achievements of Lakshmanaraja (AD 945-970), father of Yuvaraj II, the inscription states that he (Lakshmanaraja) conquered the king of Kosala and obtained an image of Kaliya of the Odra king (Odra Nripateh). The image was bedecked with gold and jewels. He then performed the worship of Somesvara apparently at Ranipur-Jharial. This took place sometime after AD 950 when the Somavamsis were at the height of power with the whole of Odra and Kosala merged in their empire. The Odra king was no more by that time but Jagannath, who is described in the

Madala Panji as the god of Odra king (Odra-rajankara Prabhu), had been installed at Kotsamalai under the patronage of the Somavamsis. At that time the Somavamsi power had extended to Bilaspur region in Chhattisgarh and although the Kalachuris coveted for the Pali region[24] near Sirpur, they dared not to invade the Kosala kingdom till about AD 1000. Then Kalachuri kings of that time were known to be devotees of *Mattamayura Shaiva* cult. The temple of Somesvara Shiva built by Gagana Shiva, from Mattamayura saint at modern Ranipur-Jharial, was then a renowned centre of that cult in Kosala.[25] It appears that Lakshmanaraja went there as a pilgrim and this was later eulogized as conquest in *Bilhari Inscription*. The king of Kosala on that occasion probably presented the Kalachuri king an ornamental replica of Jagannath, the god of Odra king. At that time also Jagannath was being painted in black colour and was affectionately known as Kalia among the devotees. Kaliya of the *Bilhari Inscription* is in fact Kalia Jagannath of Kotsamalai. The same god is still worshipped today on the *Ratna Simhasana* of Puri temple.

With all these evidences, we can say with certainty that Western Orissa was the homeland of Lord Jagannath.

NOTES AND REFERENCES

1. 'Dasgova Copper Plate', *EI*, XXXI, p. 249.
2. Mohanty, A.B. (ed.), *Madala Panji*, U.U., 1969, p. 4.
3. Panigrahi, K.C., *History of Orissa*, 1986, p. 79.
4. *EI*, XVIII, p. 244.
5. *JBORS*, II, p. 412.
6. Shastri, Vishwanatha (ed.), *Kalika Purāṇa*, Varanasi, 1972, Ch. 64, Verse 44, p. 475.
7. Sahu, N.K., *Buddhism in Orissa*, U.U., 1958, p. 147.
8. Vide Article of M.P. Dash in *Sakta Samskrutira Itibrutti* (in Oriya), ed. Orissa Cultural Forum, p. 6. Also Harihara Kanungo, *Vivartana Dharara Sri Jagannath* (in Oriya), pp. 260-61.
9. *Jnana siddhi*, 1st Canto, Verse 1 and 2.
10. Sahu, N.K., *op. cit.*, pp. 46, 48.
11. Mohanty, A.B. (ed.), *op. cit.*, U.U., 1964, p. 4.
12. Stietencron, H.V., *Advent of Vishnuism in Orissa*, 1986, pp. 12-13.
    Sahu, J.K. (ed.), *Nava Kalevara* (Oriya), p. 49.
13. Vide the two Boud Charter of Prithvimahadevi, *EI*, XXIX, pp. 22 ff.
14. 'Sirpur Stone Insc.', *EI*, XI, pp. 184 ff.
15. In Ch. XVI of *Purusottama Mahatmaya*, it is described that *Purusottama kshetra* was also known as *Nrisimha kshetra* in the beginning.
16. Vide Banpur Copper-plate of Indraratha, *JASB*, VIII, No. 4, 1966, pp. 271 ff.
17. 'Tirumali Insc.', *EI*, IX, pp. 283 ff.

18. Sahu, J.K., *Odisa Itihas*, Vol. I, pp. 167-68.
19. This tradition has been found mentioned in *Ramanuja Divya Charutai* and *Prapanamarta* (vide P.K. Mukherjee – *The History of Medieval Vaishnavism in Orissa*, 1940, pp. 27-28 and also in *Madala Panji* (*op. cit.*, pp. 49-50) in which Ramanuja has been mentioned as only Acharya and not by name. The date of his visit to Orissa being controversial, we have given our view.
20. 'Madala Panji', *op. cit., Rajbhaga Itihasa*, Chodaganga.
21. The period is also known as *Anavasara* (vide the Article of G.C. Tripathy, p. 223, Ch. XIII) and the article of A. Eschmann (p. 112, Ch. IV) in the *Cult of Jagannath* and the *Regional Traditions of Orissa*.
22. 'Bilhari Stone Inscription', *EI*, I, pp. 256 ff.
23. We follow here the book of R.K. Sharma *Kalachuri and their Times* for dates.
24. Low region was the territory around modern Ratnapur in the Bilaspur district of Chhattisgarh.
25. Vide the 'Insc. of Gagana Shiva in the Somasovara temple of Ranipur-Jharial', *EI*, XXIV, p. 239, edited by B.C. Chhabra, p. 239.

7

Recent Epigraphical Discoveries in Western Orissa

Sadananda Agrawal

Epigraphy is a pedantic term for inscriptions, or say, study of old inscriptions. An epigraph is a writing incised or engraved on a hard substance like stone, metal, wood, bone, ivory, terracotta and so forth. Again the term epigraphy usually applies to an old writing of this nature having some historical importance. Epigraphy in India has proved to be the very backbone of history, especially for the early and medieval period of any region. The epigraphical records offer valuable historical information not available from any other source and as such they play a major role in reconstructing the political and cultural history. Sometimes the discovery of important epigraphical records furnish some conclusive evidence on certain problems of history that have been baffling scholars since long. In this paper a brief note of recent epigraphical discoveries from Western Orissa, with their historical significance, has been given.

RANIPUR-JHARIAL COPPER-PLATE GRANT

This *triphali tamrasasan* was unearthed by two cultivators while ploughing their paddy field in villages Ranipur-Jharial in the year 2002 and was secured by Sri Mojiramjee Jain of Kantabanji. He was kind enough to lend the charter to me for decipherment and I am going to edit the same from the original, which will also be published elsewhere.

This charter belongs to Somavamsi king Janamejaya Mahābhavagupta who flourished during the second-half of the ninth century AD. Several copper-plate charters issued by Janamejaya are already known their total number being fourteen, and this charter adds to the total which now stand enhanced to fifteen. The importance of the charter lies in the fact that this

Fig. 1. General view of Ranipur-Jharial plates.

so far happens to be the only copper-plate grant issued by a king discovered at Ranipur-Jharial site, which occupies a prominent place in the archaeological map of India, housing the sixty-four *Yogini* temples and a cluster of other temples. This charter has been stated to be issued from Aramapati's *Vijaya Skandhavara* (lines 6-7) during his 16th regnal year on 7th day of bright half of *Bhadrapada* (lines 45-46). The following charters of Janamejaya have been issued from Arama: (a) *Gaintala Plates of Janamejaya* (R.Y. 17),[1] (b) *Sonepur Plates* (R.Y. 17),[2] and two sets of *Chaudwar Plates* (R.Y. 34).[3]

The gift village is called Tunkela situated in the *visaya* of Ksitimandapadhara (lines 9-10). Tunkela may very well be identified with modern Tukla near Khariar, situated at a distance of hardly ten miles (in straight way) from Ranipur-Jharial, the find-spot of the charter. The *visaya* or district Ksitimandapadhara is found mentioned in the *Nehna Plates* of Sarabhapuriya king Sudevaraja[4] and *3rd Gopalpur Charter* of Janamejaya.[5] Regarding the identification of Ksitimandapadhara, Prof. A.M. Sastri has expressed his inability to identify it.[6] But this author had located the *visaya* in Khariar region.[7] Now, our present record provides definite clue that Ksitimandapadhara comprised the modern Khariar and Ranipur-Jharial regions. Kosighosa, son of Ballabha Ghosa, the scribe of our charter, has been designated as *Mahapancadhikaranadhikrta* (lines 46-47). This Kosighosa has served under Janamejaya from the very beginning of his rule and has composed the draft of the charters issued in his 1st,[8] 3rd,[9] 6th,[10] 10th,[11] and 12th[12] regnal years. It is worth mentioning here that in all the previous records he has been designated as *Kayastha*, attached to the office of Mahasandhivigrahi. The word *Kayastha*, which now denotes a caste, was originally a professional term connoting a clerk or scribe in an office. It is used in all Somavamsi records in connection with their drafting. The expression *Mahapancadhikaranadhikrta* denotes an officer who judges five tenets, i.e., *Visaya, Samsaya, Purvapaksa, Uttarapaksa*, and *Nirnaya* as prescribed in *Mimamsa* and *Vedanta*. It is significant that in no other Somavamsi record of Orissa such designation is met with. Perhaps, Kosighosa was in-charge of a tribunal-like office.[13]

In this charter Brahmin Sadharana has been eulogized. It is averred from the extant records of Janamejaya that Sadharana occupied a high position in the Somavamsi administration at least from the very beginning of Janamejaya's reign and was a staunch adherent of Vaishnavism. The *2nd Gopalpur Charter*[14] tells us that Sadharana had erected a shrine dedicated to God Vishnu in his *Jala-sayana (sesasayi)* form. It is pertinent to note in this context that not only Janamejaya but all the Somavamsi kings ranging from Janamejaya to Karnadeva, without a single exception, were devout devotees of God Shiva. Our present charter lends some viability to presume that the Vaishnavite Indraratha brick temple was constructed by Sadharana. It is worth quoting here that a beautifully carved *Anantasayi* Vishnu sculpture was shifted from Ranipur-Jharial and was fixed on the outer wall of the Collector's Res. Office at Balangir by the then Collector A.N. Tiwari in the year 1969.[15]

TATARKELA CHARTER OF SILABHANJADEVA

Another most important copper-plate grant belonging to Silabhanjadeva of Khinjalimandala with the headquarters at Dhrutipura has recently been discovered from the village Tatarkela, situated near the village Bausuni of modern Boud district on the river Mahanadi.[16]

The present charter is of inestimable value for several reasons so far as the history of the Bhanjas (Dhrutipur Branch) is concerned. Firstly, this so far happens to be the only complete set of copper-plate grant belonging to Silabhanjadeva and provides some definite clue to reconstruct the genealogy of Bhanja dynasty which ruled from Dhrutipura. In this charter three verses contain the genealogy of the dynasty and mention two ancestors of Silabhanjadeva, namely, Angadi and Satrubhanjedeva (lines 3-12). Silabhanjadeva of our present charter seems to be the predecessor and brother of Ranabhanjadeva. He is known to us by a large number of copper-plate grants and ruled the kingdom for the maximum number of years as his last known record is dated in his 58th regnal year. After scrutinizing the extant records of the dynasty we have reconstructed the genealogical chart as follows:

Fig. 2. General view of Tatarkela Charter of Silabhanjadeva

1) Silabhanjadeva *alias* Angadi

2) Satrubhanjadeva *alias* Gandhata *alias* Nettabhanjadeva

3) Silabhanjadeva II (Issuer of the Tatarkela and Orissa State Museum plates)

4) Ranabhanjadeva

Earlier, Dr. Snigdha Tripathy has published another set of copper-plate grant of Silabhanjadeva[17] issued in his 11th regnal year. Unfortunately, the first plate of this charter is lost and Dr. Tripathy takes Silabhanjadeva, issuer of this charter, as the founder of the dynasty. But our epigraphical common sense would tend to suggest that the beginning two lines of the second plate were the continuation of the matter relating to the introduction of the predecessor/s of the issuer of this charter. It is pertinent to note here that both the charters have been engraved by Pandi, son of Gona. It may safely be concluded here that both the charters belong to Silabhanjadeva II. The above view of Dr. Tripathy is not at all tenable.

It is revealed from *Madras Museum Plates*[18] that a person named Seda purchased a village situated in the kingdom of Narendra Dhavala from King Silabhanjadeva. It is worth mentioning here that the Madras Museum Record has been stated to be engraved by Padmanabha, son of Pandi (engraver of present charter). Padmanabha was an inhabitant of Gandhatapati (modern Gandharadi near Boudh) and had also engraved two sets of copper-plate grants issued by Ranabhanjadeva,[19] the immediate successor of Silabhanjadeva. So, we are inclined to identify Silabhanjadeva mentioned in Madras Museum Record with Silabhanjadeva II, issuer of our present charter. It is worth noting in the present context that the *Madras Museum Plates* are a *Kraya-Sasana* (sale-deed) and executed by Seda to resale the same to three persons after some years of his purchase from Silabhanjadeva. D.C. Sircar[20] and N.K. Sahu[21] and others conjecture to identify him with Silabhanjadeva, the founder of the dynasty which, after the discovery of present record, is not tenable.

The inscription begins with the auspicious symbol of *siddham* followed by the well known Vaishnava sectarian formula *Om Namo Bhagavate Vasudevaya.* The donor of this charter is Sri Sangramamahadevi, evidently the queen of Silabhanjadeva. The grant purports to record the gift of the village Tatarkela included in Dakhinapalli. It can very well be identified with the modern village called Tatarkela situated in between Sonepur and Boudh on the south bank of river Mahanadi. Extant records of this dynasty reveal that two districts, i.e., Uttarapalli and Dakshinapalli have been formed comprising the Birmaharajpur (north side of Mahanadi) and Boudh region (south side of Mahanadi), respectively. River Mahanadi was the dividing line between the above two districts. The notification of the grant states that the village in question was donated in favour of Lord Vasudeva and learned Brahmins through *Hundis* on the auspicious occasion of *Uttarayna Samkranti* during the 19th regnal year of the king.

RASTRAKUTA CHARTERS

Discovery of two Rastrakuta copper-plate grants from the village Teresingha on the river Tel throw welcome light on the medieval history of Kosala. The first set has now been preserved at Manikyapuri Museum, Bhawanipatna, the headquarters of Kalahandi district. I am highly obliged to Sri G.P. Nanda, former Chief Commissioner of Income Tax, who extended all the facilities to edit and publish the same.[22]

This set consists of three plates held together by a circular ring. Its ends are secured under a moving and detaching seal, which is not soldered in usual fashion. Except the first plate's first side, other sides are serially numbered. The charter belongs to Dhakkarisaradeva, who has been designated as *Paramamahesvara-Rastrakuta Vamsodbhava Kulatilaka.* While Sri Vallini Mahadevi, the king's mother *(Matasri),* is the donor, the donee is Brahmin Bhatta Narayandeva, son of Bhatta Samanaga. In this charter the occasion of the grant has been mentioned as *Rathasaptami,* which appears to be most significant so far as the religious history of the period is concerned. At the present state of our knowledge, we may say that in no other Orissan epigraphic record the term *Rathasaptami* has been applied for *Magha Sukla Saptami.*[23] The seventh *tithi* of the bright fortnight of *Magha*, called *Ratha Saptami,* is sacred to the sun for its form is believed to have been revealed to the gods on this day. It is regarded as holy as the day of an eclipse and a gift made on this day is regarded as very meritorious.[24] The gift village is called Gosthapataka, which defies identification. The charter has been issued from Udayapura, which may certainly be identified with modern Udepur/Udayapur near Titilagarh of Bolangir district. J.D. Beglar[25] who

Fig. 3. Seal of Teresingha Plates of Bhanudeva

Fig. 4. First Plate, Teresingha Plates

visited Udayapur area during his tour in 1874-75 has left a graphic account of this area. Between the hillock Kumra and river named 'UNDER', there are four important villages called Kumra, Sihini, Udayapur, and Ghodar. All the places contain ruins and standing temples assignable to 8th/9th centuries AD. The ruins of an old fort are still to be seen on the bank of a small stream at Udayapur.

The upper part of the seal contains the figure of a *Garuda.* Below the figure there is a legend in one line which represents *Sri Vallini.* At the bottom, the form of a lotus with one set of petal is carved.

The numerical figures have not been written according to the decimal system of writing numeral.

The second set of copper-plate grant,[26] *Teresingha Charter of Bhanudeva* has also been reported to be found from the village Teresingha.

The charter belongs to Bhanudeva, who has been described as *Maharaja* and *Paramamahesvara.* Surprisingly neither the names of his parents nor the name of the dynasty to which he belonged is mentioned in the charter. But the seal bears the name of Dhakkarisara. Undoubtedly, this Dhakkarisaradeva, a scion of Rastrakuta dynasty, has been referred to in the *Manikyapuri Museum Plates*. It is worth noting in the present context that the donee, composer, engraver and place of issue of both the charters are identical. It is not a new thing in Orissan epigraphical records that the same king is known by two names. Dhakkarisaradeva and Bhanudeva may be equated with certainty.

The notification of the grant tells us that the villages called Tilasringa (modern Teresinga) and Koniyaralla (yet to be identified) were granted in favour of Brahmin Narayanadeva on the occasion of *Visuva Samkranti* during the 25th regnal year of Bhanudeva.

One pertinent problem of history that has been baffling the scholars since long is: ' Who were the builders of the monuments of Udayapura?' To quote P.C. Ratha:

> With definiteness it can be said that these monuments were pre-Chauhans as well as pre-Nagas. Thus it appears the ruling dynasty or the people who constructed these monuments do not exist now. With their disappearances probably worship in the temples has seized.[27]

The two Rastrakuta records lend some viability to conclude that the Rastrakutas were the builders of these monuments who flourished during the first-half of the ninth century AD.

It is averred from the *Sanjana Plates*[28] of Rastrakuta king Amonghavarsa that his father Govinda III (AD 793-817) had conquered Malava, Kosala, Kaliṅga, Dahala, Banga and Odraka and made his servants enjoy them. Mirashi holds that the Rastrakuta monarch did not depose the ruling princes of these countries, but brought them under the control of the military generals or agents appointed by him in their capitals.[29] So it is quite possible that the Rastrakutas entered Kosala with Govinda III and there is ground to believe that some of the generals of the Rastrakuta origin might have settled in Tel River Valley. During early 1978, another set of copper-plate grants belonging to the Rastrakutas[30] was discovered from the village Degoan (Tarbha) of modern Sonepur district. In this charter Mugdhagondaladeva acknowledges the over-lordship of Somavamsi king Janamejaya Mahābhavagupta who flourished during the second-half of ninth century AD. The gift village is called Kirankela situated in Telatalla *visaya*. We have identified Kirankela with the modern village of Kinerkela, on the river Tel in Kesinga P.S. of Kalahandi district. The *visaya* named Telatalla seems to have been named after the river Tel being located by the sides of it. This Telatalla *visaya* finds mention in a couple of charters[31] belonging to Yayāti Mahāśivagupta I, the son and successor of Janamejaya.

These Rastrakuta charters clearly disprove Sircar's[32] suggestion regarding the advent of Rastrakutas into Orissa in the train of the eastern expedition led by Calukya Vikramaditya VI during eleventh century AD.

A RARE SHAIVITE SEAL

One rare seal has been discovered from the village Nehena, near Khariar of Nuapada district. The same has now been preserved at Khariar Palace by Raja J.P. Singhdeo.

The upper part of the stone seal contains the emblems of a bull and trident which invariably represent Shaivite faith. There is a legend in one line in the lower part of the seal. The seal is divided into two parts by a couple of horizontal lines. The legend reads: *Saivaramesvarasya.* It means: '[The seal] belongs to the chief of Shaiva monastery.'

Fig. 5. Shaivite seal discovered from Nehena

The inscription has been engraved in negative fashion, so as to produce the legend in relief when impressed on the intended objects. We have edited the same from the original with the help of a mirror. Sri Singhdeo was kind enough to allow me to prepare the estampage, which has been reproduced here.

No internal evidence is available from the seal to determine its date. Palaeographically, it may be assigned to sixth century AD. At the present state of our knowledge we may say that this is the only Shaivite seal discovered as yet in Orissa indicating the monastic activities. This rare seal throws welcome light on the religious history of Kosala belonging to 6th/7th centuries AD. It is pertinent to quote here that the excavator of Maraguda Valley (Nuapada district)[33] has discovered the archaeological remains of a Shaiva monastery, attributed to fifth century AD. They also report the discovery of a seal containing a legend in one line which reads *Dhimatisvara.* To quote N.K. Sahu:[34]

> This monastery consisting of temples, residential buildings and recreation grounds with parks and orchards, is a gigantic complex built in five tiers. The antiquities recovered by excavation – coins, seals, icons, architectural style, etc. clearly indicate its time which is not later than the fifth century AD. This is the earliest Hindu monastery so far known in India and the name of one of its chancellor as found from this seal was Dhimatisvara.

Unfortunately, neither the photograph of the seal is published nor its present whereabout is known.

The inscriptions discovered from Western Orissa play a significant role to reconstruct the history and culture of Orissa in general. It is a desideratum that these should be edited chronologically and published by the Sambalpur University for the convenience of the scholars and interested readers as well.

NOTES AND REFERENCES

1. *Orissa Historical Research Journal (OHRJ)*, Vol. XI, No. 3, pp. 192 ff.
2. *Epigraphica Indica (EI)*, XXIII, pp. 248 ff.
3. a. *EI*, III, pp. 325 ff.
   b. *PJASB*, LI, 1882, pp. 9 ff.
4. *EI*, IX, pp. 170-73 ff.
5. *OHRJ*, Vol. XXXIX, pp. 133 ff.
6. Sastri, A.M., *Inscriptions of the Sarabhapuriyas, Panduvamsins and Somavamsins*, Vol. II, 1995, Delhi, p. 30.
7. Agrawal, S.N., *History of Sonepur*, Vol. II (Oriya) Bolangir, 1989, p. 123.
8. *OHRJ*, XXXIX, pp. 94-118.
9. *EI*, XI, pp. 93-95 ff.
10. *EI*, III, pp. 340-44 ff.
11. *OHRJ*, XXXIX, pp. 119-132.
12. *Ibid.*, pp. 133-146.
13. *Manak Hindi Kosa*, Vol. I, Prayag, 1991, p. 75.
14. *OHRJ*, XXXIX, pp. 119-32.
15. Vide a letter dt. 18.4.03, written by Sri A.N. Tiwari to this author.
16. Agrawal, S.N., *Two Copper-plate Grants from Western Orissa*, Menda, 2001, pp. 1-15.
17. *OHRJ*, XLV, pp. 14 ff.
18. *EI*, XXVIII, pp. 44 ff.
19. a. Sonepur Grant, *Journal of Bihar and Orissa Research Society (JBORS)*, VI, pp. 481 ff.
    b. Baud Grant, *ibid.*, XX, pp. 147 ff.
20. *EI*, XXVIII, p. 46.
21. Sahu, Mishra and Sahu, *History of Orissa* (2nd edn.), Cuttack, p. 130.
22. Agrawal, S.N., *op. cit.*, pp. 16-23 and plates. The paper was first presented in National Seminar on Aspects of Orissan Sculpture and Epigraphy (2-4 January 1996) held at the Dept. of Special Assistance in History, Utkal University, Vanivihar, Bhubaneswar.
23. Sahu, Mishra and Sahu, *History of Orissa*, p. 84, opine that the second Chicakole grant of Ganga king Indravarman III had been issued on the occasion of *Rathasaptami*, which is not tenable.
24. *Corpus Inscriptionum Indicarum*, IV, Pt. ii, p. 619.
25. *Archaeological Survey of India*, XIII, p. 183.
26. We have not yet availed the opportunity to examine the original plates. We have edited the plates from the photographs and eye-copies supplied by Baba Mishra and Dasrathi Acharya. The text has been published in *Kalajharan* - 2003, Bhawanipatna and a brief note has been published in *The Youth World*, Bolangir, Issue No. 19, October 2003.
27. *Journal of Kaliṅga Historical Research Society*, Vol. I, p. 103.
28. *EI*, XVIII, pp. 235 ff.
29. Sahu, Mishra and Sahu, *op. cit.*, p. 168.

30. *Journal of the Orissa Research Society*, No. 3, 1985, pp. 29 ff.
31. *Journal of the Asiatic Society Bengal* (New Series - 1905), Vol. I, pp. 7-12 and 16-23 ff.
32. *EI*, XXX, p. 138.
33. a. *Centenary Souvenir of Khadiala Sahitya Samiti*, Khariar, 1983, pp. vi-ix.
    b. Patel, C.B., *Dynastic History of Nalas*, Calcutta, 1990, pp. 200-01 and 264.
    c. Tiwari, A.N., *Reference Orissa*, Bhubaneswar, 1999, p. 146.
34. Sahu, N.K., 'Report of Archaeological Excavations in the Upper Jonk Valley in Nawapara Subdivision of Kalahandi district', (Orissa), in *Centenary Souvenir of Khadiala Sahitya Samiti*, p. viii.

8

Early Historic Urban Centres in the Tel River Valley, Orissa

Baba Mishra

I

Academic investigation to understand the ancient Indian cities date back to 1915. The early inquiry on this subject was primarily based on architectural cannons and traditional accounts. From 1972-73, however, investigation on early urban centres of India in archaeological perspective have been noticed and ample number of studies on urban centres and urbanization in early historical perspective of India, have been published.

However, works dealing with the towns and cities of ancient India makes casual reference to the early urban centres of Orissa. Brief description to Sisupalgarh and Jaugad are only discerned in plethora of research works hitherto published. Very recently, Indian archaeological society, New Delhi and a handful of scholars have harboured this subject in Orissan context for their study. As such, some preliminary reports/investigation on early urban centres of Orissa, like Sisupalgarh, Radhanagar, Jaugad, Manikapatana, Asurgarh (Narla), Asurgarh (Manamunda), Kharligarh, Budhigarh and Maraguda, etc. have come to light in the recent past.

Literary sources, moreover, reveal the existence of towns and metropolis within greater Kaliṅga, such as Kanchanapura, Simhapura, Dantapura, Tosali, Andhakapur and Teri Nagari or Rajya, etc. Epigraphic reference from 1st century AD moreover vouchsafe the existence of Kalinganagari, Sarabapura, Samapa, Tosali, Parvatadvaraka and Puskari, etc. in early medieval Orissa. Foreign testimonial, particularly the account of listing, Ptolemy and later on Hiuen Tsang, etc. refer to Che-li-Talo, Kongyu-to and Palour, etc. which were seat of royalty and port town of Orissa during the ancient and early medieval time.

The present paper, a preliminary study, is mainly concerned with a small geographical entity, Tel River Valley (south-west Orissa), where had been located at least four urban centres of early historic as per South East Asian archaeological parameter as well as of traditional Indian nation of town and city.

GEOGRAPHICAL LOCATION OF THE TEL VALLEY AND ITS URBAN CENTRES

River Tel is a major tributary of the river Mahanadi, which flows through modern Nowrangpur, Kalahandi and Bolangir districts of Orissa. The small rivers like Moter, Hati, Rahul, Sagada, Salund, Ret, Inder and the Suktel, etc. join river Tel at one point or another. The valley area, thus, encompasses the following four nuclear zones of Kalahandi,[1] Bolangir, Nuapada, Koraput-Navarangapur districts of Western Orissa and the Deobhogh region of Chhattisgarh state, viz., (i) the valley area comprising part of Navarangapur, Junagarh, Dharamgarh, Jaipatna and stretching up to Deobhogh of Chhattisgarh state, (ii) Komna zone (Nuapada district), (iii) M. Rampur, Risida, Narla and Kesinga (Kalahandi district), and (iv) Titilagarh and Sonepur-Boud (Bolangir-Sonepur districts).

These zones are interspersed by thick forests and undulated mountains. The said valley, moreover, had served as a bridge between Central India and South India. Preliminary investigation of this geographical entity has revealed the existence of the following urban centres: Asurgarh (Narala), Asurgarh (Manamunda), Kharligarh, and Budhigarh. These sites and their antiquities unfold the characteristic features of urbanism in early historic time.

II

FACTORS OF URBAN GROWTH

No doubt, the cultural process of proto-historic period gave way to urbanization in Orissa.[2] Preliminary archaeological exploration of the Tel Valley has already yielded Neolithic-Chalcolithic Iron Age cultural phase. Antiquities belonging to the proto-historic period of the valley are rich and varied. Agriculture, supported by settled community life, was converged with technology and trade during the period in between 2700 BC to 600 BC. This phase may be marked as a prelude to urban growth in the Tel River Valley.

Sixth century BC was a landmark for religious upheaval and territorial integration in ancient India. Nevertheless, Kaliṅga Janapada or greater Kaliṅga, to which the Tel Valley belonged, did not find place among the list of sixteen *Mahajanapada*s noticed in the Anguttara Nikaya. Kaliṅga and its neighbouring territories were however prosperous and were being paid glowing tribute in the Brahmanical, Jain and Buddhist literatures. At last from the 4th-3rd century BC archaeological evidence pertaining to the urban growth in the Tel River Valley has been fathomed.

Crystallizing factor of the urban growth is nonetheless a perplexing issue. Investigators of the subject have hitherto propounded some general criteria[4] for the development of towns and formation in South East Asian context like independent growth, process of colonization and political development. Allchin further adds the underlying causes of urbanization like population growth, technogical advance and agricultural surplus,[5] etc. The archaeological remains of the Tel Valley interestingly purport the above hypothesis of Allchin. Inception of craft specialization and advent of metallurgy in the Tel Valley has been documented in proto-historic and early historic context. In metallurgical sphere, the beginning of iron technology provided extra power to men. Jungles were cleared and more lands were brought under cultivation. Increase of population might be another factor of urban growth. Archaeological work in Kalahandi and Bolangir districts during the sessions 1999-2000, 2001-02 unveils the existence of a plethora of settlement sites, which lends credence to population growth.

The proposition of regional and political development and rise of feudal chieftainship[6] as primer mover of urbanization also seems to be applicable in case of the urban centres of the Tel Valley. We have epigraphic evidences pertaining to the political gravity and emanation of feudal chieftainship from two urban sites, located within the Tel Valley, viz., (i) inscribed seal-cum-pendants from Budhigarh[7] and (ii) *Allahabad Prasasti* which refers to King Vyagraraja of Mahakantara.[8] The former seal-cum-pendant (two types), dated 2nd century AD, mentions the performance of Vedic sacrifice,[9] by the king or chief for the welfare of his subject.[10] It betokens the political development as well as feudal chieftainship at Budhigarh. The latter epigraphic records adumbrate the defeat of King Vyagraraja of Mahakantara during 4th century AD, by the Gupta monarch Samudragupta.[11] Although the dynastic name of King Vyagraraja is not mentioned in the *Allahabad Inscription* of the Gupta monarch, yet it is certain that he was the overlord of Mahakantara kingdom which encompassed modern Kalahandi, Koraput and Bastar regions.[12] Asurgarh (Narla), exhibiting its strong fortification and rich antiquities, tends to demonstrate it as the capital city of the Mahakantara[13] territory, at least during the 4th-5th century AD. It thus shows that Asurgarh urban centre was the nucleus area of Mahakantara state and Budhigarh was its periphery region ruled respectively by the chief and his feudatory. At the same time, this model unveils horizontal expansion of urbanization in the Tel Valley. Also, the process of urbanization in the region was greatly influenced by internal and external trade. Literary sources and archaeological data are found in happy convergence at this point. *Astadhyayi* of Panini[14] (4th century BC) alludes about Taitilaka-Janapada, which was a major commercial centre noted for the exportation of rhinoceros hide. Taitilaka-Janapada has been rightly identified with Titilagarh,[15] a small town of the Tel Valley. Archaeological record, moreover, substantiate the above contention. *Arthasastra* of Kautilya[16] (4th century BC) further reveals a landmass known as Indravana from where precious diamonds were collected for Maurya treasury. In the South East Asia *Atlas*[17] however, Indravana has been identified with the region located in between the rivers Tel and Indravati. Needless to point out that, in the geological map of India, Kalahandi, Bolangir and Koraput districts are reckoned for the deposit of precious gemstones including diamond.

In addition, the archaeological record of Kalahandi proves beyond doubt that the commodities of high quality, such as a gate-bowl, knobbed ware, northern Bengal polish ware, precious and semi-precious stone beads and pendants, and stone of Ashokan polish, bilingual script Kharoshti-Brahmi, emboss on the seal-cum-pendant of Budhigarh, speak volume on inter-regional contact must probably through trade during the 2nd century AD.[18]

Man and environment relationship has been postulated by scholars for urban growth. According to Dhavalikar,[19] however, favourable climate was the basic factor of second urbanization.[20] The climate was congenial in the old world from about 5th century BC to 5th century AD.[21] The period witnessed the rise of empires and prosperity in different parts of the world. In Pan-Indian context, the Mauryas, Sungas, Satavahanas, Kushanas and the Guptas emerged. India witnessed at that time the growth of urban centres in all her major geographical regions.[22]

BASIC TRAITS OF URBANISM IN EARLY HISTORY

The basic traits of urbanism have been a debatable issue in South East Asian archaeology. V.G. Childe[23] enumerates ten traits of urban revolution, like magnitude of settlement, accumulation of capital, monumental public work, cultivation of science like arithmetic, geometry and astronomy, foreign trade, craft specialization, ruling class, state organized society and naturalistic art, etc. Whereas, R.J. Braidwood[24] characterized urban culture in eight ways like food production, cities, urbanization, formal political law, formal project and works, class hierarchies, writing monumental architecture, and art.

Amidst regional diversity, however, one should prefer polytheist criterion of urbanization, i.e., to consider the presence of certain features, but not necessarily of all to define the 'city' of 'Urban Centre'.[25] It has been, therefore, pointed out that refined pottery, sophisticated terracotta, granaries, coin, coin mould, etc. indicate urbanism.[26] On the other hand, classical Indian texts like Pali and Sanskrit outline rampart, moat, gate, wall, bastion, shop, trade, etc. as basic features of early urban centres.[27]

In the Tel Valley, however, urban centres like Asurgarh, Kharligarh, Budhigarh and Manamunda-Asurgarh have fulfilled these criteria of urbanism in the early historic context. They had witnessed the process of second urbanization. The spurting of these towns were due to indigenous development, yet the impact of alien forces in the course of their growth cannot be ruled out. Typology of the sites reveal that towns developed on the river banks, crossing of highways and on the confluence of rivers.

III
URBAN CENTRES

Asurgarh (Narla)

In the Tel River Valley, there are more than one Asurgarh, out of which one is located in Kalahandi district between Rupra Road and Narla Road Railway Station. Asurgarh fort, almost quadrangular on plan, has four gates, one on each side. The rampart measures about a kilometre in length. The fort is circumscribed by a deep and wide moat of 50 x 25 metres.[28] Close to the western rampart, however, river Sandul flows towards the north to meet the river Tel. Towards the north-west corner of the fort faint traces of a bridge are still visible. The said bridge was constructed to divert the water of the Sandul[29] to fill the north-west side moat of the fort. On the eastern side of Asurgarh, there was formerly an extensive water reservoir of about 200 acres of land, popularly known as Udit Sagar (also called Asurgarh). The water of the reservoir was primarily intended to fill the moat. Thus, Asurgarh reveals a unique system of water management during the ancient time. Limited excavation of Asugarh in 1973[30] and subsequent survey of the site[31] have yielded rich antiquities like sandstone pieces of Ashokan polish, wide spectrum of ceramic including NBPW (inferior variety), punch-marked coins, Kushana coins, glass bangles, terracotta figurines, four-legged saddle squerns, fragment of agate bowls, semi-precious stone beads, glass beads, coin mould, gold ornaments, iron implements of war and peace, circular brick structure, tile, brick and faunal remains, etc.

BUDHIGARH

This site is located towards the east of Madanpur village, which is about 20 km from M. Rampur of Kalahandi district. The ruins of Budhigarh cover an area of 1000 m x 506 m in north-south direction on the left bank of the river Rahul.[32] The location of Budhigarh, moreover, was on the salt route range, which was running from Utkala and South Kosala and hence to South India.[33] It was the strategic location of Budhigarh, which seems to have contributed towards the rise of township in the early historic period. The fortification of Budhigarh site is indistinct at present. Budhigarh's archaeological site, however, has revealed a spectrum of ceramics including the deluxe ware like northern Bengal polish ware. Some of the sherds of Budhigarh contain graffiti of early historic period; the others are decorated. In addition to semi-precious stone beads, glass and copper beads, glass bangles, iron objects, four-legged saddle squerns, ornament moulds, punch-marked coins, worn-out silver coins, gold coins, terracotta figurines, smoking pipes, tiles, chert seal-cum-pendant embossed with symbols and bilingual script (Kharosthi-Brahmi), chert ear-stud, faunal remains, tiles and bricks were also found. The latter measures 18" x 2" x 4". Artefactual evidence of the site, however, indicates that it was occupied at least from Iron Age to pre-Medieval period.

KHARLIGARH

Kharligarh is located at a distance of 1 km from the confluence of the rivers Tel and Rahul. It is about 10 km distant from Tusra town of Bolangir district.

The fort area, however, is about 150 acres and is protected on three sides by the river Rahul in a 'U' shape.[34] The other side (western) is protected by a rampart made of brick and stone. Inside the fort area, debris of brick and rubble are found. There are many mounds, big and small, within the fort.

There is a single gateway in the middle of the high wall on the western side. Different sizes and texture of bricks were used for construction. The common brick size, however, measures 11/2 feet x 1 feet x 4 inch (thickness). Bricks are fire-baked and prepared of well-levigated clay mixed with paddy husks. Outside the fort area, mounds are spread in a parallelogram, covering a wide tract of land. Moreover, on the left side of the river Tel, there is also an archaeological site known as 'Dhamagarh', which seems to be the granary of the Kharligarh urban centre.[35]

Antiquities of Kharligarh are rich and varied. On January-February 2001, a vertical excavation of Kharligarh was conducted by the P.G. Department of History, Sambalpur University[36] and the excavation report is in the process of publication. Artefacts of Kharligarh hitherto collected in course of the survey consisted of copper punch-marked coins, glass bangles, semi-precious stone beads, four-legged saddle squerns, iron tools, tiles, black and red ware, black slipped ware, red ware, grey ware bearing cord, applique, grid, and roof design, etc. Kharligarh has also revealed for the first time the earliest specimen of *linga* and *yoni* or votive *linga* in conjoint manner.[37] This finding lends substantial support to the development of *Shaiva-Sakta* creed in ancient Orissa. On the basis of its antiquities, the date of Kharligarh urban centre may be determined from the 2nd century BC to 5th century AD.[38]

Asurgarh (Manamunda)

It is located on the confluence of the river Mahanadi and the Tel River in the Baud, Sonepur region. Archaeological remains of Asurgarh (Manamunda) were first reported by R.D. Banerjee in 1929, who had ascribed the site as one among the 'Asura settlement'.[39]

Modern Sonepur town, which is located in close proximity to Manamunda, has been designated as Pachhima Lanka in the copper-plate of Somesvaradeva, the governor of the Somavamsi king Udyota Kesari, during the last quarter of the 11th century AD.[40] The *Mahada Plates*[41] of Somesvaradevavarman of the same period further refer to the topography in the vicinity of Lanka (*Lanka vartaka Sanidhau*).

These prima facie evidences led Prof. H.D. Sankalia and his school of thought to postulate Manamunda-Sonepur as Lanka of *Rāmāyaṇa* in 1980-1981. Subsequently, the archaeological excavation at Manamunda-Asurgarh was undertaken under the joint efforts of the Department of Archaeology, Deccan College, Pune and the P.G. Department of History, Sambalpur University in February 1981. This excavation exposed two brick structures, which were two sections of the rampart of the fort. Two trenches were laid, however, at that time, which had yielded sherds of NBPW (inferior variety), black grooved ware, black red ware and a circular brick structure.[42]

This small-scale excavation of Manamunda did not expose Ravana's Lanka of the epic. Nevertheless, the excavation unravelled the existence of fortified township in the Tel Valley, which was at least about 2000 years old.

The next phase of the excavation of Manamunda-Asurgarh was conducted in 1983 and 1990 by the P.G. Department of History, Sambalpur

University. The excavation has revealed the material culture of Manamunda-Asurgarh from 3rd century BC up to the 3rd century AD.[43] Material remains of this site chiefly consisted of ceramic assemblage, graffiti on pottery, punch-marked coins, semi-precious stone beads, iron implements, terracotta objects, tile and brick, etc.

DE-URBANIZATION

These urban centres of the Tel River Valley were disintegrated by the beginning of 6th century AD. The Chinese pilgrim Hiuen Tsang, in the early part of 7th century AD, was curiously silent about these towns and metropolis. On the other hand, Hiuen Tsang refers to the capital city of South Kosala identified with Maraguda urban centre,[44] located in the Jonk River Valley of Nuapada district. Thus, by the beginning of the 7th century AD, sites like Asurgarh (Narla), Budhigarh, Kharligarh and Manamunda-Asurgarh had lost their pristine glory.

It is a complicated task to evaluate the process of urban decay at the present state of our knowledge. Future research in this sphere will bring a cohesive detail of their decline and fall.

NOTES AND REFERENCES

1. Senapati, N. and D.C. Kuanr, *District Gazetteer of Orissa*, Kalahandi, Bhubaneswar, 1980, pp. 7-8.
2. Basa, K.K., 'Neolithic and Post-neolithic Cultures of Orissa: An Overview', in S. Pradhan (ed.), *Orissa History, Culture and Archaeology*, D.K. Print World, New Delhi, 1999, p. 27.
3. Mishra, B., P. Mohanty, D. Mishra and D. Acharya, 'The Mesolithic and Post-Mesolithic Culture of Jamuguda Padar: Dist Kalahandi Orissa', *Man in India*, Vol. 82 , Ranchi, 2002, pp. 43-54.
4. Allchin, F.R., 'Early Cities and States beyond the Ganges Valley', in F.R. Allchin (ed.), *The Archaeology of Early Historic South-Asia*, Cambridge, 1989.
5. *Ibid.*
6. Raychaudhury, H.C., *Political History of Ancient India*, Calcutta University, 1953.
7. Mohanty, P. and B. Mishra, 'Seal Matrix of Stone Bead of Budhigarh', *Puratattva*, Vol. 30, 2000, pp. 158-159. Also see, B. Mishra and M.P. Singhdeo, 'Unique Seal of Budhigarh', 2002, *Puratattva*, Vol. 32, New Delhi, pp. 152-154.
8. Sahu, N.K., *Utkal University History of Orissa*, 1964, Vol. 1, Cuttack, pp. 370-372.
9. Mishra, B. and M.P. Singhdeo, *op. cit.*, Vol. 32.
10. *Ibid.*
11. Sahu, N.K., *op. cit.*, 1964.

12. Behera (ed.), *Interim Excavation Report*, P.G. Deptt. of History, Sambalpur University, 1982, pp. 4-7.
13. *Ibid.*
14. Cited by A.C. Mittal, *An Early History of Orissa (From Earliest Times up to First Century* BC), Banaras Hindu University, 1962, p. 105.
15. *Ibid.*
16. Kangle, R.P. (trans.), *The Kautilya Arthasastra*, Book-II, Ch. II, Delhi, 1992, p. 115.
17. Eskwartzberg (ed.), *A Historical Atlas of South Asia*, Chicago University, USA, 1978, p. 16.
18. Mishra, B., M. Brandtner, P. Mohanty, and P. Yale, 2001. 'Urbanization and Trade in Early Historic Perspective of the Tel River Valley'. Seminar paper presented in the National Seminar on Archaeology of Eastern India at Konark, @001, CDI Project, Utkal University.
19. Dhavalikar, K.M., 'Environment: Its Influence on History and Culture in Western India', *Indica*, Vol. 33, No. 2, 1995, pp. 81-118.
20. Indus valley urban centres have been hailed as first metropolis or first urbanization in India. The subsequent urbanization which began in the Gangetic valley from at least 6th/5th century BC are known as second urbanization in Ancient India.
21. Dhavalikar, *op. cit.*, 1995.
22. *Ibid.*
23. Childe, V.G., 'The Urban Revolution', *The Town Planning Review*, No. 21, 1950, pp. 1-3.
24. Braidwood, R.G., *The Near-East and the Foundations for Civilization Oregano*, 1950.
25. Tripathy, D.N., *Archaeology and Tradition*, New Delhi, 1985, p. 86.
26. Sharma, R.S., *Urban Decay in India*, Delhi, 1987.
27. Bhattacharyya, T.P., *The Cannons of Indian Art*, Calcutta, 1962.
28. Deo, P.K., 'Forgotton Forts of Kalahandi' (Reprint), 1995, Part-1, *Orissa Historical Research Journal*, Vol. XIV, No. 2-3, Bhubaneswar, pp. 29-60.
29. Mishra, B. and P. Mohanty, 'The Tel River Valley Civilization (From Pre-History to Early Medieval)', 1998. Seminar paper presented in the National Seminar on River Valley Culture of India, by IGRMS, Bhopal.
30. Behera, S.C. (ed.), *op. cit.*, 1980, pp. 1-7.
31. Mohanty, P. and B. Mishra, *Early Historic Kalahandi in Orissa Revisited* (edn.) P. Pal, Marg Publication, Mumbai, 2001, pp. 17-26.
32. *Ibid.*
33. Acharya, P., 'Ancient Routes of Orissa', *Journal of Indian History*, LIXI, Part 1-3, 1981.
34. Mohapatra, R.P., *Archaeology of Orissa*, Vol. 2, New Delhi, 1986, pp. 221-222.
35. *Ibid.*
36. Prof. Sadasiva Pradhan was the director of this excavation project. His excavation report is in the process of publication.

37. Such type of *Linga* and *Yoni* in conjoint manner was first unearthed from Veerapuran excavation in 1984. The excavator has designated this object as votive *linga* and assigns the period 2nd century AD (See T.V.G. Sastri, M.K. Bai and J.V.P. Rao, 1984, *Veerapuram – A Type Site for Cultural Study in the Krusna Valley*, Hyderabad, p. 171).
38. Das, R.N., 'The Iron and other Objects from Gudaveella and Kahrligarh', *Journal of the Orissa Research Society*, Vols. 1, 2, 1982, pp. 53-58.
39. Nanerjee, R.D., 'Antiquities of Baudh State', *Journal of the Bihar and Orissa Research Society*, XIV, 1929, pp. 64-86.
40. Rajguru, S.N., *Inscription of Orissa*, Vol. IV, Bhubaneswar, 1966, pp. 268-275.
41. Behera (ed.), *op. cit.*, 1980, p. 17.
42. *Ibid*.
43. Mishra, C.R. and S. Pradhan, 1989-1990, 'Excavation at Manamunda, Dist: Phulbani', *Indian Archaeology*, New Delhi, 1989-1990-A, pp. 80-86.
44. Patel, C.B., 'A Brief Note on Maraguda Archaeological Project', *Orissa Review*, Vol. XLIX, No. II, Bhubaneswar, 1993, pp. 34-39.

9

Contribution of Guru Ghāsī Dās to the Rise of Satnāmī Cult in Chhattisgarh Region of South Kosala

Biswajit Pradhan

Like the Mahimās of Orissa, the Satnāmīs represent the poor lower class community in the area boardering Western Orissa. The area of their habitation is confined to Chhattisgarh with which the people of Western Orissa have close social association. The tradition of the Satnāmī faith came from Oudh region. Guru Ghāsī Dās is regarded as the proponent of this sect in between AD 1820-1830. There are many legends and miracles centring around him to influence the people's mind. He was a great social reformer.

The Satnāmī movement was a social revolt on the part of the lower class *Chamārs*. The fundamental tenet of the gospel of Ghāsī Dās appears to have been abolition of caste and, with it, the authority of the Brāhmaṇas. It provoked a bitter and permanent antagonism between the two Hindu classes – the caste Hindu landlords and the *Chamār* cultivators. The spread of Christianity among the *Chamārs* was in one respect aided by the Satnāmī movement, as a *Chamār* hoped also to throw off the social stigma attached to him by caste Hindus by embracing Christianity.

The Satnāmīs, a religious group in the Central Provinces, are a dissenting sect founded by a *Chamār* reformer in the Chhattisgarh area. The Satnāmī movement in Chhattisgarh was started by one Ghāsī Dās, a native of Bilāspur district between AD 1820 and AD 1830. Ghāsī Dās got inspiration from a follower of the older Satnāmī sect of northern India founded by Jagjīwan Dās in Bārā Banki district of Uttar Pradesh.[1] Thus, the Satnāmī movement was carried from Oudh into the Central Provinces by

Ghāsī Dās, a *Chamār*.[2] He was the propounder of the Satnāmī cult in the Chhattisgarh region. Chislom, an English officer, regarded Saint Ghāsī Dās as an incarnation of a divine being in human form.[3] Ghāsī Dās was born in 18 December 1756 in Girod, a small village formerly in Bilāspur and now in Rāipur district near Sonakhan forest.[4] He was a poor farm servant in Girod. His childhood days were spent in a miserable condition. In spite of his poverty he visited many sacred places. On one occasion he and his brother started on a pilgrimage to the temple of Puri, but only got as far as Sārangarh from which they returned ejaculating 'Satnām Satnām'.[5] Then he abandoned pilgrimage and began leading an ascetic's life. Ghāsī Dās next retired to the forest for a season and emerged with what he called a new revelation for the *Chamārs*. He gave up all worldly cares and dedicated himself to the propagation of the Satnāmī cult. He became a great social reformer.

MESSAGE OF GURU GHĀSĪ DĀS

The all-round development which took place during the last half of the eighteenth century and the first half of the nineteenth century in Chhattisgarh region was mainly due to Bābā Ghāsī Dās who was a follower of truth and non-violence. He was well known to the whole community, having travelled much among them, and had the reputation of being exceptionally sagacious and was universally respected.[6] The seven precepts of Ghāsī Dās included the worship of the name of one solitary Supreme God, abstinence from meat, liquor and certain vegetables like lentils, chillies and tomatoes because they resembled the colour of blood, the abolition of idol worship, the prohibition of employment of cows for cultivation and of ploughing after midday or taking food to the fields.[7] Casteism was abolished and all men were to be socially equal except the family of Ghāsī Dās, in which the priesthood of the cult was to remain hereditary.[8] The Satnāmīs worship the Sun, morning and evening, as representing the deity, crying out 'Lord Protect Us'.[9] They have no visible sign or representation of the Supreme Being. They are opposed to idolatry and are enjoined to cast all idols from their homes. Theoretically, they have no temples, public religious services, creed and form of devotion. The Satnāmīs profess to adore the so-called True Name alone, the one God, the cause and creator of all things, the *nirguṇa* or He who is void of all sensible qualities, without beginning or without end. They recognize the absolute Hindu pantheon, and although they profess to worship but one God, they pay reverence to his manifestations as revealed in incarnations, particularly those of Rāma and Kṛṣṇa.[10] Their moral code enjoins indifference to the world, its pleasure and its pain, devotion to the *guru* or spiritual guide, clemency or gentleness, rigid adherence to truth, the discharge of all social and religious obligations and the hope of final absorption into the Supreme.[11]

SOCIAL AND RELIGIOUS CUSTOMS OF THE SATNĀMĪS

Regarding the social and religious customs of Satnāmīs, it is observed that idolatry of every form is eschewed and the Supreme Being is worshipped without any visible sign or representation. All worshippers are socially equal. The religious act simply consists of muttering the name of God and asking for his blessings. A Satnāmī prostrates himself before the Sun, morning and evening, crying Satnām, the True Name or the True One.[12] Their social customs generally resemble those of other *Chamārs*. They admit into their community all except members of impure castes, such as *dhobis* (washermen), *ghasiās* (grass-cutters) and *mehtar* (sweepers) whom they regard as inferior to themselves. Their women wear nose-rings, simply to show their contempt for the Hindu social order, as this ornament was formerly forbidden to the lower caste. Another method by which the Satnāmīs show their contempt for Hinduism is by throwing milk and curd at each other in sport and trampling it under foot. This is a parody of Hindu celebration of the *Janamāṣṭami* or Kṛṣṇa's birthday, when vessels of milk and curd are broken over the heads of the worshippers. The milk and curd are eaten by all castes indiscriminately in token of amity.[13]

The creed enunciated by Ghāsī Dās was of creditable simplicity and purity, of too elevated a nature for the *Chamārs*. The religion was originally of a high order of morality. But it rapidly got degraded to its own level, when adopted by a people who were incapable of living up to it. The crude myths associated with the story of Ghāsī Dās made the religion obscure. Ghāsī Dās lived up to eighty years and died in AD 1850.[14] The number of disciples then was more than a quarter of a million. He was succeeded in the office of high priest by his eldest son Bālak Dās.[15] Bālak Dās managed things badly. He outraged the feelings of the Hindus and was finally assassinated by a party of Rājpūts in AD 1860.[16] Since the later *gurus* were extravagant, the Satnāmī movement suffered a great setback. The *Chamārs*, who had raised their social status by adopting the Satnām-*panth* preached by Ghāsī Dās, felt the need for a dignified leadership and divisions started among themselves.

However, the origin of the Satnāmī cult may be attributed to a reaction against Hinduism and the despised position to which the lower classes were relegated by the caste system. The unconscious genesis of the revolt may be taken to be social rather than religious. The Satnāmī movement represents the efforts of the lower and impure castes to free themselves from the tyranny of the caste system and the Brāhmaṇas who stand at the head of the system. So the Satnāmīs are always in conflict with orthodox Hinduism and Brāhmaṇas. Ghāsī Dās himself had been deeply impressed by the misery and debasement of the *Chamār* community.

The spread of Christianity among the *Chamārs* in Chhattisgarh is in one respect a replica of the Satnāmī movement. By becoming a Christian the *Chamār* hopes to throw off the social bondage of Hinduism. However, Ghāsī Dās created self-confidence amongst the depressed sections of the society for their fight against injustice and untouchability. They started establishing their own identity and courage to fight against injustice. Hence, the Satnāmīs originated as a religious sect but were successful in getting the status of a caste by the end of the twenties.[17]

NOTES AND REFERENCES

1. Hastings, James (ed.), *Encyclopaedia of Religion and Ethics*, Vol. XI, Edinburg, 1915, p. 210.
2. Briggs, G.W., *The Religious Life of India: The Chamārs*, Oxford, 1920, p. 79.
3. Chislom, *Report of the Land Revenue Settlement of Bilaspur District in the Central Provinces*, 1968, p. 46.
4. Nelson, A.E., *District Gazetteer, Raipur District*, Vol. A, Bombay, 1909, p. 79.
5. Russell and Hiralal, *The Tribes and Castes of the Central Provinces of India*, Vol. I, 1911, pp. 308-309.
6. Chislom, *op. cit.*, p. 45.
7. *Guru Ghāsī Dās Smrti Patrika*, published by the Satnami Vidyarthi Parisad, 18.12.1986.
8. Hasting, James, *op. cit.*, pp. 309-10.
9. Briggs, G.W., *op. cit.*, p. 222.
10. *Ibid.*, p. 223.
11. Hastings, James, *op. cit.*, pp. 210-11.
12. Sherring, M.A., *Hindu Tribes and Castes*, Vol. II, Delhi, 1879, p. 110.
13. Russell and Hiralal, *op. cit.*, p. 314.
14. *District Gazetteer of Raipur*, p. 82.
15. Briggs, G.W., *op. cit.*, p. 222.
16. *Ibid.*
17. *Gazetteer of India*, Madhya Pradesh, Durg, 1972, pp. 89-91.

10

Role of Village Panimora in the Quit India Movement

Debabandya Kabi

The district of Sambalpur in Western Orissa is known for its active participation in the nationalist movement though the extent of participation differed in different phases. A close study of the evolution of freedom movement in the Sambalpur district indicates certain distinct trends. To begin with, the leaders of the movement demanded, in unequivocal terms, the liberation of India from foreign rule. But, instead of constituting an elite class struggle, as was the feature in most parts of India, it was truly nationalistic in character. Most of the leaders in the district came from humble family backgrounds and did not have much of formal education. Few of them were rich enough to feel relaxed as to the provisions of their family members during their absence from home. Yet, their devotion to the cause was deep and their appeal to the masses impressive. Their strong organising power was highly acclaimed by prominent national leaders like Mahatma Gandhi, Jawaharlal Nehru and Thakkar Bapa.[1]

Secondly, the Harijan leaders of Sambalpur along with Brahmins, Chasas and other high caste people, constituted a solid group of freedom fighters. The fellow feeling among the members of different castes was a rare phenomenon even at the national level. Especially the 'Tanti' and the 'Meher' communities of Sambalpur district are known for their significant contribution to the freedom movement.

An analytical study shows that the entire district of Sambalpur was affected by the movement but the intensity of the struggle was felt in some key pockets like Panimora, Bargarh, Barpali, Attabira, Sambalpur, Samaleipadar, Laikera, Remanda, Lakhanpur, Riamal, Ambabhona, and

Jharsuguda. In fact, the towns of Sambalpur, Jharsuguda and Panimora in Sohela police station, Remanda in Bheden and Samaleipadar in Bijepur produced clusters of freedom fighters known for their dedication and sacrifice. The purpose of this paper is to reflect upon the activities of freedom fighters of Panimora as a case study.

The village Panimora is located eight kilometres away from Sohela township and thirty kilometres from Bargarh in the undivided Sambalpur district, but now in Padmapur subdivision of the district of Bargarh. The subdivision of Padampur has an area of 3142.5 square kilometres and has seven police stations, namely, Bijepur, Gaisilat, Jagdalpur, Melchhamunda, Padampur, Paikmal, and Sohela.[2] Panimora in Sohela, like Samaleipadar in Bijepur, occupies a place of prestige and honour in the history of freedom movement in the district of Sambalpur. Falling in line with the general trend in Orissa, there was very little participation of the villagers in the Non-Cooperation Movement. Even in the Civil Disobedience Movement the village did not have any specific contribution. But by the time the last phase of freedom movement started, the village of Panimora had become a great centre of activity relating to the movement and provided single-handedly as many as nine workers in individual *Satyagraha* of 1940 and 32 freedom workers in the Quit India Movement. All of them hailed from very humble families. None of them had much formal education and they were not at all exposed to the outside world. But, once they came into contact with nationalist leaders, they jumped to the altar of the freedom movement and dedicated their lives to the cause of the nation. An important nationalist centre was opened at Panimora where Congress workers executed the constructive programme with great vigour and earnestness. The young men of the village were attracted towards the Congress movement and devoted their time to spinning in the centre. The villagers as a whole became active supporters of the cause of the Congress. A centre for weaving was founded by the Congress workers of Panimora under the leadership of Chamaru Paradia.[3] A brief description of the activities of some of the freedom fighters of the village will be of help in giving a general picture of the nature of their participation in the freedom movement.

CHAMARU PARADIA

Chamaru Paradia of Panimora was born on 27 July 1912 as the only son of Parikishita Paradia and Kalaki Devi. His formal education ended after class V because of sheer poverty. As a poor young man he enrolled himself as a primary 4-*anna* member of the Congress in 1935.[4] He participated in the Individual *Satyagraha* of 1940. His home became a centre of activity and discussion and leaders like Bhagirathi Patnaik, Laxmi Narayan Mishra, Nabakrishna Choudhury, and Malati Choudhury visited his house several times. In 1940 Manmohan Choudhury and Dayananda Satpathy came to the village under instruction from higher authority. They discussed with several young men and their parents on topics of spinning, untouchability, etc. Ultimately they selected nine persons for individual *Satyagraha*, who took a public oath that: 'It was a crime to help the British war efforts with money or men. Non-violent resistance to all wars is the only path.'[5] All of them also wrote to the Collector informing him about the time and place where they would offer *Satyagraha*. Chamaru Paradia while offering *Satyagraha* at Saranda was arrested by the police. He was kept in Cuttack jail for six weeks. After his release, he went to Sambalpur Rastra Seva Training Camp near the Zilla School for training where Bihari Ram Tanti of Jharsuguda was the commander. After getting training he became actively engaged in constructive works. In 1942 the villagers of Panimora sent Chamaru Paradia to Sambalpur to meet the leaders and decide the exact course of action for them, but the latter could not meet anyone. After his return, the villagers discussed and decided for *Satyagraha*. For this purpose 42 people from the village went to Bargarh. A group of ten people met Fakira Behera at Balitikra and thereafter decided to divide themselves into three groups. The first group consisting of two persons occupied the Congress office already seized by the government. The second group of five went to the market to observe a 'bandh' and the third group consisting of Chamaru Paradia, Jitendriya Padhan and Purna Chandra Padhan went to the court and organized a parallel work proceedings. They were arrested and sent to Sambalpur jail for six months. On their release, Chamaru engaged himself in constructive works. He was the secretary of the District Congress Committee during the year 1945-46.

CHANDRA BHANU PARADIA

Chandra Bhanu Paradia was the son of Nakula Paradia and Chhaya Devi. He was born in 1924. He was educated up to class VII. In 1941 Gopabandhu Choudhury along with Rama Devi came to Panimora and observed the keen interest of the villagers in the Gandhian constructive programme. They selected Chandra Bhanu Paradia of Panimora and Tulasiram Giri of Samalaipadar for training at the Bari Ashram for constructive activities. There they learnt spinning, social service and Gandhian philosophy. After a training for six months, Chandra Bhanu was engaged in social service in the villages of Sarandapali and Samalaipadar. During the Quit India Movement Chandra Bhanu, along with Shyama Sundar Sahu of his village, toured different places spreading the message of the movement. They moved up to Tungibandhali village when the police intervened and asked them not to move further. They even threatened to remove Fakir Mohan Paradia (brother of Chandra Bhanu and a school teacher) from service. But Chandra Bhanu insisted on going ahead.[6] They arrived at Tabra on 24 August 1942, arranged a meeting there and spoke against the government. They asked the people not to pay 'malguzari', to burn liquor shops and attack police stations. They were arrested on 24 August and brought walking to Sohela. The next day they were taken to Bargarh and after trial taken to jail. Chandra Bhanu was sentenced to imprisonment for nine months and fined Rs. 50/-, whereas Shyama Sundara was imprisoned for 1 year, 1 month and 22 days and fined Rs. 75/-.

Chandra Bhanu worked as a teacher in the Senior Basic School at Panimora for 30 years and retired in 1981.

DAYANIDHI NAYAK

Dayanidhi Nayak was born on 7 January 1926 to father Chiman Nayak and mother Parbati Devi. He was the nephew of Chamaru Paradia. He stayed in the house of his uncle from childhood and was profoundly influenced and inspired by him. He received formal education only up to class V. On 25 August 1942, when he went to the Bargarh market, he found the place full of crowd giving slogans against the British government. But as soon as the police entered the place the crowd started dispersing. Dayanidhi requested the people not to leave the place, and started delivering speech against the government. For this he was arrested and after trial at Bargarh court, he was sentenced to nine months' imprisonment. He was kept in Sambalpur jail along with hundreds of other freedom workers. After his release from jail he engaged himself in constructive works. For excellent spinning, he was rewarded by Kailashnath Katju the then Governor of Orissa.[7]

MINAKETAN SARAP

Minaketan Sarap was born on 17 June 1926. His father, Dhanapati Sarap was a Congress worker, who inspired Minaketan to join nationalist activities. During the 1942 movement, Minaketan, who was just 16, went to Bargarh, along with Fakir Behera, Nityananda Mohapatra, father Dhanapati Sarap and others, to reoccupy the Congress office which had been seized by the government. He was arrested but being a minor, he was released soon. But, on the following day, when he resumed his activities, he was again arrested. This time, he was placed before the law court. When threatened by the Magistrate, he came forward to show his chest to be fired upon by the police. The Magistrate ultimately inflicted nine months' imprisonment on him.[8]

JITENDRIYA PRADHAN

Jitendriya Pradhan, born in 1922, was the son of Mohan Pradhan and Tulasi Devi. He was educated only up to class III. Being influenced by the general environment of his village, he accepted Chamaru Paradia as his leader and attended all the Congress meetings in the village. In 1942 he went to Balitikra to meet Fakir Behera. He was one of the participants who organized a mock trial in a parallel court at Bargarh. He was imprisoned for six months.

CHAITANYA SAHU

Chaitanya Sahu, born in 1926, was the son of Darabaru Sahu and Kokila Devi. He was almost illiterate, but was a staunch nationalist. He was one of the persons who reoccupied the Congress office at Bargarh from the British police. He was imprisoned for nine months.[9]

DIBYA SUNDAR SAHU

Dibya Sundar Sahu was born in 1916. He was the only child of the great poet Dibya Kishore Sahu and Priyabati Devi. He received education up to class V only. He became an active member of the Congress from 1937. He also participated in the constructive works of his village and in the neighbourhood. In 1939 he joined the Rastra Seva Training Centre at Sambalpur. In 1940 he was selected to offer Individual *Satyagraha* and on 18 January 1941, while giving anti-war slogans at Sohela market he was arrested. He was put on trial on 28 January 1941 and imprisoned for one-and-a-half months and fined Rs. 50/-. During the Quit India Movement, on 9 August 1942, while reading out the pamphlet directed to the *Satyagrahi*s at Bargarh, he was arrested and put to nine months' imprisonment at Sambalpur jail.[10] After his release, he devoted himself for propagation of Khadi work.

SUNADHARA SAHU

Sunadhara Sahu is also one of the surviving freedom workers of Panimora. Born in 1919, he was the eldest son of Jayaram Sahu and Umabati Devi. He was imprisoned for four months for his participation in the Quit India Movement.

DIBYA KISHORE SAHU

Dibya Kishore Sahu was not included in the list of freedom workers of Panimora. But he was the one greatly responsible for bringing national consciousness to the village through his writings. He was born in 1891 as the son of Dwarikanath Sahu and Draupadi Devi. Although he received formal education only up to class IV, he was quite proficient not only in Oriya but also in Hindi, Bengali and Telugu languages. He composed nearly 50 books, most of which are full of patriotic thoughts. He is especially known for his *Bharata Jayagan* composed in 1928 and published by the 'Mukura' Press at Cuttack. He dedicated the book in the name of Mahatma Gandhi. Through this and other books like *Swadhinata, Swarajya, Asahajoga, Ahinsa,* etc., he was able to spread the message of freedom movement in the western part of Orissa.

DAMBARUDHARA DEWAN

Dambarudhara Dewan, born in 1912, was the son of Parasuram Dewan and Gurubari Devi. He was influenced by the environment of his village and was attracted towards the principles of Arya Samaj of Dayanand Saraswati. Also, the writings of poet Dibya Kishore inspired him greatly. Eminent leaders like Laxminarayan Mishra, Dayananda Satpathy and Bhagirathi Patnaik left a deep impact on his mind through their speeches. Dambarudhara participated both in the Individual *Satyagraha* of 1940 and the Quit India Movement of 1942. He suffered imprisonment for 1 year and one-and-a-half month. He was a sincere Congress worker from 1937.[11]

JASOBANTA BHOI

Jasobanta Bhoi, born in 1909, was the eldest son of Abhimanyu Bhoi. His family hailed originally from Remanda. Abhimanyu was one among the educated persons of his time. Jasobanta studied at Bargarh High School but could not complete his matriculation because of his participation in nationalist activities. Later, he became an active member of the Congress from 1937. He participated in both Individual *Satyagraha* and the Quit India Movement. In 1942 he was imprisoned for one year and after release, he was again arrested from the jail gate and put behind the bar. He was imprisoned thrice and spent a total spell of two years and two months.[12] His father was also a freedom worker and participated in the Quit India Movement.

PHULESAR PADHAN

Phulesar Padhan, born on 28 March 1916, was the son of Ghasia Padhan and Hema Devi. He worked as a school teacher. For his participation in the Quit India Movement he was arrested from the Tabada Primary School and inflicted 18 months' rigorous imprisonment and a fine of Rs. 30/-.[13]

The list of freedom workers of Panimora, as already stated, is quite long. In a small book in Oriya named *Shraddharpana*, edited by N.K. Paradia of Panimora, the freedom workers of the village have narrated their life stories. But while describing their participation in the nationalist movement during interviews with the author, they were neither very specific about dates nor very definite about particular events, which may be due to the fact that by the time their statements were recorded, most of them had reached their old age.

By the year 1942 general consciousness had reached the remote places of Orissa as a result of various factors like the spread of education, development of the press, socio-religious reform activities of the pioneering leaders, the impact of the Mahima and the Bramho cults, etc. Participation of individuals in the freedom struggle during this phase is therefore not a very unlikely phenomenon. What appeals to one's mind, however, is how a single village, that too in such an interior part of the state, could produce such a large number of freedom fighters, especially when all of them were without much formal education, and happened to be small cultivators without a sound financial condition.

The most important character of the movement in village Panimora was the spontaneous and mass participation of the villagers. The wartime, economic depression and the consequent inflation had resulted in shortage of food, cloth and other essentials of life that had made the people hard-pressed. Even death out of starvation was not very uncommon. Ignoring such hardships of life, in the small village of Panimora as many as 35 persons had participated in the movement although the official records mention is made of 32 names as the other three were released by the government without any inflictment of fine or imprisonment.

The reaction of the villagers in Panimora to the arrest of their leaders also attracts attention. Through letters and leaflets they appealed to the police and the government officials to release their leaders and not to take action against them. Some of them resorted to destruction of government property in order to express their condemnation of the arrest of the leaders. The villagers had published a local newspaper, *Satyagrah Prachara*, where articles expressing dissatisfaction over the arrest of the leaders found a prominent place.[14]

Another striking feature of the movement in Panimora was the participation of women in large numbers. As the male members left the village to participate in different programmes of the movement, the women not only willingly bade them farewell but made arrangements for dance, music and other cultural programmes to lighten their mental pressure.

The movement in the village, as per the general pattern, was short-lived but that does not minimize the intensity of the movement.

NOTES AND REFERENCES

1. Nanda, Bhagabat Prasad, *Samkhepare Paschima Odisa re Swadhinata Sangram* (Oriya), Sambalpur, n.d., p. 127.
2. Senapati, N. and B.K. Mohanty (eds.), *Orissa District Gazetteer: Sambalpur*, Cuttack, 1971, pp. 5-6.
3. For details see C.R. Mishra, *Freedom Movement in Sambalpur (1827-1947)*, Delhi, 1986, pp. 287-88.
4. Personal interview with Chamaru Paradia on 17 February 2000.
5. *Ibid.*
6. Personal interview with Chandra Bhanu Paradia on 17 February 2000.
7. Personal interview with Dayanidhi Nayak on 17 February 2000.
8. Interview on 17 February 2000 with Minaketan Sarap.
9. Personal interview on 17 February 2000 with Chaitanya Sahu.
10. Paradia, N.K. (ed.), *Shraddharpana* (Oriya), Panimora, 1985, p. 10.
11. State Committee for compilation of *Who's Who of Freedom Workers of Orissa (Sambalpur)*, (eds.) N.K. Sahu and S.C. De, Bhubaneswar, 1967, p. 13.
12. *Ibid.*, p. 23.
13. Paradia, N.K., *op. cit.*, p. 21.
14. *Ibid.*

II

Crafts and Commerce in South Kosala from c. AD 400-1000

S.P. Nanda

South Kosala is a country with a hoary past. This region is rich in history and culture right from the early times. The *Imperial Gazetteer of India*[1] puts the country between 19° 50′ and 23° 7′ north and 80° 40′ and 83° 38′ east. The area now comprises Raipur, Bilaspur, Bastar districts of Chhattisgarh and undivided Sundergarh, Sambalpur, Bolangir, Kalahandi, Boudh districts and Athmalik subdivision of Dhenkanal districts of Orissa. Several important royal families, viz., the Nalas, the Sarabhapuriyas, the Somavamsis, the Gangas, the Telugu Chodas, the Kalachuris and the Chauhans had ruled successfully from their different headquarters leaving behind their legacies.[2]

It is significant to note that historians have traced the history of Dakshina Kosala to the pre-Christian centuries on the basis of convincing archaeological evidence and have furnished indisputable proof with regard to her rich contributions to Oriya culture. Numerous monuments, coins and inscriptions found in South Kosala bear ample testimony to the glorious achievements of the people of South Kosala,[3] and even the account of the renowned Chinese traveller Hiuen Tsang confirms the high level of their cultural attainment.[4] The discovery of large hoards of punch-marked silver coins of Asurgarh in Kalahandi district testifies to the fact that even during the pre-Mauryan period, this region was connected by trade route with Kausambi and Kasi.[5] This belief has been further strengthened by the recent discovery of a large hoard of punch-marked silver coins of the same period near the village Lukapara of Bolangir district, on the right bank of river Suktel in 1991.

The Dakshina-Kosala region was not only abounding in inaccessible mountains but also broad navigable rivers. The Mahanadi Valley was, indeed, the heart of Dakshina Kosala and it provided the mainstay of the civilization for centuries. Rising from the inaccessible mountains of South Kosala with its network of tributaries, the main river Mahanadi contributed to the agrarian prosperity which led the Chinese pilgrim to record that the country yielded abundant crops.[6] The river Mahanadi is referred to in ancient literatures like the *Mahābhārata*,[7] *Brihat Samhita*[8] and *Kapila Samhita*.[9] The Telavaha in *Serivanijja Jataka* is identified with the Tel of Orissa, which indicated that the river was imported for inland trade in ancient time. The two *Patna Plates* of Yayāti I[10] mention the name of Telatata Visaya denoting the estate in the valley of the Tel. The Ang rises from the hills of Borasambar and meets the Mahanadi near Sonepur. The Angatata Visaya is referred to in the *Patna Plates* of Janamejaya I.[11] The Mahanadi is fed by a large number of tributaries – Seonath, Hasdo, Jonk, Ib, Jira, Suktel, Bagh. Salki, etc.[12] Riverine trade of South Kosala contributed to the rise of several prosperous towns and business centres. Mallalapattana[13] (Malhar and Arang) on the bank of Mahanadi, Sambalpur referred to as Samalaka on the Mannad,[14] Dharma Nagara[15] (Dhama), Suvarnapur[16] (Sonepur), Vinitapur[17] (Binika), and Taitala Janapada (Titilagarh)[18] on the bank of Tel were some of the leading townships and business centres which flourished even before and after this period between (c. AD 400-1000).

From the epic age the country Kosala was on the highway that proceeded from the north to the south. It is known from the *Vana Parva* that Kosala and Vidarva were contiguous territories connected by highways,[19] which facilitated commercial transactions between the two countries. The territory of Kosala provided an important route to the conquerors and traders as well from Pataliputra to Pisthapura.

The account of the flourishing trade of Western Orissa region in pre-Christian era, as described in the *Astadhyayi* and the *Jataka* story, is corroborated by the discovery of a large hoard of punch-marked coins at Asurgarh and Sonepur.[20] N.K. Sahu remarks that the Sonepur-Titilagarh region appears to have been connected with towns like Dantapura, Pithunda on the one hand and Kausambi and Kasi on the other in the 5th century BC.[21] During the time of grammarian Panini (5th century BC), a territory named Taitala *Janapada* flourished to the west of Kaliṅga and that has been associated by some scholars with the modern town of Titilagarh in the Bolangir district.[22] Taitala *Janapada* was famous for trade in some commodities, described by the grammarian as *Kadru*, the meaning of which may be either horse or cotton fabric. According to V.S. Agrawal,[23] the word *Kadru* denotes some tawny coloured material, probably rhinoceros hides. Besides, salt, a daily necessity, was imported to this region through Taitala

Janapada from the coastal areas of southern India.[24] The ports through which Kaliṅga carried on her overseas trade were connected with the artery of roads within the hinterland.[25]

From the *Allahabad Pillar Inscription*[26] it is known to us that the military forces of Samudragupta in course of their march from Pataliputra had to fight against the kings of Kosala in the very beginning of the South Indian campaign. The *Aihole Cave Inscription*[27] records that Pulakesin II conquered Kaliṅga along with Kosala. These military marches of Samudragupta and Pulakesin II through Kosala indicate that South Kosala occupied a place of great importance in trade and commerce of India. In the second quarter of the 7th century AD Hiuen Tsang travelled different parts of Orissa and left an interesting account of his route. From Kaliṅga, the pilgrim travelled for about 1800 *li* (360-380 miles) to the north-west to reach Kosala and from there he went to Andhra. These sources indicate that South Kosala was linked with Pataliputra, Vidarbha, Andhra, Kaliṅga and Utkala by highways of commercial importance. Further, a military expedition led by Rajendra Chola[28] against Odra-Kosala throw sufficient light on the route system of Orissa. South Kosala was linked with several neighbouring countries by highways and naturally utilized its potentialities in trade and commerce.

In regard to the kingdom of Sarabhapuriyas, i.e., Maraguda Valley, it is stated that with its rich forest wealth, fertile soil and navigable rivers, it had all the potentialities for the development of trade and commerce. Being contiguous to Kangoda and Kaliṅga, which were famous for sea-borne trade, the kingdom of Sarabhapuriyas had the avenue to maintain commercial link with foreign countries through Palaur and Che-li-tola, which were famous ports of south-eastern India in the 6th and 7th century AD of Christian era.[29]

An important factor which contributed to the growth of trade routes in Orissa was her maritime activities.[30] A large number of copper-plate charters register grant of villages in favour of the Brahmans who hailed from other countries and settled in Orissa. The migration of these Brahmans suggests that Orissa was linked with other countries by inter-state roads. Yayāti II[31] invited a large number of Brahmans from Kanauj to perform his sacrifice at Jajpur.

Circa AD 400-1000 was the period of state formation and acculturation. Many small independent kingdoms were established by tribal chiefs who sponsored Sanskritisation under the influence of Gupta tradition. There was a vertical as well horizontal social mobility when primitive tribes adopted the Aryan caste system and social structure. At the same time the economic life adopted new aspects of earning livelihood like trade and maritime activities. Agriculture ceased to be the only source of subsistence.

The early Medieval period was significant in Orissan history which brought numerous changes in the socio-economic life. Though the society was basically agrarian, new economic developments made this period highly self-contained and prosperous. The references of *Dhanya* and *Hiranya* as taxes and *Bhu* and *Suvarna* as gifts to the Brahmans give us the clue that the commercial prosperity of the country was due to its rich agricultural products and mineral resources.

Agriculture and trade were the main activities of the Vaisyas of South Kosala. They played an important role in the trade and commerce of medieval Orissa.[32] The economic conditions of the Vaisyas seemed to be very sound. Nala epigraphic records testify to the existence of a Vaisya community.[33] It is also corroborated by the *Buddhist Jataka*.[34] It is narrated that brisk trade was carried on through the Telavaha River. *Burhikhar Copper-plate* grant[35] reveals that a Vaisya called Bota was a resources merchant of South Kosala who sold the village Sangama to Surabala of Mekala. Some of the Vaisyas were rich enough to donate lands to Brahmans and temples. Haradasa, the engraver of Gaintala charter of Janamejaya I, was the son of Ullasa, who was a merchant.[36] During the Sarabhapuriya period Achala Simha, Sri Datta and Gola Simha were some of the distinguished persons of the Vaisya community who traded in gold and other valuable goods.

India was the home of arts and crafts and her products found market throughout the world. In the words of Dionysius,

> The Indians on the other side of the Indus are variously occupied – some by mining seal for the matrix of gold, other ply the loom to weave textures of linen, other saw the tusks of elephants. Others along the courses of mountain torrent search for precious stones – the sparking diamond, or the pale green translucent jasper, or the pure topaz.[37]

Some references are available regarding the existence of industries and crafts from the epigraphic records of the Nalas, the Sarabhapuriyas and the Somavamsis. The discovery of a number of ring-stones, stone beads, copper, silver and gold coins, copper-plates, charters, etc. suggest the existence of stone and metal processing industry in South Kosala.[38] The ruins of monuments amply prove that there existed huge iron industries in different parts of the region during the period under review. Iron must have been a thriving industry as known from the finding of iron clamps in the Maraguda Valley.[39] From archaeological evidence we come to know that *Lauhakara*[40] existed in the society during the Nala rule. They earned their living by manufacturing agricultural implements as well as war weapons. Considerable progress seems to have been achieved in the field of workmanship on stones, as witnessed in the few pieces of sculptures of the Nala[41] period and the large number of figures of the Somavamsis lying scattered throughout South Kosala. The architect of medieval Orissa were skilled persons.[42] The *Rithapur Charter* [43] and the *Podagada Stone Inscription*[44] made references to the existence of a class called *Khanakas* (engraver) and they used to engrave on royal order. The discovery of monasteries, a few Shiva temples at Maraguda Valley, Ranipur-Jharial, Sonepur, Surda, and Kumda suggested the headway made by the stone industry. Discovery of stone beads and bangles from South Kosala and the precious ornamental representation of sculptural art amply indicate that goldsmiths (*Suvarnakaras*), jewellers (*Manikaras*) and bead makers were living in the society. The commodities produced by the artisans probably used to be exported through roadways and waterways. There is possibility of materials like beads, manufactured in Western Orissa, to be transported to the Cambay basin, from which place these were exported to the west.[45] The availability of gold coins of the Nalas and Sarabhapuriyas testify to the progress of smithery (goldsmith) in gold metal. A reference of *Svarnakara Achalasimha* is mentioned in the charter of Jayaraja. He seems to have been connected with the royal mint for the preparation of gold coins.[46] The techniques used in making potteries indicate the scale of technological advancement and march of civilization. The discovery of different specimen of pottery and terracotta from the definitely known Nala sites indicates that there was a flourishing potter community (*Kumbhakara*) in the society.[47] The variety of potsherds suggest that lovely and utilitarian wheel-turned shapes of vessels such as big jars, vases and goblets, etc. were made by the potters. This contention is corroborated by the early Jaina work *Uvasagadasa*, which narrates about one rich potter Sadalaputta of Kosala who had five hundred pottery industries and many a potters.[48] A few terracotta images have come to light at Nehna site of the Khariar ex-state.[49]

Forest covered a large part of South Kosala and had influenced the economic life of the people as well as the government policies. Hiuen Tsang[50] narrates that he travelled through hills and woods from Kaliṅga to South Kosala. However, neither he nor any epigraphic record provides us with any information about the forest products. Timber, firewood, and bamboo are the major produces from the forest. The quality of timber is fairly good. B. Samantarai and H. Pattanaik, while speaking on the flora of Orissa, say:

> that natural occurrence of teak is the characteristic feature of the northern tropical dry deciduous forests. This type is found in parts of Balangir, Kalahandi, Sambalpur, Khariar and neighbouring places.[51]

Khariar teak was famous and was regarded as the second-best Burma teak. It is very likely that the forests were utilized by contractors for trade in timber, bamboo, etc., which were essential commodities for everybody. Besides, in the dense forest of Kaliṅga and Kosala there were mighty elephants which find mention in literature.[52] Harshavardhan refers that the elephants were not only used for military forces but also for long journeys in inland trade. Elephant tusks were considered very valuable. *The Periplus of the Erythrean Sea*[53] states Dosarena (Orissa) as producing the best ivory exports of Orissa.[54] An inscription mentions the grant of land including the donee's privilege to (*Hastidanta*) ivory.[55]

Opulence of South Kosala is indicated by the availability of excellent diamonds in the country. The diamonds of South Kosala were so famous that Kautilya[56] has cited their significance. He clearly reveals that South Kosala had attained celebrity as an opulent country due to the deposits of a special class of diamonds called 'Sirishakusumopama', which were found in the mines of South Kosala as recorded by Varaha Mihira in his *Brihat Samhita*.[57] The grand road which connected Pataliputra with Kosala must have resulted in rich commercial transactions pertaining to diamond. Gibbon observes that the diamonds of Summelpore[58] were considered to be prized gem in ancient Rome. The state obviously monopolized the diamond mines and granted lease to the new merchants. Diamonds were valuable commodity of sale in South Kosala.[59]

We get some reference of merchant associations.[60] The development of guild system is an interesting feature of ancient economic history. The guilds[61] appear to have existed for more than fifteen hundred years, from about 600 BC to AD 1000. According to Manu,[62] the state was expected to keep a watch over the condition of craftsmen. A noticeable feature is the existence of a merchant association named Kamlavana Vanika Pratisthana at Sonepur during the reign of Janamejaya I.[63] This association has received a land grant from the king which in its turn has been bestowed on two temples. It appears that such associations carried on such religious work as maintenance, repairs and construction of temples under their supervision for which the king used to entrust them with land grant.

Riverine traffic and bullock-cart transportation were common and popular in this region. The merchants transported their wares along the perennial stream of the rivers. Water routes were more economical and convenient. Vinita Pura and Suvarnapura are situated on the banks of the rivers Mahanandi and Tel, which were of immense importance to Orissa's trade in Medieval period.[64] As the country of South Kosala being surrounded and filled with several hillocks, mountains and dense forests, it necessitated the transport of goods on the back of elephants and the animals across the valleys of the country. Probably, the bullock-carts were used for transporting consumer goods over short distances.

In the early phase of social life, barter system was prevalent. But as time passed economic life became more complicated. So man introduced coins as the medium of exchange. Hiuen Tsang[65] gives us information on the large scale circulation of cowries in Orissa as money along with metallic money in different parts of Orissa. These were used in commercial transactions in Orissa down to the advent of the Britishers.[66] Punch-marked coins were in circulation till 4th century AD. The popularity of metallic coins took a new turn in the Gupta period when Aryanisation spread to Orissa.[67] Even some smaller dynasties like the Nala[68] and the Sarabhapuriyas[69] issued gold coins. Discovery of hoards of gold coins is a clear proof of active trade and commerce through the medium of money. Discovery of gold coins of these two ruling dynasties in different parts of Orissa, Madhya Pradesh, and Maharashtra is an evidence of commercial contact of Kosala with neighbouring states. No gold coins of the Somavamsis has come to lime-light as yet, but some of the historians have tried to proved the prevalence of gold coins in the Somavamsi regime on the basis of the word *Hiranya*,[70] which literally means gold. Some scholars suggest that *Rupya* referred to silver coins [71] during the Somavamsi period. In spite of the prevalence of monetary exchange, common people seemed to have taken resort to barter exchange in their day to day living.

The epics give vivid description of the traders and the articles of trade which they carried. There had been a movement of goods in different parts of the country with a rich variety and dimension of production. Different states had relations with each other and there were various trade routes inside the country for purposes of trade. Trade was an integral factor of prosperity. In fact, we get a glimpse of the economic condition of South Kosala from the copper-plate charters, numismatic evidence, and literary sources. The aforesaid analysis gives us a picture of the economic condition of this region which made rapid strides due to the trading activities and commercial transactions in neighbouring countries like Vidarbha, Kaliṅga, Kangoda, Utkala, and Andhra. South Kosala being a repository of diamond mines attained celebrity in the commercial world. The merchants took resort to riverine trade and transported goods on boats across the rivers and others of the business community transported surplus paddy and other goods through bullock-carts on regular roads, which connected South Kosala with neighbouring countries.

NOTES AND REFERENCES

1. *Imperial Gazetteer*, Vol. X, p. 202.
2. Sahu, N.K. (ed.), *NAHO*, Vol. II, 1971, pp. 9-23, 45-48.
3. *Ibid.*
4. Sahu, N.K. *et al.* (eds.), *History of Orissa*, 1985, pp. 28-30.
5. Sahu, J.K., *Historical Geography of Orissa*, p. 111.
6. *Ibid.*
7. *Mahābhārata*, 'Bhima Parva', 9, vide L.P. Pandeya.
8. *Brihat Samhita*, XVI-10.
9. Ganguly, D.K., *Historical Geography and Dynastic History of Orissa*, p. 92.
10. *Jataka* I, Part-III, vide Ganguly, p. 94.
11. *EI*, Vol. III, pp. 340-344.
12. Sahu, J.K., *op. cit.*, p. 229.
13. Tiwari, S.P., *Comprehensive History of Orissa*, pp. 13-19.
14. *Sambalpur District Gazetteer*, p. 3.
15. *University Museum Plate of Janamejaya I.*
16. *EI*, Vol. XI, pp. 95-98.
17. *JBORS*, II, p. 52.
18. Agrawal, V.S., *India as Known to Panini*, p. 61.
19. *Mahābhārata*, 'Vana Parva', LVIII, Vr. 22.
20. *OHRJ*, I, No. 2, pp. 27-34.
21. Sahu, N.K., *UUHO*, Vol. I, p. 233.
22. *Bolangir District Gazetteers*, p. 41.
23. Agrawal, V.S., *op. cit.*, p. 61.
24. Tripathi, R., *Crafts and Commerce in Orissa*, p. 73.
25. Das, B.S., *Economic History of Orissa*, p. 40.
26. *CII*, Vol. III, p. 13.
27. *EI*, Vol. VI, p. 1.
28. *EI*, Vol. IX, pp. 229-233; P. Acharya, 'Ancient Routes in Orissa', *OHRJ*, Vol. IV, p. 43.
29. Nanda, S.P. (unpublished thesis), p. 124.
30. Sahu, J.K., *op. cit.*, pp. 229-235.
31. Panigrahi, K.C., *Itihas O'Kimbadanti*, pp. 1-4.
32. Tiwari, S.P., *op. cit.*, p. 86.
33. Shukla, *Prachin Bastar*, pp. 122-127.
34. Patel, C.B., *Dynastic History of the Nalas*, p. 176.
35. *Studies in Epigraphy*, III, pp. 183-193.
36. *OHRJ*, Vol. XI, No. 31, p. 197.
37. Choudhary, R.K., *Economic History of India*, pp. 117-118.
38. Nanda, S.P. (unpublished thesis), p. 121.
39. Sahu, N.K., *Excavation Report – Maraguda*, p. 4.
40. Patel, C.B., *op. cit.*, pp. 181-182.
41. *Ibid.*

42. Shah, A.P., *Life and Condition of Medieval Orissa*, pp. 98-100.
43. *EI*, XIX, pp. 100-104.
44. *EI*, XXI, pp. 153-157.
45. Das, D., *Economic History of the Decant*, Delhi, 1969, p. 178.
46. *JESI*, Vol. IV, pp. 70-75.
47. Podagada, Maraguda, Kesaribeda.
48. Das, B.S., *op. cit.*, p. 58.
49. Singh Deo, J.P., *Cultural Profile of South Kosala*, pp. 39-42.
50. Watters, Vol. II, p. 200.
51. Samantrai, *Orissa Past and Present*, U.U., 1962, p. 162.
52. *Haridas Sanskrit Granthamal*, Canto IV, pp. 169-173.
53. Schoff, W.H., *The Periplus of Erythrean Sea*, pp. 49-42.
54. Minorski, V., *Hudud*, p. 86.
55. *EI*, Vol. XXVIII, Part VII, p. 327.
56. Samastry, R., *Kautilya's Arthasastra*, 1956, p. 278.
57. *B. Samhita*, VIII, p. 32.
58. Gibbon, *The Decline and Fall of the Roman Empire*.
59. Majumdar, B.C., *Orissa in the Making*, p. 78.
60. *EI*, Vol. XXIII, pp. 248-255.
61. Choudhary, R.K., *op. cit.*, pp. 193-195.
62. *Manu Smirti*, VII, 127-128.
63. *EI*, XI, pp. 95-98.
64. *JBORS*, II, p. 52.
65. Beal, S., *Hiuen Tsang*, p. 207.
66. Temple, R.C., *A Geog. Account of the Countries Round the Bay of Bengal*, 1905.
67. Tripathi, S., *op. cit.*, pp. xvii-xviii.
68. *JNSI*, Vol. I, pp. 29-38.
    JNSI, Vol. XI, pp. 108 ff.
69. *Prachya Prativa*, Vol. V., No. 1, p. 70.
    ASI, 1926, p. 230.
70. *JBORS*, II, p. 53.
71. *JASB*, Vol. I, p. 13.

12

Plunder, Diplomacy and War

The Maratha Occupation of Sambalpur

Patit Paban Mishra

From the middle of eighteenth century the authority of the Chauhans weakened considerably. Earlier, their domain extended in western Orissa, as well as in certain parts of eastern Chhattisgarh. One of the provincial dynasties of the Marathas, the Bhonsle Rajas of Nagpur fully exploited the chaotic condition prevailing in Sambalpur. For thirteen years, Sambalpur was being ruled by the Marathas. Afterwards it came under the sway of the British. This article has highlighted the factors that compelled the Marathas to acquire Sambalpur, their diplomacy in ousting the Chauhans and the Anglo-Maratha rivalry for mastery over the region.

Raghuji Bhonsle (1736-56), the political rival of Peshwa, was exerting influence southward and eastward. Karnatak and Trichinopoloy came under his influence. Raghuji then got embroiled in the affairs of Bengal, Bihar and Orissa. When the Nawab Alivardi Khan ceded the province of Cuttack to the Marathas, Sambalpur became increasingly important after 1751.[1] Communication to Cuttack became essential and Sambalpur was lying in the supply route of Raghuji from Nagpur to Cuttack. The Puri-bound pilgrims of central and northern India were using the same route. Then there was the question of profitable diamond trade. Bhawani Pandit, the Maratha Subhadar of Orissa, was suspicious of T. Motte, who had been sent by Clive to buy diamond from Sambalpur. Pandit was apprehensive of British design and thought that Motte had been sent 'to form alliances with the mountaineers, *through territories my road lay whose*'.[2] Sambalpur was thus essential for Maratha security because of its strategic location.

The chaotic condition prevailing in Sambalpur facilitated Maratha interference in the region. The *dewans* were wielding real authority and political assassination became the order of the day. A reign of terror had been unleashed by the Marathas. Rice was being harvested before January, the month of Maratha attack. The people also did not work in mines rich in gold and diamond, as it would draw the attention of the invaders.[3]

Januji Bhonsle, son of Raghuji, sent three hundred cavalry under Babu Khan to Cuttack in September 1766. The king of Sambalpur, Abhay Singh (1766-78), was asked to provide supplies for the convoy. Abhay Singh declined. Babu Khan made an abortive attack on the fort of Sambalpur. He had been earlier warned by Motte to spare that part of the town where the latter was staying. Babu Khan later on resumed his journey. The enmity of Nagpur and Sambalpur increased. The former was not able to send supplies through Sambalpur to Cuttack as the troops were being attacked by Abhay's forces. Akbar Ray, the *dewan* and *de facto* ruler of Sambalpur, attacked the Maratha artillery while it was going through the river Mahanadi. Januji Bhonsle dispatched an army to Sambalpur but Akbar Ray drove back the contingent.[4] Thereafter, the Marathas were looking for an opportunity to join the territories of Chhattisgarh region and Cuttack. Meanwhile, the king Abhay Singh had been imprisoned by the *dewan* Akbar Ray. The brother of the king Jayant Singh escaped to Berar and got himself employed in the Maratha cavalry at Garh-Mandal.[5] Later on with the help of the chiefs of Chhattisgarh, Jayant marched towards Sambalpur to recover the throne from Akbar Ray.

Once again the Marathas fished in troubled waters. Taking advantage of the impending attack by Jayant Singh, Chimanji Bapu, the Maratha general stationed in Orissa, wanted the presence of Marathas in the Sambalpur region as a force to be reckoned with. He was helped by the chiefs of Sonepur Sobha Singh, who invited Bapu to come to Sambalpur and place him (Sobha) on the throne after the defeat of Akbar Ray.[6] Simultaneously, Sobha Singh was trying to mediate between Jayant Singh and Akbar Ray. Chimanji as well as Jayant attacked Sambalpur. Akbar Ray was baffled at the invasion from both the sides. But Bapu's plan did not succeed as Akbar Ray and Jayant Singh came to an understanding. Jayant Singh was proclaimed as king in June 1781. Chimanji went back to Chanda blaming Sobha Singh for the trouble.

In the later part of nineteenth century, civil wars became responsible for the decline of Sambalpur.[7] Raghuji Bhonsle II (1788-1816) made a systematic plan of pillaging the kingdom of Sambalpur. The Marathas demanded *chauth* and *rusad* from Jayant Singh. The *dewan* of Sambalpur,

Govind Mohan Singh agreed to pay thirty-two thousand *cutcha* rupees to the Marathas annually from the year 1794.[8] This state of affairs was broken in 1799. The brother of Raghuji II, Vinko II was going to Pun through Sambalpur. He felt humiliated as the *dewan* did not meet him. From Cuttack Bhup Singh was sent to punish the king Jayant Singh. After imprisoning the king of Boudh Chandra Sekhar Bhanj, Bhup Singh attacked Sonepur. Its king Prithvi Singh Deo was held captive. After waiting for four months in the rainy season, the Marathas attacked Sambalpur. The fort of Sambalpur was besieged. For five months the Maratha soldiers were unable to penetrate the fort. An officer named Chindaji Bhonsle accidentally discovered that the Samlaigate of the fort was vulnerable.[9] After taking over of the fort, Jayant Singh and his son Maharaj Sai were captured. Both were sent to Chanda as captives. In April 1800 the kingdom of Sambalpur came under Maratha occupation and Bhup Singh governed the country on behalf of Raghuji II.

Sambalpur became a military fief of Bhup Singh. The people suffered because of his misrule. The Maratha soldiers earned their livelihood by plunder.[10] The *zamindars* and tributary chiefs were indignant because of the high rate of taxation. Bhup Singh clearly understood his position; at Nagpur he had hardly any supporter, as he was not paying attention to the summons of Raghuji. The opposition to Bhup Singh's misrule was mounting in Sambalpur. An agreement was finally reached with Ratna Kumari, the chief queen of Jayant Singh.[11] Bhup Singh agreed to administer the country not as a subordinate to Raghuji but in consultation with the queen. In order to chastise the recalcitrant governor, Nagpur dispatched army to Sambalpur. Bhup Singh ambushed it at the strategic Singhora Pass joining the Gandhamardan and Barpahar ranges. While returning from victory, he looted a village named Garbhana and incurred the wrath of the village chief Chamara Gauntia.[12] The chief collaborated with the next Maratha contingent to take revenge on Bhup Singh. He concealed the Maratha troops at the Singhora Pass and duped Bhup Singh by saying that the Maratha soldiers from Nagpur were plundering the area.

When Bhup Singh came to the Pass, he was attacked by the army. He narrowly escaped and retreated to Sambalpur. Along with Ratna Kumari and another queen of Jayant Singh, Mukta Kumari, Bhup Singh stayed at the Kulabira village. Raghuji sent Tantia Pharnavis as governor to Sambalpur in 1802.

In the beginning of the nineteenth century, Sambalpur became involved in Anglo-Maratha conflict. The Governor-General Lord Wellesley had an ambitious view in raising the British paramountcy. The pre-eminence of the Marathas was shattered. Baji Rao signed the subsidiary treaty with the East India Company on 31 December 1802 at Bassein. Raghuji became aware of the fact that independence of the Marathas ended by the said treaty.[13] In October 1803 the British had occupied the province of Cuttack and Balasore so as to join the northern Sarakars with Bengal. On 29 November 1803 the British defeated the forces of Raghuji at the battle of Argaon. On 17 October he signed the treaty of Deogaon. Cuttack, Balasore and the territories west to Wardha were coded to the British.[14] The territory of Sambalpur was to be retained by the Raja of Nagpur.

The news about the treaty of Deogaon was received by British officials only in January 1805.[15] After occupation of Cuttack the British had desired to seize Sambalpur as it would strengthen the defence of Cuttack. The hinterland of Cuttack would also connect the northern Sarkars and Bundelkhand. The motive of the British was clear from the letter[16] of the commander of British troops Lieutenant Colonel Harcout to the British Resident at Nagpur, M.S. Elphinstone – joining of Birbhum with Bidar and strategic importance of Sambalpur as springboard of attack to Cuttack, Ranchi and Nagpur. The transit of goods through land routes as well as river Mahanadi would also be facilitated. The Commissioner of the *Subah* of Orissa John Melville and Harcourt, the Commander, took the initiative in forming an anti-Maratha alliance with the kings of Sambalpur, Sonepur and Boudh. Ratna Kumari of Sambalpur, Laxmi Priya of Sonepur and Jagadiswar of Boudh signed an agreement with the British. They became allies of the East India Company by paying five gold *mohur*s annually.[17] With the help of Ratna Kumari and Bhup Singh, Colonel Broughten occupied Sambalpur on 2 January 1804. The Maratha governor Tantia Pharnavis retreated to Nagpur.

The news about the treaty of Deogaon reached Sambalpur only after 14th January. The British Commanders were reluctant to leave Sambalpur. Broughton wrote to the Chief Secretary John Lumbsen on February 1804 that territories conquered by him should not be given to Bhonsle.[18] The British moved diplomatically. The British Resident at Nagpur informed Raghuji that the Company had no interest in retaining Sambalpur. It would be given back to the Marathas if the chieftains and *zamindar*s would relieve the British from the obligation of protecting them.[19] The Company was determined to retain Sambalpur. On 26 March 1804 Broughton enquired from Ratna Kumari and others about their intention of going back to the Maratha rule. They declined to return to oppressive administration of Raghuji and desired British protection by paying a stipulated amount. The Governor-General Wellesley decided about the final course of action.

Threatened with a war, Raghuji recognized that Sambalpur had come under British protection and ratified it formally as part of the 10th Article of the treaty of Deogaon. Completely disregarding the earlier agreement signed with Sambalpur, Sonepur, Boudh, etc., the British annexed these territories. Broughton was directed on 4 October 1804 by Edmonstone to make preparations for protection of Sambalpur.[20] The British troops stationed at Sambalpur were reinforced in November 1804 to prevent any impending attack from the Maratha.

The British occupation of Sambalpur was short-lived. Lord Cornwallis and his successor Sir George Berlow relinquished the policy of annexation and followed a policy of non-intervention. Sambalpur was to be restored to the Marathas. The commander of Ramgarh battalion, Captain Roghsedge came to Sambalpur in January 1806 to assess the situation. The rule of the Marathas was so tyrannical that there was a general aversion to go back to the administration of Raghuji. The chieftains and *zamindars* did not agree to come under Maratha rule. They accepted provision in the territory of the Company. Ratna Kumari acquiesced to the British proposal of compensation either in the form of cash or territory. She was promised release of her husband and son from the Maratha confinement after Sambalpur was restored to the Marathas. The king of Raigarh, Jaujar Singh did not want to go back to Maratha rule at all. Roghsedge suggested the return of Sambalpur to the Marathas.

The Governor-General G.H. Barlow gave back Sambalpur and Patna except Raigarh to the Marathas.[21] The agreement with Raghuji became effective from[22] August 1806. The *Subahdar* of Ratnapur Keshav Govind was sent by Raghuji to bring Sambalpur under Maratha rule. Some chieftains of Sambalpur region under the leadership of Jaujar Singh and Bhagat Bariha of Padampur resisted Keshav Govind.[23] Bhonsle was not able to deploy a large contingent because of Pindari problem in his domain. The British refused to help him. Raghuji demanded from the British that the king of Raigarh was not to be protected by the British. The Company charged Nagpur that the husband and son of Ratna Kumari had not been released from Chanda prison. There was also strain to the treasury of Nagpur. The loss of territory by the treaty of Deogaon had resulted in decrease of revenue from a crore of rupees. Raghuji decided to proceed through diplomacy for the acquisition of Sambalpur.

The Marathas encamped at Sauri Narayan on the banks of Mahanadi. Januji Bunsar, Antaji Nayak and Narahari Nag came to Sambalpur on behalf of Raghuji for negotiation with Ratna Kumari. Keshav Govind sent a *saree* to the queen as present.[24]

The demands of Ratna Kumari were control over internal administration, fixation of annual tribute and release of Jayant Singh and Maharaj Sai. Chotguru and Padmanav Buxi went to Nagpur as emissaries of the queen. They made it clear that Ratna Kumari was not surrending the fort of Sambalpur unless her demands were met.[25] Nothing concrete came out of the discussions. On November 25, 1803 the brother of Raghuji, Nana Saheb came to Sambalpur.[26] There was an agreement between the queen and Nana Saheb about the past arrears and future amount of revenue to be paid by the queen. This was solemnized in the Samaleswari temple situated in the fort. Ratna Kumari did not remain alert because of the agreement. All of a sudden the Maratha troops under Ramachandra Bagh crossed the Mahanadi and took over the fort. The Marathas became the masters of Sambalpur once again by this act of treachery. Ratna Kumari escaped and proceeded towards Chota Nagpur. The minister of Raghuji, Yaswant Rao Ramachandra informed the Resident that Sambalpur had come under Maratha possession and asked the British to refuse asylum to any fugitive from Sambalpur.[27] Ratna Kumari sought British protection after reaching Hazaribagh. Nana Saheb asked the Resident for her surrender but the British insisted on release of her husband and son. Roghsedge met the queen on 2 June 1809 and was granted a pension of six hundred rupees per month.

The Marathas ruled Sambalpur for nine years. Raghuji was determined to have his authority established in Sambalpur. He did not listen to the demands of the *zamindars*, who urged that they were to be excluded from the Maratha domain and given an equivalent part in British territories. Even his brother Nana Saheb demanded from the British inclusion of Boudh as it was a vassal kingdom of Sambalpur. It was refused because the strategic Baramul Pass was located in this region. Nana Saheb was warned to refrain from interfering in Boudh.[28]

Raghuji had lost a large part of his territory. This was compensated by severe demands on the inhabitants. The Resident at Nagpur Sir Richard Jenkins described:

> From this spirit of meanness and rapacity, as well as from his un-warlike character, Rughojee was not unfrequently called, in derision, the great Bunneh ... [29]

There was disorder, dissension, and disturbance in Sambalpur. The tyranny of Maratha soldiers created a reign of terror in Sambalpur. When the aim was maximum exaction, they excelled in plunder. At the sight of the Marathas people hid in the jungles.[30] The general lawlessness led to the rise of a group of looters and majority of them were from Gond tribe. This type of plunder was known as *Gondmaru* (or disturbance by the Gonds) in local parlance.[31] The Gonds were enjoying large number of *zamindaris* under the Chauhan rule and they were loyal to the Chauhan kings.[32] O' Malley observed,

> Though the loose tribal system of the Gond rulers gave rise to prosperity in times of peace, it did not knit the strength of the people together when united action was called for. It was this defect of the system which laid the country open as an easy conquest for the Maratha invaders. When this invasion came the Gonds had to take to inaccessible strongholds in the hills from which they carried on a wild marauding campaign ...[33]

The Gonds struck fear to the heart of the people and their oppression was like that of the Marathas. As the Maratha rule was for a short time and a troubled period for the Bhonsles, Sambalpur did not have any proper Maratha administration. There was no direct evidence of actual process of the administration except that it was tyrannical. It could be surmised that as Sambalpur was lying eastward of Chhattisgarh Subah of the Marathas, Raghuji might have implanted that type of administration in the Sambalpur region.

The Marathas had failed to consolidate their position after Wellesley's departure. Lord Hastings, who became Governor-General in 1813, resumed the aggressive policy of Wellesley. Raghuji was no match against the formidable British imperialism. The Pindaris under Mir Khan also created havoc in his territory. Moreover, Raghuji's penchant for money resulted in withholding the pay of his soldiers and giving them loan at a large interest rate.[34] He also took revenue advances from the collectors and was busy in profitable business alliances. Another factor that led to the weakness of Nagpur's authority was dissension in the family of Raghuji. His death on 22 March 1816 was marked by disorder and intrigue. Bala Sahib, the imbecile and paralytic son of Raghuji, succeeded with the title of *Parasoji*. The cousin of Bala Sahib became the Regent of the State. He was next male heir to the throne. However, Raghuji's widow Baka Bai was against this decision.

Appa Sahib signed the treaty of subsidiary alliance on 27 May 1816. He sacrificed the independence of Nagpur for his self-interest.[35] The rivalry with Baka Bai drove Appa Sahib to the British camp. After murdering *Parasoji* he became the head of Bhonsle state on 1 February 1817. Hereafter, Appa changed his policy of subservience to the British. He had secret meetings with other Maratha powers and was warned by the Governor-General for his anti-British activities.[36] In the third Anglo-Maratha war, the Maratha Confederacy was routed in the battle of Sitabaldi on 27 November 1817 and surrendered to the British on 16 December.[37] By the provisional agreement signed on 6 January 1818, Nagpur ceded to the British Sambalpur,

Sarguji, Narnalla, Jabalpur, etc.[38] The grandson of Raghuji II, Bajiba Gujar (Raghuji III) administered a small kingdom as a puppet of the British.

Sambalpur once again came under British suzerainty in 1817. The Marathas were so much hated by the local people that they had to ask for British protection after surrendering Sambalpur fort for safe passage. Richard Jenkins obtained the release of Jayant Singh and Maharaj Sai from Chanda prison in 1817 and the former was reinstalled as king of Sambalpur. The Maratha occupation of Sambalpur for thirteen years (1800-1804 and 1808-1817) did not leave any permanent imprint in Sambalpur except in the memory of the people as a period of pillage and plunder.

NOTES AND REFERENCES

1. The first Maratha invasion had taken place at the time of Chatra Sai (1690-1725) as a result of palace intrigue only; there was no concerted Maratha policy towards Sambalpur. The next contact with the region had been described by Gopal Telenga, an employee of the King Ajit Singh (1725-66). See Gopal Telenga, *Adhyatma Rāmāyaṇa,* Oriya (Calcutta, 1919), p. 37. Telenga had stated that the Marathas were afraid of the Chauhan king and their revenue minister Bhaskar Pandit was giving Ajit Singh presents. But the account of Telenga had doubtful validity as he was employed in the army of Ajit Singh.
2. Motte, T., 'A Narrative of a Journey to the Diamond Mines at Sumbhulpore in the Province of Orissa', in L.S.S. O'Malley, *Bihar and Orissa District Gazetters*, Sambalpur (Patna, 1932), p. 45. Halics added.
3. *Ibid.*, p. 54.
4. Mallick, R.C., *Sankshipta Kosala Itihas*, Oriya (Patna, 1931), p. 192.
5. Dube, P., *Jayachandrika*, Canto III.
6. *Ibid.*, Canto VI. See also P.C. Rath, 'History of the Chauhans from Jayachandrika of P. Dube', *The Journal of Bihar and Orissa Research Society,* (Patna), December 1942, p. 460.
7. Sahu, N.K. and J.K. Sahu, 'History and Culture of Orissa', Vol. I, unpublished manuscript, Sambalpur University, 1978, p. 534.
8. *Selections from Nagpur Residency Records*, Vol. I, p. 54.
9. For details see, *ibid.*, p. 34.
10. Das, Siba Prasad, *Sambalpur Itihas,* Oriya, Sambalpur, 1969, p. 305.
11. Sahu, N.K., 'Ratna Kaumri', *Saptarshi,* Oriya (Sambalpur), Vol. I, March 1972, p. 27.
12. O' Malley, *op. cit.*, p. 27.
13. Dighe, V.C., 'Provincial Maratha Dynasties', in R.C. Majumdar (ed.), *The Maratha Supremacy*, Bombay, 1977, p. 247.
14. Duff, James G., *History of the Maratta,* (Rev. edn.), Vol. II, (New Delhi, 1971), p. 292.
15. *Records*, n. 8, p. 37.

16. *Ibid.*, pp. 52-53.
17. *Ibid.*, p. 35.
18. *Ibid.*, p. 52.
19. *Ibid.*
20. 'Letter from Edmonstone to Broughton', Archival Cell, Sambalpur University, History Department.
21. Aitchison, C.U., *A Collection of Treaties, Engagements and Sunnuds Relating to India and Neighbouring Countries*, Calcutta, 1876, p. 79.
22. *Records*, n. 8, pp. 88-90.
23. Dighe, *op. cit.*, p. 248.
24. Das, *op. cit.*, p. 324.
25. *Records*, Vol. I, n. 8, pp. 63-64.
26. Mishra, P.P., 'Ratna Kumari', *New Aspect of History of Orissa*, Vol. V., Sambalpur, 1965, p. 11.
27. *Records*, n. 8, p. 76.
28. *Ibid.*, Vol. II, p. 85.
29. Duff, *op. cit.*, p. 423. See also O'Malley, *op. cit.*, p. 29.
30. Das, *op. cit.*, p. 330.
31. *Ibid.*
32. Senapati, N.M. and B.K. Mahanti, *Orissa District Gazetteers: Sambalpur*, Cuttack, 1971, p. 117.
33. O'Malley, *op. cit.*, p. 85.
34. Duff, *op. cit.*, pp. 422-423.
35. Sinha, R.M., *Bhonsale of Nagpur: The Last Phase (1818-1854)*, Delhi, 1967, p. 16.
36. *Poona Residency Correspondence*, Vol. V, p. 449, Referred in S.N. Qanungo, 'Decline and Fall of the Maratha Power', R.C. Majumdar (ed.), *op. cit.*, p. 501.
37. Qanungo, *ibid.*, p. 506.
38. Sinha, *op. cit.*, pp. 30-31.

13

Stellate Brick Temple of Patalesvara at Budhikomna

Jeeban Kumar Pattnaik

INTRODUCTION

South Kosala presently constitutes Chhattisgarh and the western part of Orissa. In South Kosala, the architectural movement has accelerated and popularised by the liberal ruling dynasties from 6th to 11th century AD. The temples of South Kosala served as a land bridge between the north and the south and assimilated many features from different quarters and developed into a sub-regional manifestation of North Indian architecture in consonance with the canonical texts of North and South India.

The uniqueness of South Kosala architecture is a group of temples constructed after a star-shaped ground plan which is rarely found elsewhere in India. These temples were featured by seven triangular offset projections with the provision of a passage in the eighth offset projection. Such a scheme of ground plan had been achieved by intersecting two squares at the regular intervals. As many as eleven temples of this type documented so far revealed an interesting account of their beginning, growth and development in the territory of South Kosala during 7th-10th century AD. Again, on the basis of building materials they were divided into three varieties, viz., (i) brick temple, (ii) brick and stone temple, and (iii) stone-built temple. They were dedicated to Vishnu or Shiva and oriented generally to the east or west and never towards north or south. The Patalesvara brick temple at Budhikomna is one among such a group of religious edifices.

Budhikomna is a small village in the *tehsil* and district of Nuapara in Western Orissa. It is approximately 40 km away from Khariar road railway station and 7 km from Udyanabandh on the Khariar-Raipur road. In the outskirt of the village there is an ancient brick temple facing west. The temple dedicated to Lord Patalesvara Shiva enshrined as a *Shiva linga* on a rectangular *Yonipitha*. The significance of the temple was first brought to notice by the State Department of Archaeology, Government of Orissa which had undertaken major works of renovation and structural repairs of the ancient structure.[1]

The entire structure is made of burnt bricks except the doorways, lintels, pillars, pilasters and the ceiling slab. The bricks used in the temple measure 37 x 22 x 7.5 cm, i.e., in proportion of 5:3:1.

The temple, on plan, originally had a sanctum, an *antarala* and a frontal rectangular pillared hall. At present, the *mandapa* is non-existent except for the stone pavement and the pillared bases at places.

On plan the sanctum externally is star-shaped with an arrangement of seven angular offset projections with a passage. The *antarala* occupies the eighth angular offset projection. Each axis of the intersecting squares measures 3.9 m and falls into the category of well developed stellate temple cognate of South Kosala.

Externally, the temple is *pancharatha* with offset projection like *kanika* (equivalent to the *Karna* of the Chhattisgarh stellate temples) and *anaratha* (equivalent with *pratikarna* of the Chhattisgarh temples). On plan, the Patalesvara temple at Budhikomna resembles the Shiva temple at Dhobini and ruins of a temple at Kansil. However, the major angled facets of the temple at Dhobini are featured by *bhadra* and *karna*, but in case of the temple at Budhikomna, all major angled facets are known as *kanika*s and the temple is devoid of any *raha* or central projection (equivalent to the *bhadra* of the stellate temples of Chhattisgarh) like that of the temple at Kansil. As the central offset angular projection in between the *kanika*s of each arm has no distinction from *kanikas*, it becomes the *kanika* of the other square, when the projection is reoriented. The *raha* becomes non-entity. These *kanika*s are bi-facial and have acute-angled features. However, in between the *kanika*s there is a minor projection called *anaratha.*[2] The *anaratha* is bi-facial and is obtuse angled.

Internally, the sanctum of the Patalesvara temple is square and measures 1.95 sq m like that of the temple at Dhobini.

The vestibule leading into the sanctum is a rectangular chamber measuring 1.10 x 1.56 m internally.

On elevation, the temple rises straight right from a brick pavement without any trace of *jagati*, a departure from the traditional Chhattisgarh temples which are invariably constructed over a lofty *jagati*. However, the temple measures 13.5 m in height and in vertical plan, the temple is divided into three sub-divisions of *bada, gandi,* and *mastaka*.

The *bada* or the wall portion of the temple is further sub-divided into three components, namely, *pabhaga* or the base mouldings, *jangha* or the straight wall, and *baranda* or the waist portion of the structure.

In case of Orissan temple, the *vedibandha* of Chhattisgarh is substituted by *pabhaga* mouldings, viz., *khura, kumbha* and *patta* in early temples, and a set of five mouldings, viz., *khura, kumbha, patta, kani,* and *basanta* in case of later temples. However, in the Patalesvara temple of Budhikomna an altogether new feature is noticed in the making of the base mouldings which is unlike either of the *vedibandha* of the temples of Chhattisgarh or the *pabhaga* of the temples of Orissa. It has got only three base mouldings of the similar type which may be termed as *pada* (*khura* type), *khura,* and *basanta* (inverted *khura*). The *pada* is relieved by the carvings of *tanku* and the *khura* by *chaitya* arch motifs. The *basanta,* however, is devoid of any decorations. The *pabhaga* measures 1 m in height.

The *jangha* above the *pabhaga* vertically measures 2.10 m in height. The vertical divisions of the *jangha* are composed of the *kanika*s and *anaratha* corresponding to the stellate ground plan of the temple. The *jangha* is sub-divided into two equal halves, namely, the *talajangha* and the *uparajangha* by a horizontal *bandhana* moulding. The thickness of the *bandhana* is 16 cm. The *kanika* offsets of *talajangha* consist of pilasters and in between the space of pilasters is the *chaityamundi*. Within the medallion of *chaityamundi,* sculptural motifs like human/divine or animal figures are carved in low relief. In other words, the sculptural motifs of medallion of *chaityamundi* vary from place to place in the *talajangha.*

The *anaratha* projection with *talajangha* is featured by plain bifacial pilasters with its bases.

In between the *talajangha* and *uparajangha,* the dividing line is the *bandhana.* It is featured by a projecting plain moulding that continues all along.

The *uparajangha* is featured by pilasters having neither *chaityamundi* nor any sculptural decorations. The *kanika* of the *uparajangha* is featured by two outer pilasters on edges along the two additional smaller pilasters in between the space of outer pilasters on edges. These smaller pilasters have inverted (upside-down) pyramidal capital converged into corbelled stages. At the summit, the two capitals turn inward in a convex curve for a drooping bud at the centre. The arrangement of pilasters of the *uparajangha* is more or less similar to those of the Shiva temple at Dhobini. The *jangha* of the temple is intervened by the crowning part of *simhakarna.* The *anaratha* is capped with inverted pyramidal capital.

Unlike the Chhattisgarh style of *kapotapali* mouldings of the *baranda,* the *baranda* of the Patalesvara temple at Budhikomna is characterized by a set of two *khuras* being separated by a recessed *kanti.* The mouldings are relieved with *chaityamundi* designed in low relief or *kanika* at regular intervals. In case of Chhattisgarh temples the *chaityamundis* in the *karna* of the *baranda* are of larger dimension, often accommodating floral and human figure motifs. The *anaratha* of *baranda* is as usual plain with a series of horizontal mouldings and devoid of any decorations. However, the *baranda* of Patalesvara temple, like those of Chhattisgarh temples, serves as one of the *bhumis* of the *gandi* or the *sikhara.*

The *gandi* is curvilinear in appearance and is horizontally divided into six *bhumis* including the *baranda* as mentioned above. Each *bhumi* is composed of a heavy *baranda* surmounted by right-angled quarter *amalaka* in the *kanika.* The *anaratha* of the *gandi* is relieved with a series of horizontal plain mouldings like those of the *baranda.*

The *bhumi barandas* of the Patalesvara temple are provided with *tankus* in an effort to break the monotony of the plainness of the entire superstructure. The top *bhumi* projects upward like a turret continuing silhoutte of the *mastaka* having all the basic components as noticed in the larger *mastaka* of the temple. Except for the quarter *amalaka* which demarcates the *bhumi* divisions, there are as such no decorative motifs on the *kanikas* or *anaratha* offsets of the superstructure. Each offset *kanika* terminates independently by a miniature *mastaka* around the neck portion of the central *mastaka* that surmounts the *gandi.*

The *mastaka* above the *gandi* has been totally renovated by the State Department of Archaeology. The renovated *mastaka* consists of *bisama, amla* and *khapuri,* and the metal *kalasa.*

The interior walls of the sanctum have been coated with lime plaster. The walls are plain except for a niche in the southern wall. The *Shiva linga* upon a rectangular *Yonipitha* with *pranala* opening to the north is enshrined in the centre of the square chamber. Interestingly, there is an inscription engraved in proto *devanagari* script on the right jamb of the door. It reads:

> NA SREE BA LA PRA SA DA LA TRA BRA HA MA NA U PRA NA NA (MA)? BA? KA (KRA) MA NA

It hardly conveys any meaning, possibly a name. From the style of its execution it is evident that the inscription is of a much later date than the date of construction of the temple. However, it is the only inscribed example in the whole stellate group of temples of South Kosala.

The *Sandhisthala* or the junction between the sanctum and the vestibule has a series of horizontal mouldings extending up to the *bada* portion of the temple. The upper portion of the *antarala* is featured by a *sukanasa*, which rises up to the fourth *bhumi* of the *gandi*. The facade of the *sukanasa* is *triratha*. It serves as the base for four superimposed *angasikhara*s. Since the *angasikhara*s have been completely renovated, decorative features in them are beyond recognition.

Externally, the *antarala* walls are serrated by a series of horizontal mouldings. The *antarala* is pierced by a doorway made of sandstone and appears to be in situ. The door-jambs originally had two vertical segments, i.e., *dvisakha*. Presently the divisions are blocked by modern renovated supporting walls. However, like that of Chhattisgarh temples, the door-jambs are carved with large sculptures of standing river goddess in alto-relievo. *Ganga-Yamuna* on their respective mounts occupy the right and left jambs respectively. The figures are badly weather-beaten. Their features are obliterated and beyond recognition. However, both of them hold pots in their upraised right hand with the left arm hanging downward. The figures are in *samabhanga* pose. The inner segment of the door frame is decorated with creepers and lotus medallion with scroll motifs.

The lintel of the doorway that measures 1.83 x 0.25 m is relieved with the figures of *Gajalaksmi* or *Abhisekalaksmi* at the centre being flanked by *navagraha*s on either side. Laksmi being annointed by two elephants on either side is seated in *Padmasana*. The *graha*s on her right are Ravi, Soma, Mangala, Budha, Brihaspati, and on her left are Sukra, Sani, Rahu and Ketu; they are seated in *ardhaparyankasana*. Ravi is seated in *padmasana* carrying two full-blown lotuses. Soma, Mangala, Budha, Brihaspati and Sukra display a common pot in their upraised right hand and a rosary in the left. Sani carries a sword in his right hand, while the attributes in the left hand are indistinct. Rahu is represented by a bust and Ketu by a human head with the tail of a snake. The objects in the two upraised hands of Ketu are not clear.

Navagraha slab adoring the door lintel is found in all later temples of Orissa. The earliest example of the *navagraha* slab in Orissa temple is noticed on Muktesvara temple at Bhubanesvara dating back to 10th century AD. However, at Parasuramesvara, a 7th century temple of Bhubaneswar, the concept of *navagraha* was yet to come. Here the lintel slabs of the door-jamb are relieved with eight *graha*s – Ketu and ninth planet being absent. In Western Orissa, the Patalesvara temple of Budhikomna has the distinction of possessing the earliest example of the *navagraha* slab by incorporating Ketu in the list of *graha*s.[3]

Apart from these structural details, one of the most important features of this temple which deserves to be mentioned is that the temple, both internally and externally, was originally plastered with stucco, a phenomenon not found in Orissan temples. Though most of the stucco plaster have disappeared, some decorative terracotta-cum-stucco plaster have escaped from wanton destruction. They are displayed in female figure, *dhyani naga* or *dhyani yaksa* under the snake canopy depicted in low relief within the medallions of *chaityamundis* of *talajangha*. The figures resemble with that of the brick temple at Pujaripali in Raigarh district of Chhattisgarh. However, in the Orissan temple such miniature *chaityamundis* are not meant for housing any sculptural figures; rather, miniature decorative motifs are depicted. It is a feature probably borrowed from Chhattisgarh region or from an eastward expansion of the Chhattisgarh art tradition.

Besides the terracotta-cum-stucco art pieces, there are a few fragmentary stone sculptures kept in front of the temple near *nandi mandapa*. Among the best preserved specimens, there are seated male figures holding flowers, an architectural fragment relieved with elephant frieze. A sculptural fragment of a rider on a horse-back deserves special mention. These aforesaid sculptures very likely once adorned the stone-paved pillared *mandapa* of the temple.

The soffit of the door-frame is carved with creepers on the inner side and a lotus medallion with scroll motif on the ceiling, like the carvings in the temples of Chhattisgarh. *Grasamukha* motifs are also depicted on the underside of bracket placed in the upper corner of the doorway.

The Patalesvara brick temple at Budhikomna is one of the most developed and perfect example of the stellate temple of the group. On plan, it is *pancharatha* externally and square sanctum internally like that of Shiva temple at Dhobini and the ruined temple at Kansil. It maintains the standard proportion of the exterior arms of the square, i.e., 3.9 m and the arm of the sanctum 1.95 m, just half of the external arm. The vestibule is a rectangular chamber which is in contrast to the ruined temple of Kansil, where the vestibule is oblong.

Among the whole group, it is the solitary example which has been constructed without a platform, a typical early Orissan feature. The temple of South Kosala under review are constructed over a platform *jagati*; it marks a departure from such a practice.

In the treatement of *pabhaga*, some new features are marked. Firstly, the *pabhaga* is of three mouldings in contrast to the four or five mouldings of Chhattisgarh and Orissa. Secondly, in the *vedibandhas* of Chhattisgarh temples, the lowermost mouldings are generally devoid of any art motif or decoration in the South Kosalan temples. But at Patalesvara temple reversed arrangement has been done. The lower mouldings of *pada* and *khura* are decorated while *basanta* – the top moulding – is devoid of any decoration like that of Orissan temples. In this regard, the temple at Budhikomna has the proximity with Orissan architecture and marks a departure from Chhattisgarh tradition.

In respect of the vertical offsets, it strikingly resembles the Shiva temple at Dhobini. The temple at Budhikomna has five angular projections. But it differs from the former in the treatment of its central offsets which accommodate only a *chaityamundi* unlike the *ghanadvara* of the Shiva temple at Dhobini. The *kanika*s of the temple at Budhikomna are identical to each other in their architectural pattern and decorative embellishment from bottom to top. This is a feature certainly later than that of the temple at Dhobini.

The division of *jangha* into *talajangha* and *uparajangha* is like those at the Siddhesvara temple at Palari. But the very division of *jangha* of the *bada* of the Patalesvara temple, marks the temple similarly with the 10th century temples of Orissa. The *bada* of brick temple at Budhikomna is *panchangabada*. It consists of *pabhaga talajangha, bandhana, uparajangha,* and *baranda*. Such type of division is absent in Chhattisgarh.

Unlike the temples of Chhattisgarh the brick temple at Budhikomna displays a curvilinear outline of the *gandi*. The temples are bold, squat and curvilinear outlines are not well articulated. Again in the treatment of *bhumiamla*s they exhibit a contrast arrangement from those of their Chhattisgarh counterparts. On the superstructure of Chhattisgarh temple, the *bhumiamla*s are quarter in size and circular in shape. But in the temple at Budhikomna, the *bhumiamla*s are right-angled and not circular. They are placed on the vertical plane of *kanika*s. On the Siddhesvara temple at Palari, these quarter circular *amla*s are found on *karna* division and smaller ones on *pratiratha*, while on the Shiva temple at Dhobini, these circular *amla*s are found on both *karna* and *bhadra*.

Further, unlike Chhattisgarh tradition of four *bhumi* division, it has six *bhumi*s as identified by the crowning *amla*s, where *amla* serves as the base for each *bhumi* division.

The superstructure of Patalesvara temple is almost bereft of any decoration except the *kanika* offsets where the designs of *chaityamundi* are carved in contrast to the temples at Palari, Kharod and Dhobini. The superstructure of the temples in Chhattisgarh is heavily studded with sculptural, floral and geometric designs. However, the *chaityamundi*s of *kanika* offsets on the superstructure of Patalesvara temple are smaller sculptural motifs in close affinity with Orissan temples.

In the carving of the diminutive river goddess on door-frame is also seen a departure from traditional sculptural art of South Kosala. The depiction of *Gajalaksmi* on *dvaralalatabimba* proximates Orissan practice. In Chhattisgarh, the crest figures are either *Anantasayi* Vishnu or Lakulisa or Uma-Mahesvara or Vishnu on *garuda* but rarely *Gajalaksmi*. In addition to this, Laksmi in *padmasana* provides a valuable clue for its antiquity. Because *Gajalaksmi* in *padmasana* feature is found in Orissan temple of 9th or early 10th century AD to be substituted by *lalitasana* in all the later and post 10th century temples of Orissa.

It is further attested by the *navagraha*s slab on the lintel as already discussed earlier. However, the depiction of the *graha*s in *ardhaparyankasana,* unlike Orissan standardized *padmasana* pre-dates Patalesvara to all other 10th century temples of Orissa. It is further confirmed by the incipient exposition of both *navagraha* panel and the *Gajalaksmi* motifs.

On stylistic ground, Donaldson assigns the temple to the close of 9th century AD.[4] D.R. Das places the temple in 11th century AD based on the epigraphical evidence in the temple.[5] However, the inscription in question, palaeographically does not go along with the architectural scheme of the temple.

However, a close scrutiny of the building materials, architectural features, layout of the stellate ground plan and sculptural decoration of the temple as mentioned above confirms to a date to the last quarter of the 9th century or to the beginning of the 10th century AD.

CONCLUSION

The study reveals that South Kosala, situated between the two principal art traditions of Central India and coastal Orissa, had a hoary past that played a vital role to serve as the experimental ground for temple building where many conceivable forms, styles and designs were experimented. This experimentation was solely based on distinct regional tradition and art idioms. Among the South Kosalan temples, the temples' stellate order was not only unique but also second to none in the contemporary pan-Indian context. These stellate temples found due support and acceptance from the mass and patronage from the regional ruling dynasties. Keeping in view its architectural pattern and sculptural traditions the Patelesvara temple, Budhikomna is one among such distinct cognate may be considered as the connecting link between the architectural tradition of Chhattisgarh region of Central India and Orissa for its striking resemblance to both traditions in respect of architectural features, sculptural embellishment, and artistic idioms.

GLOSSARY

Amalaka or *amla*	: Fluted disc resembling *amalaka* fruit (*embolic myrobalan*) crowning top of *gandi* spire.
Anaratha	: A vertical wall projection between *Kanika* (corner projection) and *Raha* (central projection).
Angasikhara	: Miniature replica curvilinear of the temple.
Antarala	: Space between sanctum and *mandapa*.
Bada	: Vertical portion of the temple above *pista*.
Baranda	: Springing level of the superstructure of the temple.
Bandhana	: Band moulding between the two *jangha*s.
Basanta	: Horizontal bend with ornamentation of foliage or creeper; top moulding of the *pabhaga*.
Bhadra	: Central offset (wall division) like *Raha paga* of Orissan temple.
Bhumi amla	: Fluted disc demarcating one *bhumi* from another at the *kanika* projection.
Bisama	: Top moulding of the *gandi*, generally undecorated.
Chaityamundi	: Ornamented motif resembling the window of the Buddhist rock-cut *Chaitya* hall in the shape of stylized horse shoe.
Dvisakha	: Two *sakha*s (vertical division).
Gandi	: Trunk curvilinear spire or pyramidal roof above the *bada*, *sikhara* and below *mastaka*.
Grasamukha	: Gorgan face or head also known as *grasa* or *kirtimukha*.
Ghanadvara	: False door-like object on the body of the temple.
Jagati	: Plinth/platform.
Jangha	: Shin. Vertical portion of the temple between *pabhaga* and *baranda*.
Kani	: Projecting edge or profile.
Kanikapaga	: Corner segment of the temple.
Kapotapali	: Cyma eave cornice.
Karna	: Angle, corner, corner wall division.
Khura	: Cyma recta, first basic element of *pabhaga* in the form of a hoof.
Kumba	: Water pot. Also moulding having the water pot.
Mastaka	: Head. Crowning element of the temple.
Pabhaga	: Division corresponding to foot. A set of lower-most moulding of the base of the temple.
Pata	: Flange, plain board stone band.
Pada	: Base moulding of *pabhaga*.

Pancharatha	: Temple with five projections.
Panchangabada	: *Bada* with five elements.
Pranala	: Sacred drain water chute (fall).
Pratiratha	: Thin projection between major *pagas* on *saptaratha* and *navaratha* temple.
Raha	: Central vertical projection of the temple.
Sukanasa	: Nose of parrot. Integrated projection of *gandi* in front of temple.
Talajangha	: Lower shin.
Tanku	: Heart shape design on the edge of *pidhas* or mouldings.
Uparajangha	: Upper shin (thigh).
Vedibandha	: Basal wall moulding consists of *khura, kumbha, kalasa, antarapatra* or *antarapatta* and *kapotapali.*
Yaksha	: A demon god associated with fertility.

NOTES AND REFERENCES

1. Das, D.R., *Stellate Temple of Orissa in Aspects of Indian Art and Culture,* S.K. Saraswati Commemoration Volume, J. Chakravorty and D.C. Bhattacharya (eds.), Calcutta, 1983, p. 10.
2. Donaldson, T.E., *Hindu Temple Art of Orissa,* Vol. I, Leiden, 1986, p. 213.
3. *Ibid.,* Vol. II, p. 582.
4. *Ibid.,* Vol. I, p. 215.
5. Tiwari, A.N. (ed.), 'The Unique Brick Temple at Budhikomna', in B.K. Rath, *New Dimension of Tourism in Orissa,* Bhubaneswar, 1976, pp. 55-58.

14

War Strategy of Veer Surendra Sai

Jagdish Mishra

Surendra Sai is the glory of Orissa. He occupies a unique position among those great men of action that have crowded the columns of history in golden letters. The sacrifice of his family for the cause of the motherland was a rare example of history. Much before 1857, the year of First War of Independence, he had sparked the fire of revolution on the soil of Sambalpur. The war strategy that he followed in it against the English draws special attention.

Surendra Sai who was born on 23rd January 1809 was the son of Dharma Singh, the descendant of the fourth Chauhan king of Sambalpur Raj, Aniruddha Sai. In 1827, after the death of the eleventh Chauhan king of Sambalpur Raj, Maharaja Sai, who was issueless, Surendra placed his legitimate claim on the throne of Sambalpur. As the scion of direct line his claim was justified. However, the English ignored the established royal convention and that of Surendra's claim for the throne. They enthroned the widow queen 'Mohan Kumari' of the deceased king Maharaja Sai. This act greatly displeased the *zamindars* of Sambalpur Raj. Thus, the English in 1833 enthroned the 'grand old' *zamindar* of Barpali Narayan Singh on the throne of Sambalpur.

> His accession to the throne was a part of British plot to annex Sambalpur Raj with British empire soon after his death.[1]

It disappointed those claiming their rights on the throne and they became rebellious. Among them the most outstanding was Surendra Sai. He began his struggle against the British Raj, backed by the Gond *zamindars* of Sambalpur kingdom. However, during the course of struggle in 1840, for the murder of Rajput *zamindar* of Rampur, Durjaya Singh, Surendra, and his uncle Balaram Singh with his brothers were arrested after a small battle at Deheripali near Budharaja. They were sentenced to life imprisonment in the Hazaribagh, Jail.[2]

In 1857, the revolutionaries of the great revolt broke down the prison and released all the prisoners. Surendra and his brothers being freed marched towards Sambalpur to begin struggle afresh in a consolidated way.

In the meantime, in 1849, after the death of Narayan Singh, 'Doctrine of Lapse' was applied to Sambalpur. It is said that, after the death of the king for a few days Sambalpur was ruled by widow queen Mukhyapana Devi.[3] But ultimately it became a district of the British Raj. The administrative system changed accordingly. Its land revenue in between 1849 to 1854, rised to five times in two settlements.[4] As per record it was enhanced from Rs. 8,800/- to Rs. 74,000/- per annum.[5] The *zamindar*s and *gauntia*s got alarmed by this. They thought their land will be usurped. No attempt was made by anyone to sympathise their grievances. The infuriated *zamindar*s had nothing to do as there was no one to lead them. The arrival of Surendra Sai gave a new life to their rebellious attitude. Surendra Sai organized them. At Sambalpur on 31st August 1857 he declared his 'Ulgulan', i.e., armed rebellion began before a large public gathering.[6]

As a part of his war strategy he chalked out the techniques. He had confidence on the strength of the masses. He wanted to get their support, and for this, he along with other royal members visited village to village, and met influential personalities, *zamindar*s and *gauntia*s.[7]

In his struggle against the British Raj, Surendra Sai received the selfless and dedicated help of the *zamindar*s of Lakhanpur, Balabhadra Singh Deo with his three sons Kamal Singh Deo, Nilambar Singh Deo and Khageswar Singh Deo and that of Ghens, Madho Singh with his three sons Hatte Singh, Kunjal Singh and Bairi Singh. Besides the *zamindar*s of Kolabira – Karunakar Naik; Kudaboga – Abhari Singh; Bheden – Manohar Singh; Kharsal – Dial Sardar; Mundo Mahul – Ananta Singh; Pahar Srigida – Janardan Singh; Patkulunda – Pitambar Singh; Loisingha – Chandra Gartia; Machida – Dhana Singh; Kharmunda – Markanda Bariha and the *Gauntia*s of Rampell – Loknath Panda; Arda – Mrutyunjaya Panigrahi supported and fought with him from the core of their strength.[8] Moreover, the indirect help and cooperation given to him by the *Gauntia*s and subject of many other villages had shaped the 'Ulgulan' to a great extent. The names of Krushna Chandra Singh, Raja of Khariar and Uma Rao Sai, and Raja of Bendra Nuagarh deserve mention in this regard. This indirect and secret cooperation was a noble tactic of Surendra Sai to take shelter, to get *rasad* and to collect information about the English army and administration to prepare a plan, policy and structure of his armed rebellion.

Under the leadership of Surendra Sai, the revolutionaries had adopted Guerrilla warfare against the British Raj. Of course on many occassions open battles were fought. It is a war tactics of its own class to strike with lightening speed where the defeat of enemy seems impossible even with mighty power. However, many factors worked behind such tactics.

First the then Sambalpur was full of dense forest, hilllocks, mountain peaks, ravines and upland. All these were obstruction in their own ways to good communication. Moreover, due to the absence of large (battle-fields) plain land due to hilly and upland nature, open battle of traditional line was not always possible.

Secondly, both party lacked a large army force. The English considering it a local uprising had deputed a few battalion of soldiers. Of course it was sufficient for the revolutionaries. On the other hand, in spite of peoples' support Surendra was lacking in economy and opportunity to build up a vast and sophistically trained army. Since the rebels were poorly equipped, they were no match for English in open encounter, and, thus, they resorted to a war of hide and seek, i.e., Guerrilla warfare.

Thirdly, the revolutionaries were fighting with traditional weapons like bow, arrow, spear, sword, axe and also guns. But the English soldiers fought with developed armaments like gun and barrel. They were well equipped with training in different techniques to fight in different situations. Morever, the faith of invincibility and fortune of rising star had made them one of the best army in the world of that time. Availability of guns, weapons and other requirements were not a matter of problem. Thus, a face to face war between the remote and traditional method of warfare of the revolutionaries and sophisticated English army was not only unthinkable but practically impossible. Such war environment resorted them to follow Guerrilla tactics against the British Raj.

Finally, the supporters of Surendra were mostly *adivasi* class of tribal nature. That is why it is said that the 'Ulgulan' of Surendra Sai was a tribal rebellion. The tribal people were perfect in primitive war tactics. Guerrilla warfare was a part of it. It means, the Chauhan scion Surendera Sai had followed the same war tactics that the Maratha hero Shivaji had followed against the mighty Mughals with the help of *Mawali* tribe. He brought awakening among the people of Sambalpur Raj as great hero Shivaji did among the Marathas.[9] It is needless to say that the geography of Sambalpur added by ill-equipped remote method of warfare of the revolutionaries largely contributed to influence the war tactics of Veer Surendra Sai. Because the territory of Sambalpur was filled up with dense forest, the peaks and ravines favoured them most. The English failed to search them. Moreover, the hardy mountaineer inhabitants of the region were able to take shelter in the rock caves and dense forests, and adapt themselves accordingly which was a dream for the English army. Thus, to ruin the English army and administration Surendra Sai decided to follow Guerrilla war tactics.

The armed rebellion of Surendra was controlled from different centres. All of them were either hill caves or dense impregnable ravines and forts. The most outstanding among them were Barapahada, Debrigarh, Singoda Ghatti, Barpatti, Papanga Pahad, etc. They were lacking in good communication to stop the soldiers or their fires. Dense forest had converted the guns and barrels to a handicapped weapon. The soldiers were not expert and acquainted in climbing the hills and peaks. Even many of them did not know how to climb mountains. On the other hand, the revolutionaries had tied large pieces of stone in 'Shiali Lata' – a plant rope. When the soldiers were attempting to reach them the tiding plants were cut by them. As a result, large stones were pelted at their bodies resulting many to death.[10]

With an objective to suppress the revolutionary activities, the English soldiers in different times were invading their hidden centres. But instead of getting success they suffered incalculable damage. Because when and where few English soldiers were looked upon, the revolutionaries were assembling in rapid action through secret information to attack them.

An important aspect of Surendra's war diplomacy was the burning down of post offices and police stations with damage caused to road and communication. The *zamindar*s and *gauntia*s favouring the English were terrified with a show of force. The intention was to discourage them to extend help to the British authority.

The revolutionaries had control over Sambalpur with a radius of five kilometres. The capital town itself was under direct attack.[11] The revolutionaries were divided into different divisions to keep watch on the English soldiers coming to the forest and ravines under their control. On 4th November 1857 with a battalion of soldiers J.B. Nucker reached Jharghatti to capture Surendra, Udanta and Karuna Naik, the *gauntia* of Kolabira. They were surrounded by hill ranges, from three sides, i.e., from the front, left and right. Taking advantage of it Surendra and his followers who were hiding there attacked them suddenly. It resulted in the death and injury of one each. However, when the soldiers pervaded the attack, Surendra fled away leaving huge amount of rice, wheat, etc.[12]

Surendra wanted to destroy the moral strength of the British army. It is quite clear from the murder of Dr. Moor at Jujomura on 18th November 1857. He and his company Dr. Henson were deputed by Ganjam Collector to treat the (unhealthy) ill soldiers at Sambalpur.[13] Dr. Henson who fortunately escaped for life also witnessed the fatal end of many soldiers going to protect him in their return journey to Sambalpur. It shocked and humiliated the company administration. The obstruction made in the transport and postal communication of Cuttack-Sambalpur added fuel to the fire.[14] Even it was a dream for Capt. Leigh to get reinforcement from any sides since all road communications were cut off.[15] It made Leigh mentally so weak that he requested his higher authority, Capt. Dalton, in a personal letter to give him a low salary job with less responsibility. It was followed by another one just two days later describing the critical situation of Sambalpur. He mentioned there about the burning of post offices, obstructions in postal communication from Bombay to Calcutta, and illness of sepoys with their fear and unwillingness to perform duties.[16]

Consequently, to establish law and order Sambalpur was shifted to Cuttack division on 5th December 1857 because it was difficult to administer Sambalpur from faraway Chota Nagpur division. Moreover, Chota Nagpur Commissioner was always engaged and busy otherwise for which he failed to devote time to Sambalpur.

Surendra's struggle was mainly regulated by non-Brahmin tribal Gond and Binjhal *zamindars*. Of course, a few Brahmin *gauntia*s sided with him. These *zamindar*s were exploited because of Brahmin patronization of royal power. Even their *zamindari*s were confiscated and given to Brahmins and royal servants as rent-free land.

Forts played a prominent role in the armed struggle of Surendra Sai. Debrigarh in Barapahad was the centre of all. Situated in the impregnable ravines with twelve towers at the top, it was 2267 ft. in height. In the past it was the hiding place of many kings at the time of danger. The 'Khandjore'[17] stream passing near the fort was working as a defence and supplied water to the revolutionaries. The stone wall surrounding the fort and its secret exit way was its strategic defence for protection. From the top of the peak they were able to remain vigilant towards the movement of the enemies and follow accordingly. Since it was centrally located, Surendra himself made it as his important stronghold. From here he was going to different other centres and returning back in one night to regulate the affairs of the rebellion. The Barabakhra hill caves were situated at the feet of this mountain. As many as 400 people can take shelter here with water facility throughout the year.

Pahar Srigida was another place of strategic defence. At its entrance point there was a stone wall 7 ft. in height and 30 ft. in width. Another wall was present in the left side of its halfway. The front jungle was reclaimed to have a clear vision of the movement of the enemies and to gun them down easily.[18]

The Barpatti, Jharghatti and Singoda Ghattis were also surrounded either by stone or earthen walls. Barpatti was the combination of a number of hills. It was situated in the Mundei Loisingha of Sambalpur subdivision. Its highest peak situated near Budhapali was 2,331 ft. in height. 'Maula Bhanja' was situated near Rengali station while Jharghatti was situated 60 km away from Sambalpur. The Sambalpur-Ranchi Road passes through it. It was the stronghold of Udanta Sai who had constructed a chest-height earthen wall around it.

Singoda Ghatti was another important place of defence. It was situated on the way from Sambalpur to Raipur. Besides, the forts of Manikgarh and Junagarh at different times were used by the revolutionaries. At Manikgarh they had constructed two walls for their defence. About Junagarh Ghatti, Major Foster writes,

> it is an escaping way of dangerous ravines and hill ranges flanking to different direction. Guarding on it is practically impossible.[19]

All these forts were impregnable. However, the revolutionaries were acquainted with them while the English knew nothing. It caused heavy damage to English garrison attempting to attack there.

The houses of *zamindars* and *gauntias* were also centre of arm invasion. Well-laid tactful plan for fighting battles were made inside it. The walls of the houses were made with holes in such a way that the revolutionaries were able to see the outside and to check the advance of the enemies. It also helped them to estimate the situation and escaping from the back door if necessary.

In such a situation the British soldiers were completely helpless. The attack of Capt. Leigh on 17th December 1857 to a Ghatti, four miles away from Sambalpur indicates it. The stone Ghatti surrounded with dense forests forced him to retreat. How the natural self-defending feature of the Ghattis helped in carrying out the armed struggle is important to remember here.[20]

The last but not the least tactics of Surendra Sai was the blockade of Sambalpur.

> Like a seasoned diplomat and military leader he decided to guard the passages to cut down reinforcement and fight the British forces here and there with uncanny Guerrilla speed and precision.[21]

To check the external help and coming of the English soldiers from outside to Sambalpur he blocked all road communication to the town. Nagpur-Sambalpur Road was blocked at Singoda Ghatti under Ghenss *zamindar* Madho Singh and his three sons. Its second road was checked by Kharsal *zamindar*, Dial Sardar. Pahar Srigida road was blocked by its local *zamindar* Janardan Singh. Udanta Sai checked the Sambalpur-Hazaribagh Road at Jharghatti. A group of revolutionaries remained at 'Maula Bhanja' hill near Rengali to resist any help coming from Ranchi. The people of Loisingha stayed at Barpatti to resist any reinforcement from Cuttack. It was also under the direct command of Surendra Sai. Papanga hill was under another group of revolutionaries while Barapahad was under the *zamindar* brothers of Lakhanpur. In this way Sambalpur was completely isolated from the outside world. Of course later on all these Ghattis were freed by the English, which largely contributed to their success in suppressing the 'Ulguan'.

In addition to it, many times face-to-face battles were fought. One example was Surendra's fighting with the English in 1840 near Budharaja hill. Another example was his fighting with Capt. Wood at a place near Kudopali in December 1857. In the battle 53 rebels along with the brother of Surendra, Chhabila Sai fell dead. Another example is his fighting in 1860 at Manikgarh near Khariar.

These were the various war tactics followed by Surendra Sai against the English. By his Guerrilla war, self-defending techniques, and blockade of roads, he was able to continue his armed rebellion for forty years, i.e., from 1827 to 1863. Without doubt his war tactics were epoch-making not only in Sambalpur but also on the soil of Orissa and India as well.

NOTES AND REFERENCES

1. *Kosal Khabar*, Vols. I-II, Jan.-Feb. 1997, p. 13.
2. Letter from the agent, Sambalpur to the Secretary to Govt., No. 43, dt. 23.10.1840, State Archives, BBSR.
3. Dash, Shiva Prasad, *Sambalpur Itihas* (Oriya), Sambalpur (2nd edn.), 1969, p. 358.
4. *Ibid*.
5. *Kosal Khabar*, Vols. I-II, Jan.-Feb. 1997, p. 13.
6. *Utkal Prasanga*, No. IV, Nov. 1997, p. 46.
7. Dash, Shiva Prasad, *op. cit*., p. 355.
8. *Utkal Prasanga*, No. IV, Nov. 1997, p. 46.
9. Dash, Shiva Prasad, *op. cit*., p. 380.
10. *Ibid*., p. 361.
11. *Ibid*.
12. Letter from Capt. Leigh to Naucker, No. 98, dt. 4.11.1857 (Board of Revenue Record), Sambalpur.
13. Dash, A., *Veer Surendra Sai*, Cuttack, 1936, p. 101.
14. Letter from Capt. Leigh to Capt. Dalton, No. 85, dt. 28.11.1857 (Board of Revenue Record), O.C.O, 11.

15. Letter of Cuckborne to the Secretary of Bengal Govt., dt. 5.12.1857 (Board of Revenue Record).
16. Personal letter of Capt. Leigh to Capt. Dalton, dt. 1.12.1857 and dt. 3.12.1857, (Board of Revenue Record), O.C.O., 11.
17. Dash, S.P., *op. cit.*, p. 365.
18. Dash, A., *op. cit.*, p. 110.
19. Letter from Major Foaster to the Secretary of Bengal Govt., dt. 12.11.1860, M.P. Secretariate Record, Judicial dept., 1860, file no. 7.
20. Letter from Capt. Leigh to Capt. Dalton, No. 90., dt. 17.12.1857 (Board of Revenue Record), O.C.O., 11.
21. *West Orissa – A Study in Ethos*, SU, 1992, p. 248.

15

Svarnavati, Bhogavati and Ratnavati

Some Light on Inter-State Relation (10th-12th Centuries AD)

Jadumani Mohapatra

Located on the eastern slope of the Central Indian plateau, Dakshina Kosala has played a significant role in shaping the course of events of the country in the early centuries of the Christian era and the early Medieval period. Holding a strategically important position, it controlled the highway leading from the Uttrapatha to the peninsular India. Mutual relations between a number of dynasties ruling over Dakshina Kosala and the neighbouring tracts of land from different political headquarters in the early Medieval period form an interesting study. In this paper we have focused on some aspects of the mutual relations between different ruling dynasties holding control over the three metropolises, namely, Svarnavati, Bhogavati and Ratnavati.

SVARNAVATI

Variously named as Suvarnapura,[1] Svarnapura,[2] Paschima Lanka,[3] Sannavati[4] (Svarnavati), and Sunapura[5] in epigraphs and literature, this metropolis was on the confluence of the Mahanadi and the river Tel. At present it is known as Sonepur and is the headquarters of the district named after ancient Suvarnapura. For several centuries from the beginning of the Christian era, this metropolis has played an important role as the capital city of a number of ruling dynasties and as the cradle of Orissan art and culture.

From 9th century AD to the middle of the 11th century AD, it became the cause of dissension between the Somavamsis and the Kalachuris vying for the political hegemony over Sakala Kosala. Later on, the Nagas of Chakrakotta and the Gangas of Utkala established their authority over the tract of land of which Svarnavati or Suvarnapura was the headquarters. In the middle of the 14th century AD, the Chauhans established their rule over this part of Dakshina Kosala.[6]

BHOGAVATI

Bhogavati, identified with modern Barsur on Indravati in the Bastar district of Chhattisgarh, was the capital of the Chindaka Naga rulers of Chakrakotta. In their epigraphs the Chindaka Nagas have mentioned themselves as *Bhogavatipuravaresvara.*[7] The Naga kingdom of Chakrakotta was established in the last quarter of the 8th century or in the first quarter of the 9th century AD with the support of the Somavamsis.[8] Manoeuvring the contemporary political situation in the neighbouring principalities, they could successfully maintain the territorial integrity of their kingdom until finally it was conquered by the Matsyas of Vaddadi and the Kakatiyas of Warangal in the second-half of the 14th century AD.[9]

RATNAVATI

Ratnavati or Ratnapura finds frequent mention in the inscriptions of the Kalachuris of Dakshina Kosala.[10] In Brahmagupta's *Navasahashanka Charita* we find mention of Ratnavati identified with Ratnapura or modern Ratanpur, 16 miles north of Bilaspur.[11]

The Kalachuris who held Ratnapura as their metropolis were lineal descents of the Haihayas of Tripuri who in their turn claim descent from Karttavirya Sahasrarjuna of Lunar Kshatriya race. Towards the close of the 10th century AD, a collateral branch of the Kalachuris of Tripuri began their rule in Dakshina Kosala with their headquarters at Tummana, which was later on shifted to Ratnapura. From the Ratnapura headquarters they ruled over this territory for nearly two hundred years, passing through many ups and downs in their political career. In the first quarter of the 13th century AD their power was crushed by Anangabhimadeva III (AD 1211-AD 1238), the Ganga king of Utkala who snatched away the tracts of land in the middle Mahanadi Valley from them.[12] Being relegated into a century of political oblivion they reappeared in the politics of Chhattisgarh region till the Bhonsles of Nagpur brought them under subjugation in the 18th century AD. From the time of Samudragupta's South Indian military expeditions, Dakshina Kosala began to figure frequently in epigraphs and contemporary literature. As already mentioned, because of its strategically important location Dakshina Kosala attracted the attention of many ambitious princes in the early Medieval period. The Nalas, the Sarabhapuriyas, the Panduvamsis, the Vanas, the Somavamsis and the Kalachuris held sway over this land at different periods of time suffering occasional debacle at the hands of their adversaries in the north, west and south. The Chalukyas, the Rastrakutas, the Cholas in the south, the later Guptas, the Pushyabhutis, the Haihayas (of Tripura), the Paramaras and the Pratiharas in the north and north-west were keenly interested in the politics of this part of India. From 9th century AD onwards Dakshina Kosala was divided into two distinct zones – east and west. The Somavamsis strengthened themselves in the delta part of the Tel and Mahanadi rivers and the Ib River Valley in the east while a collateral branch of the Kalachuris of Tripura occupied the western part of Dakshina Kosala. At this time the Chindaka Nagas gained the aid and assistance of the Somavamsi princes.[13]

The Somavamsis and the Kalachuris entangled themselves in hostile relationship for the title of *Sakalakoshaladhipati.*[14] The Nagas of Chakrakotta fished in this troubled water. The growing power of the Kalachuris of Tripuri who expanded their area of influence in the east by conquering territory in the western part of Dakshina Kosala and placing them under the disposal of the collateral members of their family forced the Somavamsis of Shripura to move into the Tel-Mahanadi basin, shifting their political headquarters first to Murasimapattana and subsequently to Aramakataka and Vinitapura. They finally consolidated their power over Suvarnapura and the adjoining tracts of land. In this mission they must have been assisted by the Chandrika Nagas of Chakrakotta because the *Orissa Museum Plates* of Yayāti I Mahashivagupta testifies to the fact that there was cordial relation between the Somavamsis and the Kalachuris. At least three Kalachuri princes of Tripuri, namely, Shankaragana II Mugdhtunga (AD 890-AD 910), Lakshmanaraja II (AD 945-AD 970), and Gangeyadeva (AD 1015-AD 1041) are known to have crossed sword with their contemporary Somavamsi kings Mahashivagupta Yayāti I (c. AD 885-AD 925), Mahabhavagupta Bhimaratha (AD 925-AD 960), Mahashivagupta Yayāti II (c. AD 1023-AD 1040), respectively. Their successful expeditions against Kosala, Odra and Utkala have been boastfully narrated in the *Bilhari Stone Inscription* of Yuvarajadeva II,[15] *Rewa Stone Inscription*[16] and *Goharwa Plates*[17] of Karna, and the *Amoda Plates*[18] of Prithvideva I (KE 831) of Tummana. In the second-half of the 10th century AD the Kalachuris of Tripuri tightened their grip over the western part of Dakshina Kosala. Kalingaraja (AD 1000-AD 1020), a lineal descent of the Tripuri house, took possession of Tummana, which was a previous headquarters of his ancestors. His son Kamalaraja (AD 1020-AD 1045) fought for his overlord Gangeyadeva during his campaign against the Somavamsis ruling over the eastern part of Dakshina Kosala and Utkala. From him onwards the Kalachuris of Dakshina Kosala became conspicuous in Central Indian politics, finally severing their feudal connection with Tripuri during the rule of Jajalladeva I (AD 1090-AD 1120), the fifth known ruler of Dakshina Kosala branch.

It was at this juncture that the Chindaka Nagas grew powerful in Chakrakotta with their capital city at Bhogavatipura. Yashorajadeva, the Telugu Choda general of the Chandika Nagas, conquered the eastern part of Dakshina Kosala for his master Someshvaradeva (c. AD 1068-AD 1110) by killing Dharmaratha, the Somavamsi prince-viceroy stationed at Suvarnapura. It is known from the *Kuruspal Stone Inscription*[19] that Someshvaradeva had killed the kings of Orda and one Madhurantaka, defeated Virachoda and Vajra, burnt the city of Vengi, devastated Bhadrapattana, Lanji and Ratnapura and acquired the sovereignty of Kosala (Dakshina Kosala) by conquering *Lakhastakam Sannavatya Aametam gramanam.*[20] The *Navasahashanka Charita* of Padmagupta has the information that the Paramara king Sindhuraja alias Navasahashanka had killed one Vajrankusha and Ratnachuda of Ratnavati who were the enemies of his ally, the Naga king of Bhogavati[21] with whom Sindhuraja established matrimonial relation later on. In his *Kuruspal Stone Inscription* Someshvaradeva of Chandrika Naga family has claimed victory over a number of principalities including Vajra and the prince of Ratnapura. Possibly he had sought the assistance of the Paramara king Navasahashanka in these military campaigns which form the subject matter of Padmagupta's work.[22]

When Jajalladeva I (AD 1090-AD 1120) became powerful in Ratnapura, he retaliated the humiliation suffered by one of his predecessors at the hands of the Nagas of Bhogabatipura, by defeating its king Someshvaradeva and taking him captive after a bloody battle. The Naga king was later on released from imprisonment at the behest of Rajalla, mother of Jajalladeva I. Someshvaradeva had become too old in age when he suffered reverses at the hand of his Kalachuri adversary of Ratnapura. Meanwhile, in AD 1111 Anantavaraman Chodagangadeva of Kaliṅga invaded Utkala. He defeated its ruler Karnakeshari but reinstated him as a subordinate ally and rushed back to the south for safeguarding his own principality from the hostile Chodas.[23] The political changes thus effected in Utkala by the conquest of Ganga the king worried Jajalladeva I, who had a craving for the possession of the entire Dakshina Kosala. He had subdued Someshvaradeva of

Chakrakotta, the overlord of the Telugu Choda rulers of Suvarnapura. Svarnavati was the easternmost extremity of Dakshina Kosala. To complete the occupation of the whole of Dakshina Kosala and apprehending Chodaganga's westward expansion of his conquest Jajalladeva I immediately mobilized the Kalachuri army and routed Someshvara III Bhujavala, the *Chodakula Kamala Vikasha Bhaskara Sakala Koshaladhiashyara.*[24] His General Jagapaladeva brought to submission the Mayurikas (Bhanjas) in the train of this invasion.[25] Jagapalladevea did not survive long to consolidate his conquest. His son Ratnadeva II succeeded him.

Soon after his accession Ratnadeva II (AD 1120-AD 1135) began consolidating his possession over the newly conquered territories. Chodagangadeva (AD 1077-AD 1147) and his son Jateshvara Madhu Kamarnava (AD 1147-AD 1156) miserably failed to recover the Kosala portion from the occupation of the Kalachuris. In AD 1130 Ratnadeva inflicted a crushing defeat on Chodagangadeva, which has been attested by the *Ratnapur Stone Inscription* of Prithvideva II (*Vikrama* year 1207)[26] and the *Mallar Inscription* dated KE 919.[27] The *Ratnapur Stone Inscription* of Prithivideva II (KE 915)[28] and the *Kharod Stone Inscription* of Ratnadeva III (KE 933)[29] testify to the fact that Prithvideva II's General Brahmadeva defeated and imprisoned Jateshvara, the Ganga king of Utkala after a fierce battle fought in Talharimandala. The Gangas accepted the fait accomplice. The Svarnavati region of Dakshina Kosala was lost to the control of the Kalachuris of Ratnapur only to be reconquered by Anangabhimadeva III (AD 1211-AD 1238) before sometime in AD 1220. In this battle fought in the fearsome groves along rivers, Anangabhimadeva III's Minister-General Vishnu fought valiantly and crushed the power of Pratapamalla alias Jagadekamalla (AD 120-AD 1225), the Kalachuri ruler of Tummana. This victory, recorded in the *Chatesvar Temple Inscription*, decided the fate of the eastern portion of Dakshina Kosala, which came under the control of the Gangas of Utkala.[30]

The Svarnavati tract of land remained under the occupation of the Kalachuris for nearly a period of one hundred years. During this period they organized the new territorial possession into Samanta Mandala and Madhya Mandala and placed them under their trusted military generals as feudatories.[31] During Prithvideva II's rule, his eldest son Jagaddeva himself took charge of the consolidation of Kalachuri power in the east. He allowed his younger brother Jajalladeva II (AD 1165-AD 1170) to succeed his father at Ratnapur. But the untimely death of Jajalladeva II compelled Jagaddeva to hasten back to the capital city and assume power in AD 1170. The preponderance of the Kalachuris of Ratnapur rested mainly on the valour and prudence of their worthy ministers and military generals like Sahilla, Jagadapaladeva, Brahmadeva and Purusottama. Most of the Kalachuri records boastfully narrate their achievements as great conquerors and builders. During Prithvideva II's rule Jagadapaladeva, who had acquired the name Jagatsimha, along with his master took over the Naga territory of Chakrakotta and occupied Bhramarabhadra,[32] a part of the Naga territory. Thereafter, the Nagas of Bhogabatipura possibly became a subordinate ally of the Kalachuris of Ratnapura. To commemorate this victory Jagadapaladeva set up the city of Jagapaslapura in Chakrakota.[33] Brahmadeva had mastered the *Shakambharividya* from his preceptor Delhuka. He has ascribed most of his success to the efficacy of this science of *tantra.*[34]

From the time of Anangabhimadeva III, Western Orissa and Eastern Chhattisgarh region came to be known as *Paschimadesha* and a *Samanta* was posted at Suvarnapura.[35] The Gangas did not effect noticeable changes in the administrative set-up of this region. The *Mahallaka*[36] system of chieftainship introduced by the Kalachuris during their rule over 'Sakala Kosala' continued to be in force even during the rule of the Gangas. The *Mahallaka*s enjoyed considerable autonomy in their respective domain and were under the obligation of paying certain feudal dues to the *Mandaladhipati* or the *Samanta*. In 14th century AD the Gangas of Utkala became weak. As a result, the *Mahallaka*s in the western part of the empire became more powerful. In the middle of the century Ramaideva, a scion of the Chauhan family of Manipuri, overthrew the oligarchy of eight *Mahallaka*s and established the Chauhan rule in Patna.

NOTES AND REFERENCES

1. Vakratentali charter of Mahābhavagupta Janamajaya I, *EI*, XI, p. 94, L. 1 of the text.
2. Baud plates of Solonabhanja, *EI*, XXVI, p. 277, L. 5 of the text; Gangadhar Mishra's *Koshalanandam*, Sonepur court, 1929, p. 93.
3. Sonepur plates of Kumara Somesvara, *EI*, XII, pp. 23 ff. Two inscriptions from Kelga, i.e., XXVII, p. 325, L. 6 of the text.
4. *Sanavatyam Telatata visayiya Lutaruma grame*, etc. Cf. Patana plates of Mahashivagupta Yayāti (RY 28), *IO*, IV, Bhubaneswar, 1966, p. 198, pl. II, 1st side, LL. 29-30; *Lakshastakam Sanavatyam sametam gramanam yah Koshalanamaharsit.* Cf. Kuruspal stone inscription of Someshvaradeva, *EI*, X, pp. 25-31. Hiralal and following him L.P. Pandeya has interpreted the expression *Sanavatyam* as 'ninety-six villages' of Kosala country. Cf. R.B. Hiralal, *Inscription of Central Provinces and Berar*, 2/e, 1932, p. 161; L.P. Pandeya, 'Cholakula Someshwaradeva – The Lord of Kosala (Mahakoshala)', *OHRJ*, VIII, 3 & 4, pp. 147-150. V.V. Mirashi writes in his introduction to the *Inscription of the Kalachuri-Chedi Era:* 'Sanavati as the

name of a territorial division occurs in a grant of Mahashivagupta Yayāti.' To him Sannavati refers to a tract of land having 96 villages within its boundary. Cf. *CII*, IV, I, p. cxxiv, note 2. S.N. Rajaguru editing the Patana plates of Mahashivagupta Yayāti (RY 28) has interpreted the expression in lines 29-30 as 'village of Luttaruma of Talatata Visaya or district in Sanavati', indicating thereby that Telatata Visaya was located along the bank of river Tel in Sannavati which evidently refers to the metropolies of Suvarnapur on the conflunce of river Tel and Mahanadi or the delta in which Suvarnapura was situated. The appropriate nomenclature should be Svarnavati. In the early Medieval period there were many cities with the name ending 'vati'. Bhogabati and Karnavati are a few cases in point.

5. Panigrahi, K.C., 'Sonepur Stone Inscription of Bhandeva', *OHRJ*, X, 1962, pp. 1-10, L. 2 of the text; *EI*, XII, pp. 150 ff.
6. Sahu, N.K. *et al.*, *History of Orissa*, 7/e, Cuttack, 2001, p. 246.
7. Narayanpal stone inscription of queen Gundamahadevi, *EI*, IX, pp. 371-319.
8. Orissa state museum plates of Mahashivagupta Yayāti I, *IO*, IV, p. 160, LL. 5-7 of the text; N.K. Sahu *et al.*, *op. cit.*, 2001, p. 161.
9. Senapati, N. *et al.* (eds.), *Gazetteer of India: Orissa: Koraput*, i/e, Cuttack, 1966, p. 54; *OHRJ*, VII, I, p. 77.
10. Raipur plates of Prithvideva I (KE 821), *CII*, IV, 2, p. 400, L. 17.
11. *CII*, IV, I, Map no. 3 facing page cxvi; *ibid.*, p. cxix; *op. cit.*, IV, 2, p. 399; N.L. Dey, *The Geographical Dictionary of Ancient and Medieval India*, New Delhi, 1994, p. 168.
12. Chatesvar temple inscription, *EI*, XXIX, p. 133., Vrs. 14; J. Mahapatra, *The Bhanjas of Khinjali Mandala*, Sambalpur University, Ph.D. Thesis, 1987 (unpublished), pp. 127-128.
13. *IO*, IV, p. 160, pl. XIII, Vrs. 2.
14. *Ibid.*, pp. 160, 165.
15. *CII*, IV, I. pp. 204-224, pl. XXXV.
16. *Ibid.*, pp. 252-275, pl. LXIV, Vrs. 9.
17. *Ibid.*, pp. 252-263, pl., Vrs. 17.
18. *Ibid.*, 2, pp. 401-409, pl. LXIV, Vrs. 9.
19. *EI*, X, pp. 25-31; *OHRJ*, VIII, I, pp. 78-79.
20. Supra., fn. 4.
21. Islampurkar, Vaman Sastri (ed.), *Navasahashanka Charita of Padmagupta*, Bombay Sanskrit Series, Bombay, 1895, Extract English Translation, *JBBRAS*, XXVI, 153.
22. Cf. J. Mahapatra, *Two Gold Coins of Jajaladeva.* Paper presented at the 63rd session of the Indian History Congress, Guru Nanak Dev University, Amritsar, 2002. If the Naga king Sankhapala of Bhogabati, as mentioned in the *Navasahashanka Charita*, be identified with Someshvaradeva who sought military assistance from Sindhuraja then the chronology of both the families can be readjusted to established their contemporaneity. In this connection V.V. Mirashi's opinion on Navasahashanka military exploits be considered.

According to him this invasion of the Paramara king be placed 'towards the end of the first decade of eleventh century AD in the closing years of Sindhuraja reign'. He further concludes that Vajrankusha was not a demon king, but a chief of the aborigines, perhaps Gonds whose capital must be looked for in the hilly regions not far from the Narmada at a distance of 50 *gavyuti* (50 *gavyuti* = 150 *koshas* = 200 miles). Vajrankusha is identical with Vajjka (Vajuvarman), the lord of Komo Mandala. He was a powerful chief as his matrimonial alliances with the Kalachuris is mentioned in several Kalachuri records. His daughter Nonalla had married Ratnaraja of Tummana where the hermitage of Saga Vanku was there and where the shrine of Vankeshvara Shiva, the tutelary deity of the Kalachuries of Dakshina Kosala was erected later on. Cf. *CII*, IV, I, pp. cxxi; also p. cxix, note 4.

Mirashi's proposed identification seems to be correct. But his doubt about the identification of Ratnavati with Ratnapura on the ground that Ratnapura was founded by Ratnadeva I and hence it could not have been in existance in this period, could be explained on the basis of the tradition recorded by J.D. Beglar in the *Mahābhārata*. Ratnapura has been mentioned as Manipura and as the capital of the Naga king. As *mani* and *ratna* are synonymous to each other, Padmagupta by his poetic imagination might have used the name Ratnavati which became Ratnapura after Ratnadeva I established his capital there in the middle of the 11th century AD. Possibly one of his ancestor had captured this metropolis by expelling the Nagas from Ratnavati.

23. *The Bharati*, I, Madras, 1925, pp. 101-120; *JAHRS*, I, pp. 113 ff, Vrs., 30 of the inscription.
24. *Journal of Kaliṅga Historical Research Society*, III, 3, pp. 229-230; *OHRJ*, VII, 3/4, pp. 148-149; Khorad stone inscription of Ratnadeva-II (KE 933), *CII*, IV, 2, p. 537, Vrs. 6.
25. Mohapatra, J., *op. cit.*, 1987, p. 119; *CII*, IV, 2, p. 454, Vrs. 9.
26. *CII*, IV, 2, p. 486, Vrs. 5.
27. *Ibid.*, p. 514, Vrs. 4; *ibid.*, IV, I, p. cxxvi.
28. *Ibid.*, IV, 2, p. 505, Vrs. 16.
29. *Ibid.*, p. 537, Vrs. 9.
30. *EI*, XXIX, pp. 121-133. Vrs. 14; *IO*, V, I, pp. 51-63, Vrs. 14 of the text; P.K. Mishra (ed.), *Comprehensive History and Culture of Orissa*, I, I, New Delhi, 1997, p. 264; N.K. Sahu *et al.*, *op. cit.*, 2001, p. 174.
31. Ghotia plates of Prithvideva II, c. 9.9., IV, 2, pp. 478-483; Amoda plates (second set) of Prithvideva II (KE 905), *ibid.*, pp. 491-495. Samanta Mandala now survives in Samantpur village situated a few kilometres north-east of Bolangir town. Madhya Mandala was possible constituted of modern Patnaghar, Kantabanji and Khariar region in Western Orissa, its headquarters being located around villages Madhyapur and Mandal in Belpara block of Patnagarh subdivision, in Bolangir district. The donated village Avala may be identified with the present village of Ainlabhata, not far away from Mandala.

32. *CII*, IV, 2, pp. 450-457.
33. This township can be identified with modern Jagdalpur in Bastar district of Chhattisgarh.
34. Bilaigarh plates of Prithvideva II (KE 896), *CII*, IV, 2, pp. 458-462, Vrs. 15.
35. Sonepur stone inscription of Bhanudeva I, *OHRJ*, X, 4, pp. 1-10.
36. *CII*, IV, I., p. cxiv.

16

Ancient and Early Medieval Trade in South Kosala

Rama Manjari Sahu

The significant cultural and political growth of South Kosala in different periods of history was possible due to the convenient topographical position of this region in the map of India. As a gateway between the North and South India, it became the homeland of many ancient tribes during the prehistoric period and the seat of political power of many ruling dynasties during the historic era. Synthesis of the Aryan and non-Aryan cultures could be possible due to the interactions of the prehistoric and historic tribes. As a part of culture, trade and commerce flourished immensely in South Kosala contributing a lot to Orissan trade as a whole during the ancient and early Medieval period.

Existence of routes along the river valleys, the waterways, rich archaeological finds, chance discovery of inscriptions and coins, existence of precious and semi-precious stones, quick growth of trade urban centres during different periods of history indicate the brisk trade activities of the people of South Kosala. Of course, here we have focused our attention on the eastern part of South Kosala, i.e., Western Orissa.

ROUTES

The earliest routes were discovered by the prehistoric men who moved from place to place along the river valleys in search of food and fodder. The upper reaches of the Mahanadi and her tributaries must have provided convenient roads to the microlithic tribes of this region. The prehistoric rock engravings and microlithic implements are found in the undivided districts of Sambalpur, Bolangir and Koraput. The Ang and Tel basins are replete with microlithic implements in the places like Manamunda, Haladipali, Khari, Chilpa, Khemanmal, Mahuapali, and Sarsara.[1] Scholars believe that an ancient route existed connecting 'Tosali' (ancient capital of Orissa) with Central India. It ran from the coastal region of Orissa through the Mahanadi basin and pass of Barmula, Boudh, Manamunda near Sonepur, then the bank of a river and reached Sripur and finally Vidisa and Ujjaini.[2]

The expedition of Samudragupta indicates the existence of routes from Central India to South Kosala and other parts of ancient Orissa. The troops of Samudragupta marched either through modern Rewa and Jabalpur region[3] or through Bilaspur via Surguja and reached Chhattisgarh and Western Orissa. From South Kosala, Samudragupta marched to Mahakantara, identified with former Kalahandi district and hill tract of Ganjam district.[4]

Crossing the Mahanadi or the Tel River, he entered into Amathgarh and Asurgarh areas of Kalahandi district. The antiquity of Asurgarh shows that the route touching this place was carved out much before the march of the Gupta army. The artefacts of this place reveal a cultural sequence from the 3rd century BC to the 5th century AD more akin to the cultural sequence of Sisupalgarh.[5]

Along with the other finds, the recovery of Chunar sandstone with Ashokan polish (250 BC), N.B.P fabric and the silver punch-marked coins suggest the link of this place with the *Uttarapatha* (Grand Route of India) by a feeder route.[6] The discovery of Chunar sandstone clearly indicates the contact of Asurgarh with Mirzapur district of north-western India as this artefact is not yet available elsewhere in India.[7] The similarity of some of the punch-marked coins of Asurgarh with those found at Palia and Bijnor near Kausambi and the similarity of texture and fabric of some pottery type of Asurgarh with those found at Ahichhatra further indicate that there was brisk intercourse between Asurgarh, Kausambi and Ahichhatra in Northern India during the days of the Mauryas.[8] Therefore, Asurgarh was situated on the highway that ran from South Kosala to the coastal regions of Orissa since the ancient days. By this route Samudragupta reached the coastal belt of Orissa.

A route between Kaliṅga and Kosala passed through the famous Kalingaghati which connected Boudh with Ganjam district. Perhaps this route was referred to as the Dharmaraja Kalingamarga in the *Kama Nalinakshapura Copper-plates* (AD 909) of King Samantavarman.[9] Scholars opine that this Dharmaraja Kalingamarga was the new name of the old Kaliṅga-Kosala route renovated by Dharmaraja II of Sailodbhava dynasty.[10] It was the same route that was traversed by Tiveradeva of South Kosala during 7th century AD who had come to the village called Phasi (near Chilika Lake) and was defeated there by the Kongoda ruler Dharmaraja.[11]

During 7th century AD, Hiuen Tsang visited Kongoda, Kosala, Udra and Kaliṅga and perhaps he followed the earlier route which led him to Kosala from Kongoda. At that time the capital of South Kosala – western-south Sarabhapura – was identified by the scholars with the Maraguda Valley of Kalahandi district.[12]

S.C. Panda believes it to be one of the important metropolis of ancient India.[13] From South Kosala Hiuen Tsang went to Andhra southwards and it implies that a route existed between South Kosala and Andhradesa.

The route that ran along the Mahanadi delta made it possible for cultural migration side by side with the trade transactions. The Gupta Plastic idiom of Sripura was transmitted to the Lalitagiri, Ratnagiri and Udayagiri complex by this route during the early Medieval period. D.R. Das suggests that there might be some relay-stations on the Kosala-Kaliṅga Highway to transmit the cultural trend from the uplands of M.P. (undivided) to the Mahanadi Valley. Boudh (in Boudh district) and Barneswarnasi (Cuttack) may be regarded as such relay-stations.[14]

The discovery of two 'Kaliṅga Janapada' or the 'local' punch-marked coins at Sisupalgarh proves the link of this place with South Kosala region as such type of works were profusely available only in South Kosala and formed its earliest coinage system.[15]

TRADE CENTRES

The archaeological discoveries and the inscriptions speak about the growth of many trade urban centres in South Kosala during the period of our study. Proto-historic and early-historic sites excavated in the middle Mahanadi Valley witnessed the use of a large number of urban and rural settlements characterized by the accuracy of a variety of ceramic industries including the fine black and red polished ware potteries. These sites reveal the existence of crafts like manufacture of beads of glass, precious and semi-precious stones, glass bangles, iron tools, punch-marked and cast coins of copper, silver and terracotta figurines, wells, etc.

The inscriptions bear the names of urban settlements like Sarabhapura, Suvarnapura (Pattana), Vititapura, Murasima pattana, Yayatinagara, etc. having the suffixes like 'pura', 'nagara', 'pattana' denoting towns and cities. Some of the political headquarters had trade potentialities when we consider their location and archaeological importance and the settlement pattern around them.

ASURGARH

We have already discussed how the excavated sites of Asurgarh lay along the ancient Kosala-Kaliṅga route and the place reveals the objects that belong to a period from the 3rd century BC to 5th century AD. This place was connected with the *Uttarapatha.* Samudragupta after the conquest of Kosala came by this route and defeated the king of Mahakantara. The antiquities found from the debris constitute iron objects, silver and bronze punch-marked coins, precious and semi-precious stone beads, potteries of different kinds and a broken piece of Chunar sandstone with Ashokan polish.[16] The brick structure found in ruined condition seems to be a religious shrine belonging to the 5th century AD. N.K. Sahu opines:

> Asurgarh was without doubt an important political and commercial centre, situated on the high road joining South Kosala and Mahakantara with Kaliṅga.[17] Huge amount of punch-marked coins were available in several mounds as the local people of Asurgarh inform. But due to ignorance they sold them to the merchants or melted them for ornaments.[18]

The punch-marked coins might have come to this place by way of trade and commerce through various mercantile guilds. In the later period the punch-marked coins were minted locally as evident from the terracotta coin moulds found from the excavation at the level attributed to about 4th century AD.[19]

SARABHAPURA

Sarabhapura, the capital of Sarabhapuriyas (6th-7th centuries AD), identified with Maraguda Valley, was a political, religious and trade centre as known from the artefacts and the ruined structures found from the excavated sites. The inscriptions corroborate the fact that it was an organized royal establishment and a trade centre at least from 4th century AD till AD 1350.[20] The copper-plates, coins, seals, sculptures, ruins of a fortified township give the conclusive proof of an ancient and medieval metropolis. Scholars express that there should not be hesitation in accepting the Maraguda Valley as an ancient city *(pura)* like that of Hastinapura and Pataliputra in view of evidence of continuous habitation, royal and administrative settlement, religious establishment, and strategic and advantageous military provisions associated with different ruling dynasties.[21]

SUVARNAPURA PATTANA

Suvarnapura of the *Somavamsi Charters* is being identified with modern Sonepur in the Suvarnapur district on the confluence of the rivers Tel and the Mahanadi. It was also called Suvarnapura Pattana in Jatisinga and *Dunguri Plates* of Mahāśivagupta Yayāti. A 'pattana' generally denotes a trading place where traders come for commercial missions. The very location of Suvarnapura on the confluence of the rivers Tel and Mahanadi suggests it to be a port town.

The singular reference to a 'Merchant's Association' is found in the *Somavamsi Charters*.[22] This association migrated from Khadirapadraka to Suvarnapura and received donation of the village Gotteikella from King Janamejaya I. The existence of a guild at Suvarnapura (Sonepur) during the reign of Janamejaya I suggests that at least some merchants of the period organized a guild and were patronized by the Somavamsi rulers.

A good number of punch-marked coins are found from Sonepur. Similar coins were found in other places of South Kosala. At Sisupalgarh, two similar types of coins were found and attributed to 2nd century AD.[23] As their coins were exclusively found in South Kosala region, S. Tripathy suggests Janapada coins instead of coinage of Kaliṅga Janapada.[24] The discovery of such coins at Sisupalgarh suggests trade relations between the western tract or South Kosala region with coastal Orissa. However, the discovery of punch-marked coins attributed to an earlier period than the rule of Somavamsi at Suvarnapura indicate that it was a commercial centre much before it became Somavamsi capital. Kalachin coins (AD 9 MC) and coins of the Yadavas of Devagiri (AD 12th) were also discovered at the vicinity of Sonepur. From the neighbourhood of Sonepur, *Ganga Fanams* (12th-13th century AD) were also found indicating that those coins entered into this area through trade and commerce.[25]

The archaeological discoveries from a place close to Sonepur known as Manamunda, situated on the National Highway from Bolangir to Boudh, further proves the commercial importance of this place. The pottery discovered from Manamuda is attributed to 2nd century AD.[26] Therefore, Suvarnapura continued to be a thriving centre of trade from the pre-Christian centuries till the Somavamsi period.

MURASIMA PATTANA

During the reign of Janamejaya I (AD 882-AD 922), four sets of copper-plates were issued from Murasima Pattana.[27] This political headquarters had also trade importance as the suffix 'pattana' indicates. This place has been identified with the modern village of Murasima of Bolangir district. It was situated on the banks of river Ang. The *Kalibhana Plates* of Janamejaya I describe the charm and the nature of this settlement. It had palatial buildings (*prasada, attalika*), pleasure gardens (*vihara*) with *Vapi, Kupa* and *Tadaga*. The term *Vipani Janapadasya* appears on the copper-plate as it was a centre of exchange Vipani of the kingdom Janapada.[28]

COMMODITIES

Though we do not get a clear picture of the commodity structure of the market places yet we can deduce the nature of the commodities from the archaeological discoveries, literature and inscriptions.

From the excavations of Asurgarh and Manamunda we find that potteries of the ancient period were available in these two places either brought from outside or manufactured locally. From different layers of Asurgarh decorated potteries of indigenous fabric, the most common ones being dull grey and grayish black in colour, red glazed Kushana potteries, black polished potteries of very fine fabric and metallic texture, potsherds of terracotta colour of Ahichhatra types were found. The pottery discovered from Manamunda is datable to the 1st and 2nd century AD.[29]

The beads of precious stones like chalcony, agate, cornelian, crystal and coral were discovered in large numbers from the Asurgarh excavation. A terracotta mould of the preparation of beads and ornaments was found from this place. Beads of quartz, cornelian, and steatite have been discovered from the debris of Manamunda.[30]

Iron objects of large quantities have been discovered from both Asurgarh and Manamunda like knife, dagger, spearheads, arrow-head, axe, nail, etc. Therefore, the material culture of the excavations indicate the earliest trade in ceramic products, precious stone-beads and iron objects. The presence of a mould for beads and ornaments at Asurgarh proves that beads were also locally manufactured and then supplied to other places.

The *Brihat Samhita* of Varaha Mihira (AD 6th) mentions that the finest and softest quality of diamonds were found in the country of Kosala.[31] Diamonds were found from the Mahanadi Valley of Sambalpur district, which was a part of South Kosala. Diamond mines were there at Hirakud of Sambalpur where the present Hirakud dam has been constructed. The fame of Sambalpur diamonds attracted the attention of Robert Clive who sent T. Motte to Sambalpur to collect them.[32]

Ivory was another precious commodity of early Medieval period. Two craft items, *Hastidanta* and *Baghacharma*, are mentioned in the grants of the Somavamsi kings in connection with the transfer of rights to enjoy these two valuables to the donees.[33] So *Hastidanta* (ivory) and *Baghacharma* (hide of a tiger) constituted articles of trade. Crafts and industries existed during the different periods of Orissan history. Many occupational groups are found to be mentioned in the *Somavamsi Charters* such as *Vanika*,[34] *Tathakara*,[35]

Suvarnakara,[36] *Suvarnabithu,*[37] *Purasresthi,*[38] *Sutradhar*[39] and *Gauda.*[40] So industries of gold, brass and stone existed during the early Medieval period. The *Sonepur Plates* of Mahābhavagupta-II Janamejaya refer to pearls.[41]

Salt might be a chief item of trade as Western Orissa, a land-locked territory, needed it for day to day use supplied by the salt merchants of Coastal Orissa. By the Kosala-Kaliṅga route salt and cotton products were exported to South Kosala and silk clothes and forest products were imported to Kaliṅga.[42]

CONCLUSION

The ancient main route joined North India with South-eastern Sea Coast from Kausambi via Bharhut through the present districts of Satna, Shahdol, Bilaspur and Raipur.[43] Important towns like Bandogarh, Kharod, Sarabhapura and Sripura were located on this route.[44] The region of South Kosala had close contact with Kaliṅga from a very early period. After the rise of Somavamsis during the 5th century AD, the contact grew considerably. The trade contact is evident from the circulation of imperial type of silver punch-marked coins which were found almost in all parts of Orissa. Those coins were introduced in Orissan markets during the Mauryan supremacy.

The Malhar excavation brought it to light that Tantragayana form of Buddhism grew up in South Kosala from about c. AD 700 and continued about AD 1000. This cult also developed in Orissa during the same period.[45] N.K. Sahu opines that the presiding deity of Suvarnapura was being revered by the Tantric Buddhist and has been referred to in some Tantric *Sadhanas*.[46] The Lankapuri of the Tibetan Buddhist literature can therefore be no other than Suvarnapura.[47]

Amongst all trade urban centres of the early Medieval period reveal religious importance. Sirpur (Sripura), Maraguda Valley (Sarabhapura), Sonepur (Suvarnapura), Binka (Vinitapura), etc. had religious monuments and shrines. Of course, during this period, the temple complex boosted up trade and vice versa. South Kosala saw all sorts of religious cults flourish on its soil as it was the chess board of different ruling dynasties and invaders from outside. The cultural migration was possible when the invaders, merchants and preachers trekked the same routes during different periods of history.

The Somavamsi ruler made Kaliṅga a prosperous territory in all aspects and the South Kosala region as an integral part of the Somvamsis saw its zenith in trade and commerce. The reference to *Vanika Purasresthi, Vanika Sthana* (Merchant's Association) and the royal patronage extended to the merchant class as known from the epigraphs are enough evidence for such an inference. The reference to different occupational groups also prove the growth of art and crafts.

The circulation of different types of coins, often minted locally and brought from outside by invaders, also prove the commercial importance of South Kosala. The use of gold and silver coins by the people and merchants prove the high purchasing capacity and affluence of the people in general. Barter system and use of cowry shells as currency might have existed no doubt, but metallic currency speak highly of the brisk commercial activity.

Thus, the South Kosala region, which is rich in prehistoric culture as evident from the discovery of prehistoric tools and rock art, rock engravings, and pictographic art, is also proud of her thriving trade activities through the ages.

NOTES AND REFERENCES

1. Mohapatra, R.P., *Archaeology in Orissa,* Vol. I, New Delhi, 1966, p. 1.
2. Pattanaik, S.K, 'Routes in Ancient Orissa', *Journal of Orissan History,* Vol. XI, 1991, pp. 13-19.
3. Sahu, N.K., *Buddhism in Orissa,* Calcutta, 1958, p. 432.
4. Acharya, P., 'Studies in Orissan History', *Archaeology and Archives,* Cuttack, 1969, p. 447.
5. Rajaguru, S.N., *Odisara Itihasa* (in Oriya), Vol. I, Cuttack, 1985, p. 233.
6. Lahiri, N., *The Archaeology of Indian Trade Routes up to* AD *200,* Delhi, 1992, p. 322.
7. *Ibid.,* p. 373.
8. Mohapatra, *op. cit.,* p. 236.
9. Rajaguru, S.N., *Inscriptions of Orissa,* Vol. I, Part-II, Bhubaneswar, Orissa State Museum, p. 264.
10. Sahu, N.K., *Odia Jatira Itihasa* (in Oriya), Vol. I, Bhubaneswar, 1977, p. 234.
11. Rajaguru, S.N., *Odisara Itihasa* (in Oriya), Cuttack, 1985, p. 391.
12. Panda, S.C., 'The Metropolic of South Kosala Maraguda Valley', *New Aspects of the History of Orissa,* Vol. VII, 1997, Deptt. of History, Jyoti Vihar, Burla, pp. 33-34.
13. *Ibid.,* p. 33.
14. Das, D.R., 'Ratnagiri School: Its origin', *Journal of Indian History,* Vol. XXVI, 1976, p. 248.
15. Tripathy, S., *op. cit.,* p. 4.
16. Sahu, N.K. (ed.), *Interim Excavation Reports.,* P.G. Department of History, Jyoti Vihar, Burla, 1982, pp. 1-8.
17. *Ibid.,* p. 7.
18. Tripathy, S., *op. cit.,* pp. 22-23.
19. *Ibid.,* p. 23.
20. Panda, S.C., *op. cit.,* p. 33.

21. *Ibid.*, p. 35.
22. Rajaguru, S.N. (ed.), *Inscriptions of Orissa,* Vol. IV, pp. 136-138.
23. Tripathy, S., *op. cit.*, p. 5.
24. *Ibid.*, pp. 3-4.
25. *Ibid.*, pp. 90-111.
26. Sahu, N.K. (ed.), *Interim Excavation Reports*, P.G. Department of History, Jyoti Vihar, Burla, 1982, p. 16.
27. Rajaguru, S.N. (ed.), 'Kalibhana Plates of Janamejaya Mahāśivagupta and Patna Plates of the Same Ruler', *Inscriptions of Orissa*, Vol. IV, pp. 101-104.
28. *Ibid.*
29. Pradhan, Sadasiba, 'Megalithic Problem of Orissa in the Light of Manamunda Excavations', 1990, in the *Journal of Orissan History*, Orissa, History Congress, Vol. XI, 1991, pp. 40-43.
30. *Ibid.*, pp. 41-43.
31. *Brihat Samhita*, Ch. VIII, V. Subramanyam Shastri and M. Ramakrishna Bhat (eds.), Bangalore, 1947, p. 392.
32. Motte, T., 'A Narrative of a Journey to the Diamond Mines at Sambalpur', *OHRJ*, Vol. I, No. 3, Appendix II, p. 42.
33. Mishra, B. (ed.), *Journal of Bihar and Orissa Research Society*, Vol. XVII, Part-I, 1930-31, p. 15, lines 28-21 and *Epigraphica Indica*, Vol. XXVIII, pp. 321-28ff.
34. *Orissa Historical Research Journal*, Vol. XI, No. 3, pp. 192-97 ff.
35. *Epigraphica Indica*, Vol. XI, pp. 95-96 ff.
36. *Indian Historical Quarterly*, Vol. XX, 1944, pp. 236-45 ff.
37. *Journal of Bihar and Orissa Research Society*, Vol. XVII, pp. 1-15 ff.
38. *Epigraphica Indica*, Vol. IV, pp. 254-59 ff.
39. *Inscription of Orissa*, Vol. IV, pp. 245-52 ff.
40. *Epigraphica Indica*, Vol. XII, pp. 237-42 ff.
41. *Inscriptions of Orissa*, Vol. IV, pp. 130-137.
42. Sahu, N.K., *Odia Jatira Itihasa* (in Oriya), Bhubaneswar, 1977, pp. 324-325.
43. Bajpai, K.D., cited in *The Political History of the Somavamsi Kings of South Kosala and Orissa* by S.R. Nema, New Delhi, 1978, p. x.
44. *Ibid.*
45. *Ibid.*
46. Sahu, N.K., *University History of Orissa*, Vol. I, Bhubaneswar, Utkal University, 1964, p. 139.
47. *Ibid.*, p. 139.

17

Borasambar in the South Kosala Tract

Early State Formation

Bhaktapuran Sahoo

In the early and medieval period of history, a large number of tribal states and principalities with multi-ethnic regional cultures had developed in Central and Eastern India. It is true that these state systems have withered away but their contributions have led to the growth and development of regional vigour in our national culture.

From early times, the western and hill portion of Orissa with inaccessible forest tracts nurtured a large number of forest kingdoms and petty principalities inhabited by aboriginal races like the Sabaras, Binjhals, Gonds, Kondhs, Bhuyans, etc. Each of the tribes was divided into several groups and each under its own chief or headman. In the course of their history these states and principalities had acknowledged the supremacy of some great power at one time or the other, and enjoyed internal autonomy of the real sort. Mention may be made of the imperial dynasties such as the Satavahanas, Chedis, Guptas, Somavamsa, Kalachuri, Telugu-Choda and the Ganga who occupied these forest kingdoms situated within South Kosala (Chhattisgarh and Western Orissa) and extracted command and tributes from them. With the waning of the imperial power of the Gangas over Western Orissa, powerful adventures mainly from Rajput stock, from Northern and Western India penetrated into this region, and by virtue of their superior intelligence and military skills, overthrew the tribal chiefs in a most calculating manner or reduced them, in some cases, to complete subjugation to feudal lords. Borasambar in the districts of Bargarh is a typical example in this context.

TOPOGRAPHY OF BORASAMBAR

The Borasambar tract of Bargarh district in Orissa is situated in 20.58° North latitude and 83.00° East longitude. It lies to the south-west of Bargarh. To the east of Borasambar is Agalpur, Nuapada-Khariar in the west, Patnagarh in the south, and Saraipali of Chhattisgarh in the north. The Gandhamardan range runs along its southern boundary. It is bounded by high hills on the north and the intervening plain is drained by the river Ang, a tributary of the Mahanadi. During the British period the Borasambar *zamindari* extended over 2178 sq km and consisted of 476 villages.[1]

SOURCES

Till this date no systematic effort has been made by scholars to reconstruct the history of Borasambar state. Source materials for the early history of Borasambar are not many. The Ang River Valley area with its tributaries has yielded flake, blade, microliths, scrapers, points, polished celts and potteries of Neolithic Age[2] and these indicate a prehistoric culture of Borasambar. But the chequered history of the region has remained neglected until now. There is lack of adequate epigraphic or literary sources bearing directly on its history. Only some stray and passing references to its medieval history are found in the writing and dispatch of some British officers. During the long span of their reign, none of the rulers of Bariha dynasty of Borasambar could find a poet-laureate or court-historian to write a trustworthy account of their achievements.

Until recently in the beginning of the 20th century, Rajendra Singh Bariha, one of the scions of the Bariha dynasty, and ex-*zamindar* of Borasambar under British protectorate, could prepare the genealogy of his family utilizing the family traditions handed down for generations in the book *Nrusimha Mahatmya* published by him in 1908. This text was compiled by Rajendra Singh Bariha on the basis of an earlier work called *Nrusimha Charita* of Jugadasa, a Kondh poet of the locality who is believed to have flourished in the second part of the 16th century AD.[3] The *Nrusimha Mahatmya* seems to have preserved essential names and events memorized in narrative tradition of the family legends, and description of incidents may or may not have changed, but its contents have to be used after careful examination. And the regnal years assigned to individual rulers in the genealogy section should not be taken literally. In addition to this, certain legends relevant to our study should be utilized after critical analysis. When there is complete lack of historical data, 'Legends or even myths are given as much credence as is compatible with the nature of events.' The legends current among the tribal people are assumed to have been handed down from generation to generation in basic form, though minor modifications might have occurred at one time or the other in the past.

LEGENDS RELATING TO THE ORIGIN OF BORASAMBAR STATE

According to the traditional account,[4] Goddess Vindhyavasini, the presiding deity of the Vindhya, had twelve sons known as *Bara Bhai Bentakara* (twelve archer brothers). Once while they were out in the forest for hunting, they happened to witness an unbelievable scene of fighting between a *Varaha* (wild boar) and a *Sasaka* (hare). They chased the *Varaha* which was found too adept in changing its colours (*Maya Varaha*). The elder Bentakara shot an arrow which miraculously reached as far as Puri in Coastal Orissa and struck at the great door of the temple of Lord Jagannath. Nobody could pull it out from the door. Even the Gajapati king harnessed his royal elephants but he could not succeed. The Bentakaras in search of their arrow reached Puri and pulled it out very easily. The Gajapati king was very much pleased with them and in appreciation of their feat gave them the Borasambar estate of Bargarh district declaring them as its rulers and the title of 'Bariha', symbolizing the strength of a wild boar, was conferred on them.

Regarding the origin of Borasambar state, there is another legend[5] current among the Binjhals. Accordingly, one Rajput king, namely, Humeru (apparently Hamiradeva), fled from his paternal state (Ranthambhor) being defeated by the Muslim ruler Allauddin Khilji (of Delhi) and took shelter in the Gandhagiri (Gandhamardan mountain situated on the borders of Bargarh and Bolangir districts). Obtaining the blessing of Goddess Durga, he built there a strong fort and was able to raise an army. After sometime, he proceeded to the north to avenge the defeat at the hands of Allauddin Khilji. On account of a wrong news, the queens of Humeru drowned themselves in a deep well in order to end their lives. But the youngest of them, Ashabati, who was pregnant at that time, was rescued by the goddess of the well, Jalkamini Devi. The widow queen roamed in the dense forest in a helpless condition. At Ramodgarh, she was traced by a Binjhal chieftain who gave her shelter and treated her like a sister. Humeru returned from the warfront and when he could not find his queens, committed suicide by jumping into the well. (This version of the *Nrusimha Mahatmaya* is found somewhat in a different manner in other versions of the legends wherein it is told that a Chauhan Rajput princess in her advanced stage fled from Northern India to Gandhagiri mountain after her husband and relations had been killed in a battle with a Muslim ruler of Delhi).

At the home of the Binjhal chieftain, the legend goes to say, the widow queen gave birth to a son. The child named Ramadeva (Ramaideva in popular tradition) was brought up with utmost care in the Binjhal household. At that time, the neighbouring Patna kingdom (former *Malliks* or chieftains) were ruling over territories controlled by eight forts, after its *Ranaka* (feudal lord) Raja Harinath Deo of the Ganga lineage died without an heir. The *Malliks* used to place a lemon on the throne considering it as *Ranaka* and by rotation they exercised all powers of the *Ranaka* for a day. They were power-mongers who never wanted the end of their rule. They used to select candidates for the throne but by stratagem they were killing them at the shrine of the Goddess Patanesvari.

One Chakradhara Panigrahi, a Brahmana of Patna (Patnagarh) while on his visit to Borosambar came to know about the widow Rajput queen and her son Ramaideva. With the consent of the Binjhal chief the Brahmana took the mother and the son to his home and trained him in the art of statecraft. Some years later, the *Malliks* elected the Brahmana Chakradhara Panigrahi for the throne. But instead of himself, he sent Ramaideva with secret planning and the latter in a dare devil manner killed the *Asta-Malliks* inside the temple of Patanesvari. Thereafter, the chief of Borasambar organized the coronation ceremony and put the turban (*Raj Pagadi*) and anointed the *Raj Tika* (mark of royalty put on the forehead) to Ramaideva, who thus became the founder of Chauhan rule in Patna kingdom. In appreciation of the services of the chief of Borasambar rendered to his widow mother in distress, Ramaideva bestowed the Borasambar state on him. It is since then, the household of the Bariha ruler of Borasambar is recognized as 'Mamughara' (maternal uncle's home) of the Chauhan rulers of Patna and the Bariha ruler has been enjoying the sole right of affixing the *Raj Tika* to the new king of Patna at the time of coronation.

CRITICAL APPRAISAL OF THE LEGENDS

The little that we know of the manner in which the state of Borasambar was formed, is available from the text *Nrusimha Charita* of the Kondh poet Yuga Das of the mid-16th century and *Nrusimha Mahatmya* of Rajendra Singh Bariha of 1908, both of which record legends preserved in the oral tradition. The information that is available from these sources is contradictory and often confusing in so far as the origin of Borasambar state and the Bariha dynasty are concerned. The first legend tells us that the Borasambar state and the Bariha dynasty are the handiworks of the Gajapati king of Puri, the sovereign ruler of Orissa, while the second one makes us believe that it was created by Ramaideva, the first Chauhan ruler of Patna. A critical analysis of the legends along with an insight into the analogous political developments in other tribal tracts of Western Orissa will certainly reveal the hitherto unknown historical process responsible for the origin of the State of Borasambar in the early period. Certain ancient customs, the beginning of which is unknown, such as the installation ceremony of the Chouhan king of Patna and the role of Bariha ruler of Borasambar in it, the special status accorded to the Barihas by Ramaideva, the founder of Chauhan dynasty at Patna, etc. can be taken as circumstantial evidences in the absence of direct evidence of the foundation of Chauhan rule at Patna.

That the ruler of Bariha dynasty of Borasambar was instrumental in raising Ramaideva on the throne of Patnagarh and became a feudatory state to the Chauhan adventurer, yet a historical event of this magnitude which does not find mention in any epigraphic record of contemporary of later period except its existences in the legends, obviously in mutilated state, through generations, is indicative of an extraordinary political situation that prevailed in this part of South Kosala in early Medieval period. In the relevant legend there is no mention of any fight between the Banjhal (Bariha) chieftain and the Rajput adventurer, but it is not known under what circumstances did he welcome an alien power over Patna kingdom of which he had been the overlord, subjugating himself and his people to an alien authority and reducing him to the lower status of a *Samanta* (vassal/*zamindar*) from his anciently autonomous status. These very vital issues of Borasambar history need investigation in their proper perspective.

In the absence of sufficient source materials, we shall have to take into account the process of early state formation in the neighbouring of Borasambar and elsewhere in the tribal zone of Central India. It is to be noted here that since prehistoric times, the Vindhya has become the abode of numerous forest tribes of autochthonous origins like the Savaras, Pulindas, Kiratas, etc., a fact which is known from the epic *Mahābhārata*,[6] *Brihat Samhita*[7] of Varaha Mihira and *Kathasaritasagara*[8] of Somadeva. The Vindhya has been described as one of the seven *Kulaparvata*s of *Bharatavarsa* of Jambudivipa.[9] It is believed that the Savaras, Binjhals, Kondhs, Bhuyans, etc. have originated from one great Vindhyan tribe. These indigenous tribes of the historic period are the descendants of the early men of the prehistoric age in Orissa and Central India. With the passage of time many of them and their subgroups migrated to the north, east and south of the Vindhya and built settlements after forests lands. They had built their dwelling houses invariably at the foot of inaccessible ranges of hills and later on they built mud-forts.[10] Remnants of such mud forts have been traced at several places of South Kosala region and Bindra-Nuagarh region, the Gonds in Phulijhar,

Sarangarh, Raigarh and Surguja of Chhattisgarh, the Bhuyans in Gangpur, Bamanda and Bonai region and the Kondhs in Sonepur, Baud and Athamallik region had established their principalities.[11]

As per the genealogy of the Bariha dynasty of Borasambar as found in the *Nrusimha Mahatmya* compiled by Rajendra Singh Bariha, ex-ruler of the State (Accession year, 1899), 32 rulers are stated to have ruled over Borasambar in succession for a period of 1723 years prior to him.[12] If we deduct this from 1899, we get the year AD 176, the period of Surya Bariha, first ruler of the dynasty. Then it follows that the origin of Borasambar state and that of Bariha dynasty took place in the second-half of the period. But the text in hand strangely states that the Barihas of Borasambar placed Ramaideva on the throne of Patna whereas it is an established fact that Ramaideva, founder of Chauhan rule in Patna, came to power sometime in the middle of the 14th century AD.[13] Further, according to the same source, Ramaideva installed Surya Bariha on the throne of Borasambar as its first ruler but his period comes to the 2nd century AD according to the genealogy. This obviously is the historical truth and is confusing all the more.

Prima facie, the regnal year assigned by the Nrusimha to individual rulers may not be accepted with certainty, but it cannot be altogether dismissed as a mere legendary account since it is based on the family tradition of the Barihas. Hence, with some reservations, we can accept it as containing historical truth in the guise of traditional account.

Thus, both the literary tradition and legends agree to it that the progenitor of the Bariha dynasty (of the Binjhal tribe) of Borasambar principality was Surya Bariha. Like many other ancient tribes, stories and myths have been fabricated in later period to establish the divine origin of the Binjhals. The *Adipurusa* of the Binjhals were *Bara Bhai Bentakara* (twelve archer brothers) who are believed to have been the sons of Goddess Vindhyavasini, the presiding deity of the Vindhya. In all probability, the eldest of the twelve brothers, Surya Bariha was the chief of the tribe. With the passage of time the Bentakaras headed by Surya Bariha migrated to the Chhattisgarh region wherefrom they entered into Borasambar territory in the Ang River Valley. They might have obtained it either by way of clearing the forest lands or by conquering it from other autochthonous tribe. Borasambar formed the nucleus territory and each of the brothers came to possess an area consisting of certain villages.

The word 'Bara Bhai' seems to indicate the pattern of what may be called clan monarchies that originated in the division of lands or villages among the twelve members of the ruling family. Such units of 12 villages or its multiples like 24 or 48 as practice of settlement and local government are known to have existed in the early Medieval period in the Rastrakuta kingdom[14] and kingdoms of the Chahamanas, Paramaras and Chalukyas.[15]

It is interesting to note here that the number '12' has great importance in the social and religious myths of several tribes. Tradition has it that in the remote past Bara Bhai Bhuyan (twelve Bhuyan brothers) were ruling over Bengal and their whole territory was called Bara Bhuyan Muluk.[16] The Beska Kondhs are divided into twelve subgroups known as *Bara Bhaya Beska Kondh* (twelve Beska Kondh brother).[17] There is a legend current among the Bondas that their progenitors were a brother and a sister and by the blessings of *Mahaprabhu* twelve sons and twelve daughters were born to them.[18] The potter class of Bihar believes that in the beginning they had 'Barah Baran' (twelve castes).[19] The Gonds believe that their gods *Bara Bhai Gond Devata* (twelve brothers Gond *Devata*) were from Goddess Kali *Kanakalin* at Bara Pahad of Satpura mountain range.[20]

In the light of the above, it is presumed that out of the twelve Bentakara brothers, each one became the founder of one *Gotra*. This is also testified by the fact that the Binjhals have twelve *Gotara*s, viz., Sonbana, Sarai, Nag, Kharsal, Dudka, Amir, Bag, Semi, Boja, Parghania, Marhi, and Bariha. It may be said with greater credibility that each Bentakara brother was in-charge of a tract of land or village. As chieftain, he used to look after the overall administration of the area assigned to him but he was subservient to the eldest brother, Surya Bariha.

Thus, in our opinion, like many other tribes, the Barihas of the Binjhals tribe headed by Surya Bariha were able to carve out a principality in Borasambar in circa 2nd/3rd century AD in South Kosala tract, which was then under the Satavahana supremacy. Borasambar in the South Kosala tract maintained its separate political existence through the vicissitude of time even when it acknowledge the supremacy of great royal dynasties like the Chedis, Guptas, Sarabhapuriyas, Pandu-Somavamsa, Kalachuris, Telugu-Chodas, Gangas and the Chauhans in various stages of its history.

The areas covered by the tribal principalities of South Kosala, including Borasambar, were thickly covered with forest with practically no good means of communication and transport. The chieftains of these territories had to pay tribute as mark of submission and render feudal services to the lord paramount.[21] They were known variously by the titles of *Mandalesvara*, *Samanta*, *Upasamanta*, *Ranaka*, *Bhupala*, etc. depending upon the position they held. They enjoyed internal sovereignty and none of the great dynasties that had subjugated these states did interfere in their internal autonomy. Their territorial extent expanded or contracted on the basis of the capability and strength of their rulers.

The rulers of these states were frequently engaged in mutual conflict with one another. Perhaps that is the main reason why, in course of time, many military and political adventures, mostly Aryans, either being displaced from their seats of power of with and attitude of adventure, entered into these forest tracts. By virtue of their superior power, strength and diplomatic skills they overthrew the tribal chiefs, established themselves in their places or put them under subjugation (as in most cases) along with extraction of tributes and other feudal dues.

In the light of the above discussion, we are inclined to believe that the Borasambar region of South Kosala tract rose to prominence as a principality in the early centuries of the Christian era under the Barihas of Binhal tribe. The progenitor of the family, Surya Bariha, the eldest of the twelve *Bentakara* brothers, controlled the affairs of the twelve clan-monarchies set up by him, each of which was under the charge of one brother. His period may be assigned to the circa 2nd/3rd century AD.

The tribal state of Borasambar acknowledged the supremacy of great royal dynasties such as the Chedis of Kaliṅga, the Imperial Guptas, the Somavamsis, the Kalachuris, the Gangas and the Chauhans of Patna kingdom in successive manner. It occupied a strategic geographical position with Chhattisgarh in the north, Kaliṅga in the south-east, Utkala in the east, and Mahakantara and Bastar in the west. In fact, it has acted as a gateway through which one of the many Aryan infiltration had taken place in the south passed through this tract. It started from Kausambi (Allahabad) and passing through Bilaspur-Raipur district of Chhattisgarh entered along the Ang River Valley through Borasambar-Bargarh-Binka-Suvarnapur. Samudragupta in his *Dakshinapatha* campaign undertook his expedition through Ang Valley via Suvarnapur to Baud and Baud via Kaliṅga Ghat to Kaliṅga.[22]

Because of its strategic location, Borasambar had to bear the brunt of numerous wars fought by imperial powers such as the Gangas, Kalachuris, and Telugu-Chodas to establish their supremacy over South Kosala in early and medieval periods. In spite of the obvious hardships faced by the Barihas of Borasambar due to the struggle for power for supremacy, they could maintain their feudal status. Clouds of misfortune shrouded the political sky of Borasambar in first-quarter of the 14th century AD. Several Rajput rulers of Northern India being expelled from their states by the Muslim rulers of Delhi fled to the south and took shelter in the tribal zone of Chhattisgarh and Orissa. They were able to earn the sympathy and goodwill of the tribal populace and by virtue of their superior skill and hereditary qualities, took advantage of the innocence of their tribal patrons. Incidentally these Rajput adventurers were able to establish their rule at many places. In some cases several Rajputs from Northern India having come on pilgrimage to Puri stopped on their way back and carved out kingdoms. The Rajput dynasties of Athmallik, Narsingpur, Tigiria, Talcher, Nayagarh, Pal-Lahanda and Kendrapara claim such circumstances of foundation.[23]

In some cases the Rajputs had to cross swords with the natives to establish their authority. The Chauhan king Balaramdeva, before establishing his dynastic rule at Sambalpur, ousted the Savara chief from Bargarh by force and occupied it.[24] But there were some native tribes who extended astounding help to immigrant Rajput-Hindu royal families to establish new kingdoms. The relationship between the rulers of Nagavamsa and Kondhs of Kalahandi developed on this basis. According to tradition,[25] the seventh Nagavamsi king of Kalahandi was deprived of the throne which he could regain only with the military help of chief Pata Majhi of Jugasaipatna. Since then tradition has it that at the coronation ceremony the new king of Kalahandi sits on the lap of the Kondh chief of Jugasaipatna.

In the early and medieval period, the Bhuiyan chiefs of Keonjhar, Bonai and Pal Lahada anointed the Hindu rulers in their respective principalities and they became trusted vassals of those Hindu rulers. In somewhat a similar manner, a ruler of the Bariha dynasty of Borasambar, most probably Karna Bariha as per genealogical data, helped the Chauhan prince Ramaideva in occupying the throne of Patna kingdom from the Astamallikas and out of gratitude Ramaideva confirmed and accepted the Bariha ruler as his chief vassal. Above all, the Bariha ruler was given the sole right of anointing the Chauhan king at Patna kingdom at the time of coronation, and the theory that Ramaideva created the estate of Borasambar, is thus unacceptable at the present state of knowledge.

NOTES AND REFERENCES

1. *Orissa District Gazetteers – Sambalpur*, Cuttack, 1971, p. 516.
2. Tripathy, K.C., *Lithic Industry in India: A Study of South-western Orissa*, Delhi, 1980, pp. 36, 37, 52.
3. Pruseth, N. (ed.), *Nrushimha Charita* (in Oriya) of Poet Yuga Dasa, Introduction, p. 20 (reprint: Padampur, 1999).
4. *Orissa District Gazetteers – Sambalpur*, Cuttack, 1971, p. 516.
5. Bariha, Rajendra Singh, *Nrushimha Mahatmya*, Sambalpur, 1908, Chap. 27.
6. *Mahābhārata*, 'Adiparva', CL XXVII, 504.
7. Sastri, V.S. (ed.), *Brihat Samhita*, Vol. I, text chapter XIV-2, p. 173.
8. Tawney and Penzer (Eng. trans. and eds.), *Somadeva's Kathasaritsagar or the Ocean of Story*, Vol. I, pp. 102, 152; Vol. II, pp. 141-149; Vol. IV, p. 100; Vol. V, pp. 159, 164.

9. *Markandeya Purāṇa*, 57, 10-11.
10. Cobden-Ramsay, L.E.B., *Bengal Gazetteers of Feudatory States of Orissa*, Reprint, Howrah, 1950, p. 30.
11. Dash, S.P., *Sambalpur Itihas* (in Oriya), 2nd edn., Sambalpur, 1969, p. 4.
12. Regnal years of four rules are not given in the genealogy.
13. Sahu, N.K. *et al.*, *History of Orissa*, 7th edn., Cuttack, 2001, pp. 245, 266.
14. Sharma, R.S., *Indian Feudalism*, 2nd edn. Reprint, Madras, 1996, p. 85.
15. *Ibid.*, p. 88.
16. Chanda, R.P., *The Indo-Aryan Races*, Indological Book Corporation, Reprint, New Delhi, 1976, p. 199.
17. Bishi, Dolagobinda, *Prajatantra Pratibha*, Oct. 1993, Cuttack, p. 74.
18. Mishra, M.K., *Loka Samskruti Parikrama* (in Oriya), Cuttack, 1996, p. 18.
19. Saraswati, B., *Pottery Making Culture and Indian Civilization*, New Delhi, 1979, pp. 179 ff.
20. Haimadorf von-Furer, *Gonds of Andhra Pradesh*, New Delhi, 1979, pp. 179 ff.
21. Pattanaik, J., *Feudatory States of Orissa*, Vol. I, Allahabad, 1988, p. 14.
22. Acharya, P., *OHRJ*, Vol. IV, No. 3 and 4, p. 45.
23. Pattanaik, J., *op. cit.*, pp. 35-36.
24. Dash, S.P., *op. cit.*, Sambalpur, 1962, p. 300.
25. Mishra, M.K., *Paschima Odisara Loka Samskruti* (in Oriya), Cuttack, 1990, pp. 63-64.

18

Saptamatrikas in the Temple Art of Western Orissa

Prabhas Kumar Singh

The concept of *Matrikas* (*Matrugana*) or divine mothers is one of the manifestations of *Shakti*, the great goddess. We find the reference of *Saptamatrikas* in various *Purāṇas* like *Agni, Matsya, Markandeya, Linga, Varaha* and *Devi Mahatmya*, etc.[1] The *Devi Mahatmya*, the early *Shakta* text, describes the *Matrikas* such as *Brahmani, Maheshvari, Kaumari, Vaishnavi, Aindri, Varahi, Narasinghi* and *Chamunda*, and *Shaktis* (embodiments of the potent feminine powers) of the respective Brahmanical gods, who are generically named as *Matru* or *Matri* and in a group *Matrugana*, meaning mothers. Etymologically, *Matru* derives from the root *Maa*, meaning to measure or to be contained or comprised in.[2] *Matru*, thus means a mother, who contained obviously referring to the maternal potential. M.M. Williams, based on the *Rig Veda*, interprets *Matru* as to measure or to traverse, to be large or long enough to find room or to be contained in.[3] *Rig Veda* interprets *Matri* as one who measures across or traverses, and as one who has true knowledge, obviously meaning that of regeneration. *Matru* also means a mother as a term of respect or endearment.[4] When used generically, *Matrika* means all kinds of groups.[5] *Matrika* as used in the present work refers to the *Shakti* embodiments of respective gods as described in the Brahmanical literature, who in iconic sculptural portrayals are the divine mothers and warriors, used for ritual worship.

The origin of *Saptamatrikas* is shrouded in obscurity. About their origin, *Markandeya Purāṇa* states that the *Matrika* appeared in the scene to help Ambika or Durga to kill demon Raktabija who was bestowed with the quality of multiplying into demons of its stature and strength from the drops of his blood oozing from the wounds.[6] The *Puranic* accounts are not unanimous regarding their origin and numbers. The *Suprabhedagama*[7] reveals that the *Saptamtrikas* were created by Brahma to kill Nirrita. On the basis of iconographic features, the *Matrika* images have been accepted as the seven mother goddesses or divine mothers.[8] *Varaha* and *Kurma Purāṇa* put it to eight (*Asthamatrikas*). The *Varaha Purāṇa* mentions eight *Matrikas* and says that they represent eight mental qualities which are mentally bad. Accordingly, Yogesvari represents *Kama* or desire; Mahesvari, *Krodha* or anger; Vaishnava, *Lobha* or covetousness; Brahmani, *Mada* or pride; Kaumari, *Moha* or illusion; Indrani, *Matsarya* or fault finding; Chamunda, *Paisunya* or tale bearing; Varahi, *Asurya* or envy.[9]

Afterwards the destructive qualities of the divine mothers were withdrawn by Shiva, whereupon the divine mothers became worthy of prayers. The entire episode is symbolic of the struggle between spiritual wisdom represented by Shiva and ignorance symbolized by Andhakasura. In the struggle between these two process, the process of ignorance are strengthened by evil qualities like desire, anger, covetousness, etc. possessed by men.[10]

The *Agni Purāṇa*[11] mentions in detail the iconographic features of the mothers. According to T.A. Gopinath Rao,[12]

> they are female counterparts who are armed with the same weapons, wear the same ornaments and ride the same *vahanas* and carry the same banners as the corresponding male gods do.

Thus, Brahamani is represented like Brahma, Mahesvari like Mahesvara, Varahi like Varaha, and Indrani like Indra.

The *Saptamatrikas* are considered to be important Brahmanical Tantric goddesses, either worshipped in a group or in individual forms.[13] Whatever be the sources of origin, they are accepted as important manifestations of the supreme deity from the time of Indus civilization till the present day.[14] In highlighting the mother, scholar M.C.P. Srivastava rightly states, in India mother is installed on a highest pedestal of reverence by children presupposing a very important sect of Hindu religion and continues to be so.

Coming to Orissa, the popularity of *Saptamatrikas* can be seen by their profuse sculptural representation in the Orissan temples. They are not only worshipped as *Parsvadevatas*, but also propitiated as presiding goddesses. *Matrika* figures are shown standing or seated with their mounts. In most cases they are associated with babies. The concept of *Saptamatrikas* gained momentum with the rise of the *Bhaumakaras*. According to scholar B.C. Pradhan and others, the temple of Parsurameswara (7th century AD)[15] is the earliest momentum of Orissa, which bears on its northern wall of *Jagamohana*, the sculptural representation of the seven divine mothers and are not associated with babies. They are Chamunda, Varahi, Indrani, Vaishnavi, Kaumari, Maheshvari, Brahmani flanked by Virabhadra and Ganesha (all are four-handed with their attributes). The association of Ganesha without mouse with the *Saptamatrikas* indicates that this is the earliest representation of *Saptamatrikas* among the monuments of Orissa.[16]

Other earliest representation of the *Saptamatrikas* can be noticed at Ghodar (AD 7th) near Titilagarh in Bolangir district. In the temple of Vaital (AD 9th), at Belkhandi, in the district of Kalahandi, at Dasasvamedhaghata (Jajpur), at Khiching (Mayurbhanja), at Markandeya Tank, Puri, etc. In this paper representation of *Saptamatrikas* in the temple-art of Western Orissa has been dealt with.

Western Orissa, part of South Kosala of ancient and medieval period, comprising the modern districts of Sambalpur, Bargarh, Jharsuguda, Deogarh, Nuapada, Baudh, Bolangir, Sundargarh and Kalahandi have provided evidence regarding the origin and popularity of *Shakti* and Tantrism in this area. The discovery of *Yoni* at Maraguda Valley of early historical period reveals the hoary antiquity of *Shakti* worship in Orissa.[17] Western Orissa might also have witnessed the rise and fall of many dynasties such as Nalas, Parvatadvarakas, Panduvamsis, Sarabhapuriyas, Bhanjas, Somavamsis, Teluguchodas, Kalachuris, Gangas, Chauhans and the Nagas. Under the royal patronage of these royal dynasties, Western Orissa became the meeting ground of various religious creeds of diverse nature during the last two thousand years. The religious history of this region presents an interesting account of the blending of major Indian religions with the local folk and tribal faiths under the benign royal patronage. This part has a large number of temples, either in ruins or in situ, dating from the 5th century AD up to the late medieval period. The sculptural art of these temples are of very high standard and they reveal the socio-religious culture of this part. The various religious cults developed in this part in the different periods, has been expressed in the art form exquisitely in the temples. The cult of *Saptamatrikas* distributed in the form of sculptures can be observed in the different places of Western Orissa.

The earliest representation of *Saptamatrikas* in Western Orissa can be noticed at Ghodar, situated at a distance of 10 km from Titilagarh subdivision of Bolangir districts. The images are found carved in a projecting rock about 389 cm long and about 100 cm in height inside a paddy field.

Beglar wrongly identified them as *Navagrahas*. In fact, it is the representation of a set of *Saptamatrikas* flanked by Ganesha and Virabhadra.

Being weather beaten, this panel of *Saptamatrikas* is mutilated, blurred and disfigured to a great extent. Yet by minute study of that panel we can say that here the *Saptamatrikas* are guarded by Ganesha on the one side and Virabhadra on the other. All *Matrikas* as well as Ganesha and Virabhadra are associated with their usual vehicles. All are in sitting posture with their respective *Ayudhas*. Of course Virabhadra is in standing posture. The Ghodar representation of *Saptamatrikas* reveals that the Tantric form of Shaktism had gained popularity in South Kosala by 7th century AD.[18] The teachers of the Amardaka school, who lived in South Kosala and Kangoda during the period obviously contributed to the evolution of the cults of the seven or eight devine mothers. Late K.N. Mohapatra[19] and Dr. M.P. Dash have suggested that *Saptamatrikas* at Ghodar is the earliest representation of *Matrikas* in Orissan art.

Sonepur, popularly known as Suvarnapura in the early medieval period, was a stronghold of Shaktism and Tantrism. Here we can find even today a number of *Shakta* divinities including *Saptamatrikas* who are worshipped as presiding deities and in some cases as *Parsvadevatas*. In course of field study, this scholar find living temples dedicated to goddess Suresvari, Samalesvari, Khambesvari, Bhagabati, etc. In the niches of inner wall of *Jagamohana* of Samalesvari temple, one can notice *Saptamatrikas* images which are due to thick vermillion coating difficult to identify properly. Here the *Matrikas* are eight in number such as Narasimhi, Shivani, Kaumri, Vaishnavi, Varahi, Indrani, and Dakshinakali. Here Narasimhi replaces Brahmi. The addition of an eighth *Matrikas*, creating an *Astamatrikas* set, suggests a different literary tradition and strong Tantric influence.[20] The *Matrikas* here are not depicted in their conventional passive mode, i.e., with a baby on their left but as warrior goddesses who include a garland of skulls in their body ornamentation. Narasimhi, riding on a lion, holds a *Vajra* and sword in her right hands and blows a conch held in one of her left hands. Varahi, sitting in *alidha* pose stuffs a demon into her gapping mouth with her uplifted back hand. The eight-handed Chamunda stands on a prostrate corpse while other *Matrikas* are riding on their respective mounts. Shivani holds a *Vajra,* rosary, trident and *Parasu,* while the two-handed Indrani carries an *Akusa* and a *Vajra*. Vaishnavi is riding on *Garuda* and Kaumari is shown with her mount peacock. The eight-image Dakshinakali is found seated in intercourse on the corpse of Shiva. The *Matrikas* are accompanied by Mahisamardini and Hanuman.[21]

Chamunda is worshipped as the presiding deity at Suresvari temple. The six-handed image is standing on a corpse, holding a sword, rosary and a small trident in her right hands, whereas in her left lands, she is holding a skull and shield while biting the finger of her remaining left hand. She is wearing a garland of skull in her neck. Towards the north of Suresvari temple, a second image of ferocious Chamunda is found. She is four-handed standing image with hanging breasts, sunken belly and skeleton body. She holds spear and sword in her uplifted hands and a human skull in her lower left hand; she wears a garland of human skulls. A jackal under her feet is dragging the corpse upon which the image stands. In the western niche of Suresvari temple, another image of Varahi is found in the Suvarnameru temple compound; some loose sculptures are present. One among those is a six-handed Chamunda. In her upraised upper right hand, she holds a sword whereas she is seen biting the finger of her upper left hand. In her middle left hand she is holding a loping sword while her middle right hand is on her right breast. She is seen wearing a *jatamukta.* Her left leg is raised up to the knee level.[22] Archaeological remains and literacy accounts speak volumes on the rich cultural and sculptural antiquities of Sonepur. It was a seat of Tantric Shaktism and esoteric practices, the impact of which can be felt even today.

The rise of the Somavamsis in the post-Bhauma period is a significant landmark in the growth and development of Shaktisim in Orissa. Though the Somavamsis embraced Shaivism, they were deeply influenced by the Tantric form of Shaivism. In this context it may be said that Ranipur-Jharial and Belkandhi, the two great centres of Tantric form of Shaktism were located in South Kosala under the Somavamsis.

Ranipur, which is the same as Ranipadra of the *Ranod Inscription* was a *Shakta Pitha* under the guidance of the teachers of the Mattamayurya School. Two rock-cut *Saptamatrika* panels on hill boulders are located at Ranipur-Jharial and another set of two at Ghodar. One independent image of Brahmani is also found at Ranipur-Jharial.

In 1946, Late Kedarnath Mohapatra[23] conducted the excavation at Belkhandi, located on the confluence of river Utei and Tel Valley in the district of Kalahandi and discovered a famous shrine called Chandi temple, dedicated to seven mothers. Most of the loose sculptures of Belkhandi temple site are shifted to Manikyapuri Museum, Bhawanipatna. Chandi or Chamunda was the presiding deity of the shrine. It is striking to note here that another name of Mahāśivagupta Yayāti II was Chandihara. This shows that under the royal patronage of the Somavamsis, the cult of *Saptamatrika*s with the presiding deity of Chamunda became widely popular in South Kosala. The Tel Valley continued to be a great centre of Tantric form of Shaktism under the Somavamsis. Initially, the *Matrika*s at Belkhandi were arranged in the following order: Kaumari, Maheshvari, Brahmani, Vaishnavi, Varahi and Chamunda. The deity of Viresvara is found to the south-west corner of the temple. The group resembles in every respect, the well known *Saptamatrikas* statues standing on the Dasasvamedha *ghat* of the river Vaitarani at Jajpur and those on the banks of Markandesvara tank at Puri. On the basis of iconographic style, Late K.N. Mohapatra believes that the renowned Somavamsi kings to whose glorious rule built the Chandi temple at Belkhandi, the construction of the *Saptamatrikas* temples of Puri and Jajpur is also attributed.

Scholar S.S. Panda at Chandital has discovered sets of *Saptamatrikas* images,[24] in a small village in the Ghantabandha Grampanchayat area of Boudh district. According to local people, goddesses like Chandi, Naraghanta, Dakshinakali and Rudrakali are enshrined in the Chandital is also the name of the temple. Local legends ascribe the builder of the shrine to King Chandihara Yayāti II of Somavamsi dynasty, who was also the builder of Chandi temple at Belkhandi and Ranipur-Jharial. Uma-Mahesvara images also found amidst *Saptamatrikas* images at Chandital. Flying *Vidyadhras* with garlands in hands (male and female) one each are carved in the topmost corner of the slab of each *Matrika.* The first *Matrika* on the row is the image of Indrani; sitting in *Lalitasana* and wearing a *Kirita-Mukuta* on her head. Her *vahana* elephant is carved on the pedestal. Next to her is the image of four-handed Kaumari, whose head is missing, her *vahana mayura* is carved on the pedestal. Next to her four-handed image of Brahmi, whose *vahana hansa* (swan) is carved on the pedestal. Next to her is the image of four-handed Maheshwari, whose *vahana* bull is carved on the pedestal. Near this image, a four-handed image of Ganesha sitting in *Maharajalila* is placed on the platform meant for these deities. Next to Ganesha, an image of Uma-Mahesvara is kept in this shrine. The next image is a eight-handed goddess, sitting in *lalitasana* on a *visvapadma* pedestal. It is also the Maheshvari aspect of *devi*, the female counterpart of Maheshvara. Next to this deity, there is an image of six-handed Chamunda, sitting on a corpse in the *ardhaparyanka* posture. A garland of skull is worn around her waist. Her hair is tied like a *Jatabhara*. She holds a *sarpa* (long snake) in the upraised left and right hands over her head. In the lowest left hand is a severe human head. This is a unique image of Chamunda. Another image of Chamunda is also found here whose hands are broken. The last image in the extreme right side (proper left) of the platform is the two-handed image of Varahi, sitting in *lalitasana*. Her right hand is in *abhayamudra*, while her left hand is holding a baby, who is sitting on her left thigh. The baby is touching her left breast. Her *vahana* buffalo is carved on the pedestal.[25]

Thus, the *Matrikas* played a significant role in the religious life of the people of Orissa. Ganesha as their son and Virabhadra, a form of Shiva, as the guardian as well as their consort have special significance. Ganesha with the mothers is not only depicted as their son, but also represents divine knowledge and learning. As such in the worship pattern of Hindu deities, Ganesha is propitiated first. Virabhadra, though a guardian deity, is invariably depicted in a benevolent form. The alignment of the *Saptamatrikas* has a cosmological significance. Brahamani at the beginning represents creation, Vaishnavi symbolizes preservation of the universe, while Chamunda at the end represents destruction.[26] The wide distribution of *Matrika* in group or individual in Western Orissa (part of South Kosala) suggested its efflorescence of Shaktism in the medieval period.

NOTES AND REFERENCES

1. *OHRJ*, Vol. IX, No. II, p. 116.
2. Blide, V.V., *A Concise Sanskrit-English Dictionary*, First edn., Poona, 1926, p. 868.
3. Williams, M.M., *A Sanskrit-English Dictionary*, Delhi, 1963, p. 804.
4. *Rig Veda*, Vol. 41.4.
5. Blide, *op. cit.*
6. Mookherjee, R.K., *Flowering of Indian Art*, Calcutta, 1964, p. 191.
7. *ASI*, Vol. IX, p. 73.
8. Pradhan, S. (ed.), *Orissa: History, Culture and Archaeology*, P.K. Mishra felicitation volume, article authored by K.C. Mishra, New Delhi, 1999, p. 150.
9. Srivastava Kamal, S., *Hindu Symbolism and Iconography: A Study*, Varanasi, 1998, pp. 102-103.
10. *Ibid.*
11. *Agni Purāṇa*, p. 118.
12. Rao, T.A. Gopinatha, *Elements of Hindu Iconography*, Vol. I, pp. 380-381.
13. Das, H.C., *Brahmanical Tantrik Art of Orissa, Cultural Development of Orissa*, Calcutta, 1985, p. 99.
14. Panikar, S.K., *Saptamatrika Worship and Sculptures*, New Delhi, 1997, p. 1.
15. Panigrahi, K.C., *Archaeological Remains at Bhubaneswar*, New Delhi, 1961, p. 28.
16. Pradhan, *op. cit.*
17. Singh Deo, J.P., *Cultural Profile of South Kosala*, New Delhi, 1987, p. 314.
18. Vide *JKHRS*, Vol. II, No. III, pp. 167-172.
19. Mohapatra, K.N., 'Excavation at Belkhandi in the Kalahandi State', *JKHRS*, Vol. II, Nos. 2 and 3, September and December 1947, pp. 167-172.
20. Donaldson, T.E., *Tantra and Sakta Art of Orissa*, Vol. II, New Delhi, 2002, pp. 328-329.
21. Panda, S.S., 'Early Sculpture Art of Suvarnapura', *OHRJ*, Vol. XLIV, No. 1-4, pp. 60-61.
22. *Ibid.*
23. Mohapatra, *op. cit.*

24. Panda, S.S., 'Early Sculpture of the Upper Mahanadi Valley', *Orissa Review*, November 2003, pp. 53-55.
25. *Ibid*.
26. Das, H.C., *Iconography of Sakta Divinities*, Vol. II, Delhi, 1997, pp. 406-407.

19

Architectural Study of South Kosala

In the Alignment of Antiquities of Khariar Region

Brajakishore Padhi

The physical features of the land of South Kosala are responsible for much in the making of its earlier history. As per the *Puranic* base, the part at least of the story of the *Ramayana,* was acted in the land of Kosala, on the bank of Gomati, Surayu and Airavati, with its capital Ayodhya and in the kingdom of the Mithila with their chief town Janakapura. The Malla lived north of the Kosala. East of the Kosala were Videha or Mithila. The Odra lived in the present Orissa and south of these the Kalinga. Some of the Kosalas had wandered to the south and settled south of the Vindhya and on the banks of the Narmada.

The Gupta dynasty came into existence at the beginning of the fourth century AD. Samudragupta's dominions extended from the Hugli to the Jumna and Chambal, and from the Himalayas to the Narmada. He organized a great campaign in the south of India, but achieved no permanent conquest. His first attack was directed against South Kosala and the valley of the Mahanadi, after which he subdued the forest countries of Orissa, took the hill forts of Mahendragiri and Kottura in Ganjam. This information about Samudragupta is wholly directed from the inscriptions on a stone pillar still standing in the fort of Allahabad.

The present 'Nawapara' district of Orissa consummated with entire Zamindari of ancient Khariar. It is situated between 20°-21° North Latitude and 82°-83° East Longitude,[1] comprising an area of 3,857 square kilometres adjoining Bindra-Nawagarh on the west and Patna State on the east.[2] In *Nawapara Gazetteer*, Durga Prasad Tripathy[3] has written that the name Khariar seems to have been derived from a village known as Khaliapali and people of Bhatra caste were flourishing there. It is very probable that subsequently the name Khariar was derived from Khadu and Alaya (Khadu means the Bhajwaras and Alaya means above). Jitamitra Prasad Singh Deo[4] stated that there are about five rivers, namely, Menda, Kharial, Khandel, Rupnagar, and Aral in Rajasthan, which fall into Sambhar Lake. Kharial, alias Khariar, therefore keeps in memory, a river of Rajasthan, which falls into Sambhar land and is an additional proof in support of claiming the Chauhans of modern Western Orissa, who belong to one family, to be of Garh-Sambhar Chauhan's lineage. Being located in an ancient land of Sarabhapura, Khariar had a rich heritage from very early times. The antiquities and monuments of the Sarabhapuriyas, the Somavamsis, the Chhindaka, Nagas and the Kalachuris, were replanting the history of Khariar.

The river Jonk which originates from Sunabeda Plateau, falls into Maraguda Valley and flows out to meet with the river Mahanadi, after Mahanadi turns right from Sabainarayana site. Sarala Das, a famous poet of Orissa of the early fourteenth century, suggests that Lord Jagannath was brought to Puri from Sabainarayana. The site of Sabainarayana is situated at a distance of five kilometres from the Mahanadi. As this site is situated at the upstream of the Mahanadi, K.C. Mishra[5] suggested that the civilization might have progressed through the course of this river to the costal regions of Orissa from the far-away hinterland of Madhya Bharata. In the earlier days the Chauhan rulers occupied this Sunabeda Plateau is adorned by one hill fort – 'the Jumlagarh fort'. It has been constructed with large-sized brick. It has got a great ranging which is 24 inch wide. It is a square feet with a width of 882 inch on each side. There are only two gates–one entrance gate and other for going to the river where there exist two Darahs, known as 'Tel Darh' and 'the Haldhi Darh'. A big stone wall about 10 ft. to 11 ft. in height and 7 ft. in breadth surrounds the fort which are in ruins. About two furlongs eastward from Jumalgarh fort, village Jalmari is situated where there is another big Shiva temple now in ruins, locally called Chheliagarh (fort of the shepherd). It is also surrounded by stone walls and the compound is a square one with 110 ft. on either side. In the vicinity of this fort, there is another big ruined temple. Till date the village worship Goddess Kankalen or a female reduced to skeleton. When the Chauhan rulers became weak and left it, gradually the huge structures of the Jumalgarh hill-fort, that adorned the area, collapsed. Therefore, invaders were attracted to this part of South Kosala.[6] In due course, this locality became the cradle of many political activities in the history of South Kosala.

Maraguda Valley is named after the King Manik Roy, a Chauhan ruler. Along the side of the Jonk River, there rises a hill akin to the Gwalior fort with precipitous stone cuttings on all sides except on the eastern side. There are about 30 to 40 tanks in the area. There is a huge tank named Raital Sagar ranging about 150 to 200 acres in area, which can be compared with Dal Lake of Srinagar.[7] The Maraguda Valley is enriched with its archaeological site. The important images, mound sculptures and inscriptions include the images of Lord Ganesh, Jain Tirthankar, rows of elephant, ladies playing drums and doing penance, *Shakti* temple, watch tower-cum-treasure house, Pataleswara Shiva on a brick platform, Chingra Kachhar Complex, Chandan Mahal, Trisul hill, Tej Mahal, a gigantic *Shaiva* Vihar Complex, and Rani Mahal Darbar Hall. Some antiquities like Mahendraditya gold coins, Kalachuri copper coins, punch-marked coins, *Shakti Pithas*, *Shiva Linga*, carved stone slabs, iron implements, vessels, pottery, and potsherds were discovered during the excavation of 1974, 1983, 1986, 1991. The above antiquities represent early history. C.B. Patel narrated that Maraguda and Sisupalgarh, etc.[8] J.P. Singh Deo and Estimate Committee of Orissa State Assembly visited Maraguda Valley during 1976. They identified one broken sculpture of a Kalachuri king, lying on a brick mound over the embankment of Raital Sagar.[9] The brick used in these mounds are abnormal in size. It was 1 ft. 3 in. in length, 0 ft. 7 in. in width and 0 ft. $2^{1/2}$ in. in height, pointing out the sculpture discovered at Ratanapur and exhibited at Raipur Museum. This finding adds to the information that there were constant practices of temple construction in this belt during the Kalachuri predominance. Now a dam has been constructed over the river upper Jonk near Patora. It constraints the visit to these archaeological sites.

During that time the area was a prominent place and enriched for its antiquities and sculpture. Hiuen Tsang, known to have visited the town in the early part of seventh century AD, has left graphic account about it.[10]

The Khariar claps not only with the early history but also synchronize through the antiquities belonging to Stone Age. Innumerable ringstones are scattered throughout the Sundar River Valley and the foot-hills of Khariar belt. Throughout Kalahandi districts ringstones are scattered and it seems these can be traced mostly in the mountainous valleys of Western Orissa.[11] The ringstones were used mostly for weighing and are described as agricultural implements. The surface discovery of these polished stone celts or ringstones, popularly known as Neolithic celts, show the early occupation to be agriculture.

The cave of Yogimath Donger near Khariar reveals the artistic heritage of prehistoric men through the depiction of a series of paintings in natural caves. It through a flood of light, on the prehistoric life and culture of the people of this area. The painting is of the Neolithic Age[12] and it shows the domestic bulls and cows. The whole painting is in red tint colour.[13] This cave painting shows the main occupation of early men to have been food producing through agriculture. The paintings of Manik-Mada and Ushakothi in Sundargarh districts are also considered to be of late Stone Age or Neolithic Age.[14] As per the style, colour, and behaviour of the painting and thought, the philosophy of the Bikram Khol and Ulapgada rock-shelter painting come to include in the period of Neolithic or New Stone Age. It is a matter of surprise to scrutiny that both of these rock-shelters are situated at the nearby area still than there is full difference in between them. But the rock-shelter painting of Bikram Khol can be compared with the rock-shelter painting of the third cave of Laxmi Mundia Pahada. In other words, the paintings of Bikram Khol can be compared with the ones of Central India. Then if we will combine all the similar rock-shelter paintings of Ushakothi, Bikram Khol, Central India and Laxmi Mundia Pahada, automatically a new light of civilization of Neolithic Age will come to the mind basing on this.

The expression of man during the late Stone Age culture was produced through picture painting. A prehistoric cave painting was discovered on the rocky wall of a natural rock-shelter on the rocky side of Ghat Ghumar Stream, which falls into the Udanti River, on its left bank in between Dumerbahal and Baijalpur villages. The paint was in red tint colour and has become very faint. Little traces of bulls and men could be traced and, therefore, it might be assigned to the last part of Neolithic Age. This prehistoric painting with the similar painting found at Singhanpur[15] in Madhya Pradesh show that close cultural affinity contact prevailed in the early period.

Many antiquities have been discovered from various places of this locality that signify the artistic creation of early man and they are regarded as backbone of the art of historiography. Those are: *Yoni* of Chalcolithic period: find-spot Maraguda Valley; Mother Quartz having 108 projections showing naturally the significance of 108 numbers: find-spot Sinapali Block Area, Lac Bridge at Maraguda Valley; Potteries of Medieval period: find-spot Nehena and Elephant Panel, early Medieval period: find-spot Puchipada, etc.

The coins discovered from Maraguda Valley during the excavations and from different areas within this territory also form an important source of ancient history. The Maraguda Valley, Sunabeda Plateau has a veritable treasure of archaeological ruins dating back to fourth century AD.[16]

The eight ancient Shiva temple discovered from the dense forest of Maraguda is a symbolic one of Shaivism. These temples represented the *Asta Sambhu*. In some of these temples the *Shiva Lingam*s of black granite were apparently broken by people in search of gold.[17] The Shaiva monastery of Maraguda Valley was very likely found by the Nalas who ruled over that region.

Trisul Mound of Maraguda Valley exposed to bring it to light through excavation is unique. It is a five-storeyed ancient castle. The ruins have formed a mound of about 152 metres height and 244 metres in girth. A stone *yoni* without *Shakti* and an inscribed image of Goddess Durga are found. This was a Shaiva monastery with leaning to Shaktism.

The village of Maraguda and another nearby village had stone sculptures. Most possibly Buddha images were being worshipped as the village goddess. Besides some antiquities of Stone Age, clay seal of a Panduvamsi king of South Kosala and some Naga sculptures have been discovered from the nearby Raital Sagar of Maraguda Valley.

Banjari rock is also a remarkable one. The side of the Nawapara town situates it. It is a place of heaps of rocks. It is said that an inscription found on rock and is worships as Banjari.

Many temples have been erected in between eleventh to twelfth century AD. Paramananda Acharya[18] dated the inscription of the temple at Narasinghanath built in red stone in *Panch Ratha* plan, in the Borasambar *zamindari* to be AD 1421. In this temple the style of Kalachuris are traced. The temples constructed during the Kalachuri period were more beautiful than any other temple. It is described in the *Chateswara Inscription*[19] (AD 1220) that Vishnu, the Commander-in-Chief of Anangabhima Deva III (AD 1211-1230), went in an expedition towards Tummana, which resulted in the defeat of the Kalachuris. In the embankment of Tirbandha tank site of Khariar town, Kalachuri temple is constructed. It is traced that there is a structural similarity of body design and other aspects between the temple at Tirbandha site and temple of Narasinghanath. Mahadeva, situated on the right bank of Mahanadi, that is a Kalachuri temple structure[20] also has similarity with this temple.

The brick temple of Pataleswara at Budhi Komna, which is situated at a distance of about forty kilometres from Khariar town, is a unique temple. The Pateleswara temple is of two interesting squares plan, thereby making an eight-pointed star plan. There is no side deity; besides this, other temples erected in this localities during modern period like Dadhibamana temple, Sambleswari temple, Raktambari temple, etc. are also remarkable.

Some copper-plate grants have been discovered from various places of Khariar. The Sarabhapuriya king Mahasudevaraja[21] issued Khariar copper-plates of Mahasudevaraja during his second regnal year on the twenty-ninth day of *Sravana* registered in the grant of the village Navanaka near Borasambar. Navanaka has been identified with the modern village Nehena, the find-spot of the plates. It is also ascertained from *Raja Komna Copper-plate Grant* of Maharaja Padman Singh Dev that the grant of piece of land called Kandagada of Raja Komna on the eighteenth day of March, 1873. This is an Oriya record.

The antiquities of Khariar enriched the early history of Orissa being a part of South Kosala in this manner.

NOTES AND REFERENCES

1. *Topographical Map Sheet, No. 64 L/S U* (in the scale of 1"=1 mile).
2. *Report of the Orissa Committee,* Vol. 1, Reprint and Financial Appendices, p. 15.
3. Tripathy, D.P., *Nawapara Gazetteer* (Unpublished manuscript preserved at the Archive of Sambalpur University).
4. Singh Deo, J.P., 'Significance of Kharial Settlement', unpublished manuscript to be included in the proposed volume, *Khariar through the Ages*.
5. Mishra, K.C., *The Cult of Jagannath,* Calcutta, 1971, p. 17.
6. *Districts Statistical Handbook,* Kalahandi, 1978-1979, p. 5.
7. Deo, P.K., 'Forgotten Forts in Kalahandi District, Jumalgarh-Maraguda Complex', Part-II, *The Orissa Historical Research Journal,* Vol. XVI, 1967, p. 4.
8. Patel, C.B., 'A Brief Note on Maraguda Archaeological Project', *Orissa Review,* June, 1993, pp. 34-38.
9. Singh Deo, J.P., 'Temple of Narasinghanatha is a Kalachuri Structure', *The Orissa Historical Journal,* Vol. XXVII, 1981, p. 111.
10. Patel, C.B., *op. cit.,* pp. 34-38.
11. Singh Deo, J.P., *Cultural Profile of South Kosala,* Delhi, 1987, p. 19.
12. *Districts Statistical Handbook,* Kalahandi, 1978-1979, p. 19.
13. *Orissa Historical Research Journal,* Vol. XXII, No. 2, pp. 21-22.
14. Kuanr, D.C. (State editor), *Gazetteer of India, Orissa Kalahandi,* N. Senapathi (ed.), Cuttack, 1975, pp. 41-42.
15. Dutta, A.N., *Prehistoric Relics and the Rock Paintings of Singhanpur,* Calcutta, 1931, passim.
16. Champatiray, S. (ed.), 'Maraguda Valley – A Treasure of Archaeological Ruins', *Orissa Review,* Bhubaneswar, February and March 1983, p. 25.
17. Padhi, B.K., 'Modern History of Khariar', Ph.D. Thesis, 1988 (Unpublished. Preserved at Sambalpur University).
18. Acharya, P., *Studies in Orissa History, Archaeology and Archives,* 1969, p. 374.
19. *Epigraphica Indica,* Vol. XXIX, p. 125, *ibid.,* Vol. XXXII, p. 325.
20. Dikshit, M.G., *Introduction to Archaeological Remains in Madhya Pradesh* (in Hindi), p. 106.
21. *Epigraphica Indica,* Vol. IX, pp. 170-173.

20

Society and Culture under the Chauhans of Sambalpur

Samikshya Satpathy

The Chauhans, who played an important role in the history of India during the Muslim invasions in 12th century AD, gradually lost their hold in North India. A branch of this dynasty migrated to Western Orissa and established their set-up at Patnagarh of Bolangir district in the middle of 14th century AD. Gradually from this place they spread their overlordship almost the whole of Western Orissa and even some portions of Madhya Pradesh.

The Chauhan dynasty of Patnagarh faced its decline after Narasimhadeva, the last great ruler. With its decline a new region, Sambalpur became powerful under the able Balaramadeva. It is a turning point in the history of Chauhans because, after this the kingdom of Patnagarh declined and the Sambalpur region emerged as a very powerful state.

The great Chauhan dynasty of Sambalpur continued for more than 275 years. It faced its decline during the rule of Raja Narayan Singh. Narayan Singh was a most incapable ruler. During his region several uprisings took place. So, great chaos and lawlessness was prevailing all over the region. At this time on 10th September 1849, Narayan Singh died issueless. After that the Sambalpur region lapsed to the British Empire on the basis of the doctrine of lapse and the kingdom was converted to a district. Thus the Chauhan rule in Sambalpur was brought to an end and again Patnagarh emerged as a seat anchor of the Chauhans.

Though the Chauhan administration was a political organisation, its socio-cultural activities had also a deep footmark in the cultural history of Orissa. No doubt it was a feudal system, yet it bore the marks of tribal organization. During the reign of the Chauhans, we marked a cultural synthesis between the tribal life and the monarchy by conquest. This became possible because all authorities from the king downwards were satisfied with limited direct control and each grade of society got ample scope to progress and prosper.

The Chauhan rulers were patron of Oriya culture. They extended their patronage towards the men of letters in their states. The Chauhan ruler, Vaijala Deva II was popular even outside the state of Orissa due to his great Sanskrit work *Prabodha Chandrika.*[1] Another important Sanskrit work of the Chauhan dynasty was the great *Kosolananda Kavya* written by Gangadhar Mishra, the court poet of Raja Baliara Deva of Sambalpur. Gopinath Sarangi, the court physician of Raja Chatra Sai, was the author of *Chikitsa Manjari*, a poetic treaties on medicine. During the coronation of King Jayanta Singh in AD 1781, *Jayachandrika*, the historical *Kavya* in Hindi was written by Kavi Prahallad Dubey, the court poet.[2] According to Dr. N.N. Basu, Chaitanya Das, the author of *Nirguna Mahatmya* and *Vishnugarbha Purāṇa* was one among the *Panchasakha* writers of Oriya literature whose writings were based on the theosophical part of Jagannath cult.[3] Some other prominent writers of Chauhan period were Pratap Rai, author of *Sasisena*, Ratnakara Meher, author of *Saraswata Gita*, Gopala Telenga, author of *Adhyatma Rāmāyaṇa*, *Sudhasagara Gita* written by Chandramani Das and *Kapata Pasa* written by Bhima Dhivara. Among all these poets, the prominent was Bhima Bhoi, the blind poet, who wrote a number of *bhajans* and philosophical *Kavyas*. He provided a new lyricity and expressiveness to Oriya language. His poems were full of compassion with a deep feeling of identification for the sufferings of people.[4]

Another outstanding poet of this period was Gangadhar Meher. He was born in a poor weaver family in Barpali of Sambalpur region. His writing displayed spontaneity and natural freshness. He was a self-taught person, who acquired a deep knowledge in Sanskrit, Hindi and Bengali languages. His themes of writing were taken from old Sanskrit literature. He remains memorable for the rare insight he exhibited in exposing the minds and souls of his character. His masterpieces include *Indumati, Tapaswani, Kichakabadha, Uttararamacharita, Pranayavallari*, etc. He gave a new flavour to ancient themes and portrayed characters in a novel way. His writing creates an everlasting sensation among the readers. So, the Chauhan rules marked a glorious epoch in the field of learning and literature in Western Orissa.

In the field of religion, the Chauhans followed a policy of toleration and extended their patronage to all forms of Hinduism. Even a new religion was started in this period, that of the *Kumbhipatias* or the *Mahima Dharma.*

Bhima Bhoi, the blind poet, was the religious propagator of this religion. With his simple and powerful words, he creates a favourable atmosphere for this religion. He established his *Matha* at Khaliapali under the patronage of the Chauhan ruler of Sonepur. At Patnagarh the Chauhans accepted Patneswari as their chief deity and built a temple for her. At Sonepur they built Suvarnameru Shiva temple and worshipped there. One thing is marked among the Chauhan Rajas that, they honoured the deities of the people and took care of the local festivals and cultures. Their religious policy not only empowered them politically but they also became a popular figure. And their policies built up a better and healthier society in Western Orissa.

The Chauhan dynasty was mostly surrounded by the aboriginal tribes. In order to improve their social life they introduced Aryans elements and encouraged the immigration of Brahmins and other higher castes. They attracted the people of higher castes to live with the tribes, by which the life-style of the tribal people could be improved. For attracting higher caste people they offered free land and other attractive gifts and privileges. They showed paternal care and patronage for the local aboriginal to improve their social life and also improve their own customs and traditions. Thomas Motto, who visited the Chauhan court at Sambalpur in 1766, commented:

> If a state of ignorance is a state of nature. The inhabitants of this country are perfect natural.[5]

Motto thought that the people of Sambalpur tract were very lazy, treacherous, cruel and coward. To prove him wrong, the people of Sambalpur showed their courage and determination against the leadership of Surendra Sai.

Economically, the people under Chauhan dynasty were prosperous and wealthy. They were living with much simple comfort in particular village communities. No man was rich except in grain and no man was distressingly poor, beause the food supply was cheap and abundant. In Sambalpur rice was sold 54 *seers* a rupee at the close of the Chauhan rule in 1849.[6] When, the Britishers occupied this region, they knew that this was the land of prosperity and of promise.

In the sphere of art and architecture also the Chauhan rule was reached to a high level of excellence. When the Chauhans ruled over Western Orissa at that time the glorious architectural movement of Eastern Orissa had begun to decline. But the Chauhans did not lose heart; rather they wanted to maintain that tradition in their own territory. Both Nagara as well as Orissan style of architecture was found in the Chauhan time of architecture. Some *Shakta* temples were built in Nagara style of art, like that of Khajuraho in

Bundelkhand. While in their *Vaishnava* temples, influence of Orissan style of art is clearly shown. Their *Shaiva* temples exhibit a strange synthesis between both the styles of art. The Chauhans built hundreds of beautiful temples throughout their kingdom. Some of their masterpieces are the Kosaleswara and Patneswari temple, Narasinghnath temple, temples of Harisankar, Samalai temple of Sambalpur, Brahmapura temple of Sambalpur, Bimaleswara Shiva temple at Huma, Suvarnameru Shiva temple and Gundicha temple of Sonepur, etc.

At the conclusion, we can say that the Chauhans not only established an extensive and powerful kingdom but also looked after the overall cultural and social development of their territory. While in other parts of Orissa, the social and cultural developments faced decline in the 18th century due to political instability, in this part (western region) the cultural aspects reached its zenith under the Chauhans. The people were living in peace and prosperity. In all the fields – art, architecture and literature – this period showed the maximum level of improvement in Western Orissa.

NOTES AND REFERENCES

1. Sahu, J.K., *Souvenir, Fifth Oriya Yuva – Lekhaka Sammelan*, Vol. I, p. 142.
2. Sahu, J.K., 'Historical Value of Jaya Chandrika', *OHRJ*, Vol. XIV.
3. Basu, N.N., *Modern Buddhism and its Followers in Orissa*, pp. 38-39.
4. Das, C.R., 'Orissa's Cultural Heritage', in *Souvenir: Third Purva Bharat Sanskrutika Sammelan*, Bhubaneswar, 1976, p. 31.
5. Motto, Thomos, *Sambalpur District Gazetteer*, 1910, p. 52.
6. O' Malley, *Sambalpur District Gazetteer*, p. 122.

21

Yoni Tantra and Yoga of Sexual Transformation as Discovered in South Kosala

Jitamitra Prasad Singh Deo

The upper Mahanadi Valley, which comprised South Kosala, during ancient and medieval periods is not yet properly surveyed and excavated from archaeological point of view. The author has been continuing field surveys as study of antiquities from 1968 at an individual level.

Tantra is the earliest concept of spirituality and *yoga,* because *Kundalini,* is the gift of *tantra* to mankind.[1] Knowledge is of imitative, repetitive, derivative, educative and intuitive type. Intuitive knowledge can be only experienced through the rise of *Kundalini. Yoga* is the only process through which practice *Kundalini* can rise. There are ten kinds of *yoga* and they are *Jnana yoga, Raja yoga, Bhakti yoga, Karma yoga, Hatha yoga, Kundalini yoga, Tantra yoga, Japa yoga, Laya yoga,* and *yoga* of sexual transformation.

A tantric text called *Varahi Tantra* gives an elaborate description of the main subject of *tantra.* They are summarized as follows:

1. Consciousness.
2. The creation and destruction of the physical university (*Shristi* and *Pralaya*).
3. Worship of deities (*Devi* or *Deva Puja*).
4. Classification of beings.
5. The heavenly bodies – astronomy and astrology.
6. The different levels of awareness (*Loka*s).
7. The psychic pathways and centres in the human framework (*Nadi*s and *Chakras*).

8. Laws and duties in society.
9. Sacramental rites (*Samskaras*).
10. Consecration of forms of deities (*Murtis*).
11. Incantation (*Mantras*).
12. Magic circles (*Mandalas* and *Yantras*).
13. Symbolic and invocative gestures (*Mudras*).
14. Spiritual practices (*Sadhana*).
15. Worship (*Puja*), both internal and external.
16. Consecration of houses, wells, etc.
17. Description of holy shrines.
18. Magic (*Yogamaya Sadhana*).
19. Ceremonial rites and initiations (*Diksha*).
20. *Yoga*–including *asanas*, *pranayama*, meditative methods, etc.
21. Medicine of many types, including *Ayurveda* which is a herbal science combined with yogic practices.
22. Science.

To this list we would add all that *tantra* also included in alchemy, the art of living a fruitful and blissful life and the use of sexual energy as a means to unfold higher awareness.[2]

Tantra gives importance to the feminine aspect of Godhood, because mother's love and care is more than the father. Though no social sanction was received, the people continued to practise *tantra* in the rituals and continued to attach to it a philosophical content. *Tantra* was a parallel cultural current along with the philosophical one in the Indian culture.

> Other expression of the fertility rites in the philosophy of *tantra* in India. Based on the dual perception of the creation phenomenon with the participation of 'Shiva' and 'Shakti,' the germinator and the nurturer respectively, it is a highly complex system of philosophical thought. The *tantra* practices, however, involved sexual intercourse and other abhorrent methods.[3]

When the geological earth crust was under formation, in many places the mother earth formed the shape of female vulva, the external organ of generation, oval, like a cleft or female organ. *Yoni* in Sanskrit means vulva, the female organ. One such naturally formed vulva or *Yoni* of mother earth is found under a bamboo thicket near Patal-ganga, site of Nuapada district, situated in the extreme western boarder of Western Orissa. In total, eight *Yonis* are discovered in Nuapada district so far. *Yoni* symbolized triangle pointed-down *Yantra*, which is the *Yantra* of goddess Bhairavi, the fifth goddess of Dasamahavidya. So, all these eight *Yonis* discovered in Nuapada district are the manifestation of *Shakti* in its *Bhairavi* form. According to tantric literature, *Shakta Pramod*,[4] *Bhairavi* is the giver of knowledge. Triangle is the primal *Yoni*, which is *Yantra* of Goddess Bhairavi. So, it can be claimed that early or original yogic conception and its yogic knowledge had developed in central Mahanadi Valley, which comprises the Western Orissa of present, which led to the origin and development of *yoga* of sexual transformation, as known from archaeological findings of two stone sockets intersecting each other. The shape of two stone sockets owe their origin to the rock art at Yogimath Donger, situated at a distance of about ten kilometres to the east of Khariar. With this background, it can be claimed that the spiritual yogic culture, which developed in central Mahanadi River Valley, moved to east and evolved Jagannath deity.[5] While the spiritual *Tantric Hatha Yogic* culture moved to the west and evolved, *Composite Tantric Yogic Figure of Mahakala and Mahakali*, at Tala,[6] in Bilaspur district of Chhattisgarh province, with all the *Tantric Hatha Yogic* fearures of *yoga* of sexual transformation, on its entire body.

The union of male and female principles are known from findings of stone sockets in pair, or in two components, which fit into the socket very well, found at Mohangiri site of Kalahandi district by the author. One such stone socket set is found at Kharligarh site of Bolangir district. Both these sets are now preserved at Manikyapur Museum of Bhawanipatna. Two such socket sets are found at the Shakti temple ruin, within Bagaon village area, on the edge of the left river bank of Udanti River in Nuapada district. One half of such socket is traced at Patalganga site.

According to T.N. Mishra,

> Archaeological materials from the Indus valley civilization also point to the existence of fertility cult in India from the protohistoric period. The discovery of numerous phallic stones and ring-stones, the figure of a male ithyphallic horned god (probably the prototype of Shiva) and the figure of a Mother Goddess are ample to indicate the prevalence of the said cults. However, no representation of the sexual act has been reported in the art and ritual objects yielded by the Indus civilization.[7]

This proves that the 'Yoga of Sexual Transformation' was discovered and well known in upper and central Mahanadi Valley, before the Aryan spiritual culture penetration. Therefore, the earliest eight-handed Nataraja image with *Urdhvalinga* (penis erectus) of the country is found at Sirpur, on the right bank of Mahanadi River, dated to 5th century AD.[8]

This discussion on the discoveries shows that a great spiritual *tantric yogic* generation took place in South Kosala's eastern region among the early and medieval upland dwellers of Mahanadi Valley.

Agastya was the first Arya *rishi* to cross the Vindhya.[9] After Vedic rishis' contact with peninsular people, the *yoga* of sexual transformation was elaborately incorporated in *Brhadaranyaka Upanisad* of Sukla Yajurveda, as *Upanishads* listed or classified under the different Vedas in *Muktikopanishad*.[10]

From the critical study of the *Yoni Tantra*,[11] it is known that Kamakhya was not the original *Yonipitha* (site). So, it can be claimed that the *Adi* alias original *Yonipitha* (site) was situated in Nuapada district area and *yoni* cult gradually shifted to Kamakhya region in eastern India.

It can be thus claimed that *Yoni Tantra* and *yoga* of sexual transformation were discovered in the South Kosala region and these two rituals and *yogas* are the gift of South Kosala belt to humanity.

NOTES AND REFERENCES

1. Saraswati, Swami Satyananda, *Kundalini Tantra*, Bihar School of Yoga, Munger, 1992, passim.
2. Saraswati, Swami Satyananda, *A Systematic Course in the Ancient Tantric Techniques of Yoga and Kriya*, Bihar School of Yoga, Munger, 1989, p. 322.
3. Kulkarni, S.D. (General editor), Bhishma's *Study of Indian History and Culture*, Vol. I, *Beginnings of Life, Culture and History*, Shri Bhagvan Vedavyasa Itihasa Samshodhana Mandira (Bhishma), Bombay (Thane), 1997, p. 462.
4. *Sakta Pramod*, edited by Sri Venkatesvara Press, Bombay, 1951, p. 262.
5. Singh Deo, J.P., *Origin of Jagannath Deity*, (2nd edition), Gyan Publishing House, New Delhi, 2003, passim, Appendix-II and vide the plates.
6. Singh Deo, J.P., 'Composite Tantric Yogic Figure of Mahakala and Mahakali', *Riddle of Indian Iconography* (Zetetic on Rare Icon from Tala), in L.S. Nigam (ed.), Sharada Publishing House, Delhi, 2000, pp. 127-134.
7. Mishra, T.N., *Impact of Tantra on Religion and Art*, New Delhi, D.K. Printworld (P.) Ltd., 1997, pp. 101-102.
8. Sivaramamurti, C., *Nataraja in Art, Thought and Literature*, New Delhi, Publication Division, Govt. of India, 1994, pp. 159-160.
9. Kulkarni, S.D. (ed.), *op. cit.*, Vol. I, Thane, 1997, p. 218.
10. Nathan, R.S., *Our Heritage, Book-I*, Central Chinmaya Mission Trust, Bombay, 1986, Appendix, p. 120.
11. Schoterman, J.A. (ed.), *The Yoni Tantra*, Manohar, New Delhi, 1980, pp. 3, 4 and 9.

22

Situating Satrubhanja II in the History of Khinjali Mandala

J.K. Sahu and D. Chopdar

Khinjali *mandala* with its capital Dhrtipura is the earliest known kingdom of the Bhanjas of Orissa. The records of Dhrtipura reveal three names of the rulers of this dynasty, viz., Silabhanjadeva, Satrubhanjadeva and Ranabhanjadeva. No copper-plate charter of Silabhanja is available to us whereas there are two charters in the name of Satrubhanja and as many as a dozen of charters issued by Ranabhanjadeva. The two charters of Satrubhanja are the undated *Sonepur Grant* and the *Kumurkela Grant* issued in his 15th regnal year. Both the charters are edited by B.C. Majumdar, the first in *Epigraphica Indica,* Vol. XI, pp. 91-103 and the second in *JBORS,* Vol. II, pp. 429-435. Scholars working on the Bhanja rulers of Orissa have generally accepted that Satrubhanja of both the charters is one person. He bore the same name, ruled over the same territory and called himself Paramavaishnava in both the grants. A close study of these charters, however, gives rise to certain objections to this identification.

Satrubhanja in the *Sonepur Grant* is described as the son of Silabhanja whereas in the *Kumurkela Charter,* his father's name is given as Angadi. It may, however, be argued that Angadi might have been another name of Silabhanja because there are evidences of a king giving different names of his father in different records. This argument appears to be valid, but there are some other objections to it.

The *Sonepur Grant* was engraved by Sivanaga, son of Pandi. The same engraver is known to have engraved almost all copper-plate charters, issued by Ranabhanja, son of Satrubhanja, till at least his 26th regnal year. The engraver of *Kumurkela Grant* was Suvarnakara Devala who also engraved the last known charter of Ranabhanja[1] issued in his 58th regnal year. This indicates that Satrubhanja of *Kumurkela Grant* succeeded Ranabhanja and not preceded him. He is, therefore, not identical with his namesake of the *Sonepur Grant*.

In the *Sonepur Grant* of Satrubhanja there is no mention of the name of *Sandhivigrahika*. In fact, the post of *Sandhivigrahika* is not known to have been instituted by the Bhanja rulers of Dhrtipura till at least the 50th regnal year of Ranabhanja. We come across the *Sandhivigrahika* of the Bhanjas for the first time in the Sambalpur University Museum plates,[2] issued in the 52nd regnal year of the king. The *Sandhivigrahika* of Ranabhanja in the closing years of his reign was one Himadatta. In the *Kumurkela Charter* of Satrubhanja, the *Sandhivigrahika* is named as Savaradatta. It appears that Savaradatta was the successor and probably the son of Himadatta. In that analogy, Satrubhanja of *Kumurkela Grant* may be described as the son and successor of Ranabhanja.

Ranabhanja, in his last two *Baud Grants* issued in his 54th[3] and 58th[4] regnal year, describes his father Satrubhanja as Gandhata which appears to be the family name of that king. Satrubhanja of *Kumurkela Grant* also describes the family name of his father Ranabhanja as Angadi.

On the basis of these evidences, we can conclude that Gandhata alias Satrubhanja of *Sonepur Grant* was the father of Angadi alias Ranabhanja and grandfather of Satrubhanja II of *Kumurkela Grant*.

NOTES AND REFERENCES

1. *IHQ*, X, pp. 473-77.
2. *NAHO*, II, pp. 13 ff.
3. *EI*, XII, pp. 321-25.
4. *IHQ*, X, pp. 473-77.

23

Numismatic History of Ancient South Kosala

Susmita Basu Majumdar

South Kosala as we know roughly denotes the geo-political unit comprising of present-day state of Chhattisgarh (leaving apart Bastar region) and adjacent regions of Orissa especially Sambalpur, Kalahandi and Bolangir districts. This territory came into existence due to its typical composite geographical character. But it is very difficult to adjudge when this geo-political unit acquired the name Dakshina or South Kosala. However, Kosala denoting South Kosala finds its earliest mention in the literary sources; epigraphic sources do not help us in this regard. None of the indigenous powers ruling over South Kosala claimed themselves as the rulers of South Kosala prior to the Panduvamsins. This points towards the fact that none of the powers ruling here had control over the whole territory of South Kosala. The Allahabad *prasasti* of Samudragupta mentions Mahendra as the ruler of Kosala that was one of the twelve kingdoms conquered by Samudragupta during his *Dakshinapatha-vijaya*. Thus, the territory had already gained this name at least by the 4th century AD. The *Vakataka Inscriptions* mentioning Kosala definitely denoted the region of South Kosala. In this context, a clay sealing from Malhar attracts our attention towards the name 'Kosali'. It bears legend in Brahmi characters, palaeographically datable to the 2nd century AD reading *Gamasa Kosaliya,* i.e., of the village Kosali or Kosala. This shows that Malhar and its surrounding region was known by the name Kosala or Kosali during this period. We know that Malhar region was an important town in ancient times. On the basis of the above-mentioned evidence, one of the probabilities that may be suggested is that the dynasty which reigned in this region, with passage of time, could have extended its sway over the whole of South Kosala and with this the name of their village, i.e., Kosala or Kosali, was applied to the whole territory. To distinguish it from the territory of the same name, i.e., Kosala or Uttara Kosala, it was termed as South or Dakshina Kosala.

Coins procured from this region have attracted the attention of numismatists and historians time and again. The regio-specific character of the coins of this region, especially those minted in the repousse technique, have been given due attention. However, a detailed study of the early indigenous issues of this region and their contribution in reconstructing the regional history is a desideratum.

As far as the earliest issues are concerned, it may be pointed out that punch-marked coins have been reported from several sites in South Kosala like Arang,[1] Udela,[2] Tarapur[3] in Raipur district, Bar or Bayar[4] in Sarangarh, Akaltara,[5] and Malhar[6] in Bilaspur district, etc. These coins do not have any regio-specific character on the basis of which they can be regarded as local punch-marked coins of South Kosala as in case of the punch-marked series of Kosala.

Though substantial amount of numismatic evidences have been discovered throughout the length and breadth of South Kosala, it is interesting to note that none of the sites of this region have yielded any indigenous issues except Malhar[7] and Thathari.[8] Thus, for a better understanding of the history of South Kosala rather economic history of this region, a detailed discussion on the coins of these two regions is very important. Another interesting feature is the unique technique that was used to mint coins during the close of the ancient and the beginning of the early medieval times. This is the repousse technique. The coins minted in this technique are mostly of gold though a few silver and a single copper coin minted in this technique has also been found.

The earliest indigenous issues of South Kosala are those of Malhar. Malhar is a village located in the Bilaspur district of Chhattisgarh. During the excavations at Malhar, Prof. K.D. Bajpai and Prof. S.K. Pandey (1975-78) discovered few coins that are at present in the Sagar University but unfortunately they have not been cleaned yet, so a proper study of these coins unearthed in excavation was not possible. A detailed study of the coins found in surface exploration at Malhar, at different times, preserved in more than five different private collections has been done by the present author. Since these issues had been found in surface exploration, they lack the support of stratigraphy. The only possible method to arrange these coins in chronological order is to date them on palaeographical ground. Most of the coins of this region bear Malhar symbol (⩤). Since the symbol has been used by different dynasties that came to power in this region from time to time, it may be safely inferred that this symbol was either a mint mark or stood for the identity of the place, i.e., Malhar. Possibly these coins served the same purpose which the ancient city issues did. Malhar was an *isolated indigenous numismatic zone* in South Kosala from the 1st century BC to the 4th century AD, which indicates that excepting Malhar, other areas of South Kosala were not minting coins. However, this does not indicate that coins of imperial powers like the Kushanas, Guptas or other universal issues like the punch-marked coins were not in circulation in this region. As far as the question of minting their own coins is concerned it was only confined to the people of Malhar. The coins minted by them were meant for circulation in their own locality, i.e., Malhar. These coins are in base metal, i.e., copper and lead.

The coins of Malhar have enriched our knowledge and have helped us to reconstruct the early history of this region especially when there is dearth of archaeological evidences from other quarters. The earliest known ruler of this region and probably also the one who started the use of the Malhar symbol was *Silalusiri*[9] (c. 1st century BC). On the basis of the palaeography of the coin legend next in sequence may be placed the rulers *Achadasiri* and then *Dhamabhada* (c. 1st century AD). The coins of these two rulers being typologically similar to those of the first ruler possibly suggest that they belonged to the same dynasty but at present with dearth of archaeological evidences at our disposal it is difficult to conclude. Next in chronological sequence may be placed the rulers of the Magha dynasty. In this context it is worth mentioning that the *Purāṇa*[10] mentions the reign of nine Magha or Megha rulers over Kosala. This Kosala is in all probability South Kosala and out of the nine, coins of four Magha rulers have been found so far from Malhar. They are *Maghasri, Siriyamagha, Sivamagha, Para(?)magha* and two sealings that provide us with the name of the fifth ruler *Yugamagha* (c. 1st century-2nd century AD). To the next dynasty in chronological order after the Maghas of Kosala, belong the rulers *Śivasiri Silaluka*[11] and *Bhaliga* (c. 3rd century AD). The coins of all the above-mentioned rulers mostly bear the figure of an elephant on the obverse and the reverse is either blank or bears a tree in railing or the figure of a peacock. All the above-mentioned coins are dynastic in nature and bear the name of the ruler on the obverse. The next series of coins bear the figure of a stylized elephant different from the earlier conventional form on the obverse and the figure of a deity on the reverse. Hence, these coins have been termed as *Elephant: Deity type.* On some of the coins of the above-mentioned series, we find incomplete legend and the Malhar symbol, on some of the legends is meaningless whereas the others bear only dots reminding us of the occurrence of the legend and finally we have the uninscribed coins of the same variety. Thus, on the basis of relative occurrence and non-occurrence of legend these coins can be arranged chronologically placing the inscribed ones first and then the uninscribed issues. An attempt has been made by the present author in collaboration with the Saha Institute of Nuclear Physics, Kolkata to make an in-depth study of the metal contents or components present in these coins using non-destructive XRF technique. To make a more comparative and rational approach, coins of neighbouring areas have also been selected for metal analysis. In this respect it is worth mentioning that the results of this compositional analysis also indicate or rather corroborate the chronological order of the coins that had been attempted on the basis of the palaeography of the coin legend.[12] The early rulers like Silalusiri, Achadasiri and others up to Bhaliga have issued coins mostly in lead or with high percentage of lead mixed with other metals like iron, zinc and copper. Though the early rulers, especially Achadasiri and Sivamagha, had issued some coins with high percentage of copper content, these are very few in number when compared to their lead issues. These copper issues of the early rulers seem to be of higher valuation than the commonly used lead issues. Possibly, lead was easily available to the people of this region and we know that lead has a low melting point and hardens fast on cooling. These factors led the people of Malhar to use this metal for minting purposes. However, to the minting authorities of this locality nuclei, i.e., Malhar, the most important factor was probably easy availability and comparative easier processing necessary for minting lead coins.

With the introduction of the *Elephant: Deity type* coins we find a change in the monetary scenario. Lead was no more preferred; there began an experimentation procedure to make the coins more and more durable with the increase in the percentage of copper and at times zinc. This experimentation in the alloying process continued till they reached an approximate standard of 80-90 per cent copper with small admixture of other metals. However, the role played by lead as a comparatively lower valuation money was later on met by adopting different denomination of a coin standard (possibly Karshapana; 1/2, 1/4, 1/8 and 1/16th of Karshapana).

With the widening of the area of circulation resulting to an increased transaction, the people needed coins in more durable metal. The increase in the area of circulation is suggested by two factors: firstly, the discovery of these coins, i.e., *Elephant: Deity* series especially the Class V coins which are completely uninscribed are found from many sites throughout the length and breadth of South Kosala, and secondly the Malhar symbol which was found on almost all the issues of this region, gradually went out of use with the coming of this series (only the Class I coins of this series bear the Malhar symbol). These factors indicate towards the fact that the circulation of indigenous money was no more restricted to Malhar region or, in other words, it indic· :es indigenous monetization of the whole zone. The XRF analysis has not only corroborated the chronological arrangement of the coins and rulers done previously on the basis of palaeography but also allows us to draw logical conclusions in favour of the change of metal (from lead to copper) in relation to the increase in the transaction process.

The fact that Malhar was an isolated indigenous numismatic zone in South Kosala from at least 1st century BC to the 4th century AD raises our curiosity as to what was the factor that led the people of this region to mint their own money when the rest of the neighbouring areas were using the current available coinage of other dynasties that probably came into their territory through the medium of trade. Large amount of Kushana, Gupta, Satavahana, Yaudheya, Indo-Sassanian, few Roman and Western Kshatrapa coins have been found from different regions of South Kosala.[13] In all probability, Malhar was situated on the trade route connecting Kausambi via Bandhogarh to Andhra region; it was probably a resting station for the traders. The people of Malhar might have participated in this brisk trade which in turn was responsible for raising the necessity of minting their own issues for solving their internal transactional complexities. Another strong evidence, which helps us to infer that the trade route passed through Malhar, is the discovery of replica of Roman coins and Byzantine coins with pendant holes from Malhar. Moreover, Chakarbeda,[14] a village situated close to Malhar in the Bilaspur district, has yielded two Roman gold coins, aurei in denomination. Both the coins bear pendant holes. This shows that the people of this region had seen Roman coins in original and realized their importance and value. Hence, they made replicas and used them as ornaments.

The coins of Thathari are uninscribed and hence it is difficult to ascribe a particular date to these coins. R.R. Bhargava[15] and other scholars had suggested an early date for these issues (as early as 2nd century BC) on the ground that they are uninscribed but as we have already seen in case of *Elephant: Deity* type coins that the uninscribed issues have been assigned a later date in comparison to the inscribed ones. XRF analysis of the coins of Thathari has revealed that they contain high percentage of copper (92-94 per cent) which in turn reflects that when these issues were minted the process of extraction of pure copper from the ore was well known to the people of this region. Thus, on the basis of this fact we may place the coins of Thathari after the *Elephant: Deity* type in chronological order.

The discussion on indigenous ancient coins of South Kosala would remain incomplete without the repousse coins. The issue of repousse is an over-discussed problem. The coins minted in this technique have been mostly reported from ancient South Kosala. These issues are thin and light and the device and legend are embossed in relief on the obverse; the reverse thus bears the negative incision of the obverse embossing. These coins were in circulation in the later half of the 5th century AD and possibly continued up to the 8th century AD. The legend on these coins are mostly in box-headed characters leaving apart a few exceptional cases. So far coins minted in this technique bear the names of eight different rulers, viz., Prasannamatra, Mahendraditya, Kramaditya, Varaharaja, Bhavadatta, Arthapati, Nandanaraja, and Stambha. The most popular device being the *garuda* and legend, besides this bull, *chakra*, and Shiva standard are also found embossed on these coins along with the names of the respective rulers. These are found in two denominations: big and small. Coins of Varaharaja and Prasannamatra are found in both the denominations and coins of Stambha are found in the smaller denomination whereas the rest of the rulers had issued bigger coins only. The silver and copper repousse issues being lesser in number indicate that they were not minted with the purpose of circulation. The problem regarding the attribution of some of the coins like Prasannamatra, Mahendraditya, and Kramaditya still remain unsolved even after decades of their discovery. Here the author would like to raise a few questions the answer to which may in future lead us to solve the riddle in the light of more constructive historical evidences.

**In the Berhampur hoard the coins of Prasannamatra have been found associated with a coin of Vishnugupta who was a member of the later Gupta family of Magadha and a successor of Adityasena. He ruled sometime in the last quarter of the 7th century AD or in the beginning of the 8th century AD. Thus, the gap between Prasannamatra and Vishnugupta may not be a long one.

**The coins of Prasannamatra being found along with the coins of Kramaditya in the Bhandara hoard and those of Mahendraditya found with the coins of four Nala rulers, viz., Bhavadatta, Arthapati, Nandanaraja and Stambha in the Kuliya hoard may indicate towards a probable relationship between these rulers. However, above all we must remember that none of the Gupta rulers are otherwise known to have issued repousse coins (except a single coin of the standard type coin of Samudragupta). Thus, the repousse variety is restricted to South Kosala and secondly, the script used on these coins is box-headed *brahmi* specifically employed by Vakatakas and the Sarabhapuri and Panduvamsin rulers of South Kosala.

**If we regard the coins of Nandanaraja and Stambha as Nala issues only on the ground that they have been found along with other issues of the Nala rulers and have typological similarity with the rest of the coins of the Nalas, then we have to keep in mind that the same hoard also contains the coins of Mahendraditya. Then why not consider Mahendraditya too as a ruler of the same dynasty. The only difference is the motif on these coins. On the coins of Prasannamatra, Mahendraditya and Kramaditya we find the *garuda* motif whereas on the coins of Bhavadatta, Arthapati, Stambha, Varaharaja and Nandanaraja the motif is that of *Nandi* or bull. The difference in the motifs may be due to religious affinity. It is only because we have inscriptions of Nala rulers that bear the names Bhavadattta and Arthapati we consider these issues as Nala issues.

**Most of the scholars regard Prasannamatra as a Sarabhapuri ruler as the inscriptions mention the name of Narendra's father as Prasanna. However, this attribution raises a few questions like:

*Why was the complete name of the ruler avoided in the inscriptions that have much more space compared to the small flan of the coin?

*Why didn't the other rulers of the Sarabhapuri dynasty who were more powerful than Narendra issue coins?

*Why the dynasty which followed the Sarabhapuriyas in South Kosala, i.e., the Panduvamsins in which there were such powerful rulers like Mahāśivagupta Balarjuna also did not tend to issue coins?

All these questions may be answered if we assume that the rulers of a single dynasty, i.e, the Nalas minted all these issues. However, we do not have any supportive evidence in favour of this conjecture. But we know that the Nalas were initially a power of the southern part of Chhattisgarh comprising the Bastar district and parts of Orissa, especially Koraput region. Later on, they extended their sway towards the north and had built a temple of Vishnu at Rajim that was the heart of South Kosala. One of the reasons can be the pressure of the Vakatakas from the south that compelled them to shift towards the north. The provenance of the Sarabhapuriya inscriptions show that their main zone of activity was the upper part of Chhattisgarh plains, i.e., Bilaspur and northern part of Raipur district. During this period the Nalas might have occupied the rest of Raipur district and the region to the south of it and parts of Orissa. The find-spots of the hoards of repousse coins also support this conjecture. However, we will have to wait for more substantial evidences to answer these queries with certainty.

NOTES AND REFERENCES

1. Accession no. 15080-15085. Mahant Ghasidas Smarak Sangrahalaya, Raipur. Dr. R.N. Mishra presented these coins to the Museum.
2. Nigam, L.S., *Coins of Chhattisgarh*. These coins have been discovered by Shri Vinay Kumar Nigam of Saraipali who handed them over to Dr. L.S. Nigam of Raipur.

3. *Journal of the Andhra Historical Research Society*, Vol. III, p. 181; *JNSI*, Vol. XIX, p. 108 and B.C. Jain, 'Inventory of the Hoards and Finds of Coins and Seals from Madhya Pradesh', *Numismatic Notes and Monographs*, No. 5, p. 1.
4. *JNSI*, Vol. XXVII, p. 139.
5. Jain, B.C., *op. cit.*
6. Shall be discussed later in detail along with the indigenous issues of Malhar.
7. Majumdar, Susmita Basu, *Local Coins of Ancient India: A New Series, Coins of Malhar*, 2000.
8. Bhargava, R.R., 'Uninscribed Coins from Thathari (M.P.)', *Numismatic Digest*, Vol. 17, IIRNS, Nasik, 1993, pp. 11-14.
9. The coins of this ruler can be broadly divided into three categories – firstly, those on which the Malhar symbol is absent, possibly the earliest in chronological order; secondly, those with Malhar symbol; and to the third category can be assigned those coins which bear the Malhar symbol within an incuse restruck later on those coins which came back to the royal treasury in the circulation process. The above classification suggests that probably it was Silasusiri during whose reign the use of Malhar symbol started on the coins of this region.
10. *Vayu Purāṇa* (11, 373-382).
'Kosalayam tu rajano bhavishyanti Mahabalah
Megha iti samakhyata buddhimanti navaiva tu.'
11. Scholars like K.N. Dikshit and Ajay Mitra Shastri previously ascribed the coins of this ruler to Apilaka of the Satavahana family. Though P.L. Gupta read the legend on these issues as 'Rano Śiva Siri Sapilakasa' and not as 'Apilakasa' as others had done but he too ascribed it to the Satavahana dynasty. Whereas this issue bears a distinct Malhar symbol and the legend on the coin can clearly be read as 'Rano Śiva Siri Silalukasa'. Silalu as we have seen is not an uncommon name. The earliest known ruler of Malhar whose coins have been found bear the name Silalusiri. For details see Susmita Basu Majumdar, *Apilaka or Sapilaka Coin – A Coin of the Satavahanas or Local Ruler of Dakshina Kosala.* Proceeding of the Andhra Pradesh History Congress, 22nd Session, Hyderabad, 1998, pp. 19-20 and 'Local Coins of Ancient India: A New Series, Coins of Malhar', IIRNS, Nasik, 2000.
12. Majumdar, Susmita Basu, 'XRF and its entente with Numismatics', to be published in the Proceedings of the Indian History Congress, 63rd Session, Amritsar.
13. For details see B.C. Jain, 'Inventory of the Hoards and Finds of Coins and Seals from Madhya Pradesh'.
14. Aravamutha, T.G., *JNSI*, Vol. VII, 1945, pp. 6-10.
15. Bhargava, R.R., 'Uninscribed Coins from Thathari (M.P.)', *Numismatic Digest*, Vol. 17, 1993, pp. 11-14.

24

Shakta Monuments of Kalahandi District

A Part of Ancient South Kosala

Jayanti Dora

The Kalahandi, cradle land of early people of India, was a part of ancient South Kosala. It is situated in between 19° 3° north and 21° 5° north latitude and 82° 20° east and 83° 47° east longitudes.[1] The district occupies the south-western portion of Orissa. It is bounded on the north by the districts of Bolangir, Sambalpur and Raipur (C.G.); on the south by the districts of Koraput; on the west by the districts of Koraput and Raipur (C.G.); and on the east by the districts of Koraput and Phulbani. It is served by a series of rivers like the Tel, the Indravati, the Jonk, the Sunder and the Udanti.[2] Being a part of South Kosala, Kalahandi is characteristically the meeting ground of various waves of culture and faiths. Though mostly populated by tribals, it absorbed the Aryan culture from the north and harboured great religions and cults like Buddhism, Jainism, Vaishnavism, Shaivism and Shaktism along with tribal religious beliefs. Shaktism claims a hoary antiquity in this region. Through survey and excavations a number of *Shakta* monuments came to light, which speak about the growth and development of Shaktism in this area. Hence, a modest attempt is made in this present study to highlight the importance of *Shakta* monuments of Kalahandi district and their contribution to the enrichment of cultural heritage of South Kosala.

In ancient and medieval times, the territory of Western Orissa formed the eastern part of South Kosala. The territory Kosala which was an important *Mahajanapada* of North India was continued as a single unit at least up to the rise of the Mauryas.[3] But at a later period, a new kingdom called Kosala was established in order to distinguish it from the ancient Kosala *Mahajanapada*, which was located in the north. The *Ramayana* mentions that Kosala kingdom was divided into two parts between the two sons of Rama. Uttara Kosala was given to Lava, while Dakshina Kosala was bestowed upon Kusa[4] with the capital Kusavati near the Vindhyas.[5] Early Buddhist literature like *Avadanasataka* mentions both North and South Kosala during the lifetime of Buddha,[6] but it is a matter of controversy as to when and how South Kosala came into currency. By the time of poet Kalidasa,[7] it had already been recognized as a distinct political unit on the Vindhya range. The territorial limits of South Kosala always varied depending upon the ability and powers of its rulers. But South Kosala comprised the modern districts Raipur and Bilaspur of Chhattisgarh and Sambalpur, Sundargarh, Bolangir and Kalahandi districts of Orissa.[8]

No record is available on the origin of Kalahandi. The district Kalahandi was previously termed as 'Karand'. According to the Deputy Commissioner Lieutenant C. Elliot, Raipur it is known as Kharande, the Oriya name being Kalahandi. As we do not find any place or village corresponding to the name Kalahandi, it appears to be a corruption of the name Kalahandi. In the Maratha records, the word 'Karand' appears invariably. But, since 1905 the name Kalahandi is used when it formed a part of Bengal Presidency.[9] There is a local tradition that a man from Rajputna, namely, Kalahambir came to this region and ruled it for many years. Subsequently, the state was named Kalahandi according to his name. The literary meaning of the word Kalahandi is 'black pot' or 'pot of arts'.[10] The word Kalahandi occurs for the first time in the *Dadhivamana* temple inscription of Junagarh. It was issued by Maharaja Juga Shahi Deo from his capital Kalahandi Nagar in the *Yuga Era* 4819, i.e., AD 1718. This is the only inscription where the term Kalahandi is found. The ex-state of Kalahandi was probably named after its headquarter town Kalahandi. The ancient Kalahandi Nagar was identified with modern Junagarh. But later on Bhawanipatna became the headquarter.[11]

The undivided Kalahandi district of Orissa comprises the ex-state of Kalahandi, and ex-*zamindari* of Khariar except Kasipur. In 1948, all the princely states merged in the province of Orissa. The ex-state of Kalahandi together with the ex-state of Patna and Sonepur formed the district of Kalahandi with headquarters at Bolangir. The ex-state of Kalahandi along with the Nawapara subdivision which formed a part of Sambalpur district since 1st April 1936, was reconstituted as a separate district, Kalahandi with its headquarter at Bhawanipatna.[12]

As the district lies on the sides of the ancient highway from north to south, antiquities belonging to the Maurya, Kushana and Satavahana periods are found in large numbers in this area.[13] During 4th century AD Samudragupta too, led his South Indian expedition through this district. In the early and medieval periods different ruling dynasties like the Nalas, the Parvatadvarakas, the Sarabhapuriyas, the Somavamsis, the Chhindakanaga, the Gangas and the Nagas ruled over this region.[14] This territory assumed independence after the downfall of the Gajapatis of Orissa in AD 1568 under the Chauhans. Then the rulers of Kalahandi claimed authority over eighteen forts which was considered to be a symbol of independent power.

The Chauhans were ruling over Khariar since about the time of Ramai Deo, the first Chauhan ruler of Patna. In AD 1590 Gopal Ray, a scion of the Patna family, became the king of Khariar and started a line of semi-independent kings in that territory. This status of independence continued till the occupation of Kalahandi by the Marathas in the middle of the 18th century AD. It came under British occupation in AD 1818.[15]

In fact, Kalahandi is the treasure-house of archaeological remains. Also, it has magnificent scenic spots with towering hills and deep valleys. Many archaeological relics as well as prehistoric rock paintings on the walls of the caves are found in different parts of the districts which are the legacies of the past socio-cultural heritage of the people of this part. The district Kalahandi yielded various antiquities in the shape of religious monuments stray sculpture, military strongholds, numismatic finds and epigraphical records. Particularly, the district has scores of important *Shakta* monuments, of ancient and medieval periods. It is from Kalahandi district that we get the earliest evidences about the worship of Goddess 'Stambheshwari', an iconic form of mother goddess. Also, the *yoni* stones found from the Kalahandi district have been held by scholars as relics of the worship of mother goddess in the form of 'female organs'. Though its origin goes back to remote past, the exact date has not been assigned. Besides, the district is having notable *Shakta* temples like Manikeshvari, Samaleshwari, Raktamvari, etc. Also, a number of archaeological sites with *Shakta* remains are found in the district, viz., Asurgarh, Belkhand, Maraguda, etc. The *Shakta* monuments of the district are following:

SHAKTA REMAINS OF ASURGARH

The most important archaeological site of Kalahandi district is the fort of Asurgarh. It is almost square on plan and covered the extensive area of more than half square kilometre. The ramparts are about 4 km in width and 15-50 m in height. It is made of rubble and mud with brick fencing. Close to the western rampart the river Sandul flows to the north to meet the river Tel.[16]

The fort has four wide gates in four cardinal directions. There was a guardian deity in each gate. They are known as Ganga, Kalapat, Vaishnavi and Dakni on the eastern, western, northern and southern gates, respectively. According to local tradition, the fort was being surrounded by 64 *yoginis* in the early times. But during the excavation no *yogini* images were found.[17]

The most important antiquity of the district, relating to Shaktism, is the *Terasingha Copper-plate Inscription* found near Asurgarh. It reveals that a king, namely, Sri Maharaja Tustikara was ruling over this area during 5th century AD. He was an ardent devotee of Goddess Stambheshvari. The place Tarabhramaraka of the inscription, identified with modern Talbhamra village, was the headquarter of the King Tustikara. It seems that the worship of Goddess Stambheshvari was very popular in 5th century AD in this region. A shrine brought to light in the residential area of Asurgarh most likely belongs to this deity.[18]

In the excavated site of Asurgarh, a circular brick structure (40 feet in diameter), was brought to light. The structure was possibly a temple of mother goddess as known from small terracotta female figures discovered from the site. The roof of the structure was probably made of wood as indicated by grooves for wooden pillars. This may be taken as the earliest trace of temple construction in western part of Orissa.[19] It seems the practice of temple construction was already in vogue in Western Orissa before Somavamsi rule. The architectural remains of this site have been assigned to 5th/6th century AD.

SHAKTA REMAINS OF BELKHANDI

Belkhandi or Rajpadara is an important archaeological site of Kalahandi district. It is the find-spot of the famous Chandi temple and *Saptamatrika*'s images in Western Orissa. The site is situated at the confluence of the river Tel and Utei in the north-eastern corner of Kalahandi. S.N. Rajguru states that only one fragmentary stone inscription had been discovered from this place. It records the name of this locality as 'Gourabani Khondi Visaya'. It may be accepted that 'Gourabani' was the ancient name of river Utei. Palaeographically, this inscription has been dated in between 9th and 10th century AD, which was also revealed by S.N. Rajguru.[20]

For the first time this archaeological site was brought to light by J.D. Belgar in 1874-75 and 1875-76. He has described its ruined monuments as follows:

> Higher upon the extreme tongue of the land justing out of the junction of the Utei with the Tel are a number of ruins of great interest and undoubted his antiquity. The principle one is a large ruined brick temple. Its original state included a large sanction, a vestible, a *Mahamandapa* of large size, a

> *Mandapa* or *ardhamandapa* or portico. In front of the temple appears to have been an enclosed courtyard so that the whole in the plan formed.[21]

Mr. Belgar further states about the sculptures in the following words:

> I cannot speak too highly of the antiquity of the sculptures, although executed in the extreme soft yellowish sandstone and consequently great warm and injured by time and weather. Still from what little remains there is no doubt that they were executed in the best style of Hindu art with a breadth of conception and a depth of execution, which we vainly look for in the production of later ages.[22]

Again the site was excavated by K.N. Mahopatra in the year 1916. It brought to light the lower part of the Chandi temple. Also several new temples, all made of bricks of different sizes and sculptures, have been unearthed. The *Saptamatrika*s images which were found from Belkhandi closely resemble the *Saptamatrika*s images found at Puri and Jajpur. This temple of *Satpamatrika*s testifies that the *Shakta tantric* cult of *Saptamatrika*s had by that time made its way up into north-western Orissa. Among all the findings from Belkhandi, the image of *Saptamatrika*s and *Uma-Maheshvara* are most beautiful and distinguished images. All the excavated images of Belkhandi are preserved by the government of Orissa inside a small museum of the nearby city of Bhawanipatna. The images are seated in *lalitasana* with each a child on the lap except Chamunda, who is in *ardhaparyanka* pose without a child. The past popularity of the *Saptamatrika*s of Belkhandi as cult deities is demonstrated by the fact that in bygone days a mass slaughter of goats was carried out in the temple on the *Shivaratri* days.[23] The monuments of Belkhandi may be assigned to 10th/11th century AD.[24]

LANKESHVARI TEMPLE AT JUNAGARH

The temple of Lankeshvari is found at Junagarh. It was under the Nagavamsi ruler of Kalahandi up to AD 1856. Junabali was the ancient capital of the Naga dynasty. Later on they shifted their capital to Junagarh.

This temple is built in *pidha* order. It is decorated with the sculptures of female musicians and dancers of folk tradition. The image Lankeshvari is much older than the present temple. Iconographically, this image may be assigned to the 12th century AD.[25]

The image of Lankeshvari is seated in *Padmasana* pose on a lotus throne. She is four-armed. She holds *Sankha* and *Chakra* in her upper hands and the two lower hands are partially damaged. But *ayudha*-like mace in the lower right hand and a lotus in the lower left hand can be identified. Her hair is arranged in the shape of a bun. Also a braid is rolling down her back. She is boar-faced. Accordingly the image is identified as *Varahi*. The image is carved out of a solid block of black chlorite stone measuring 23 ft. 16 in. She is also wearing beautiful ornaments. Most probably she is the presiding deity of Junagarh.

The former ruler of Kalahandi used to make animal sacrifices in the premises of this temple and the town is named as Junabaligarh after such human sacrifices.[26] The spot of sacrifice is at present marked by four blocks of laterite stones. During the festivals of *Dussehra* a large number of goats and buffaloes are sacrificed here every year. But Lankeshvari is a *Vaishnavite* deity. Hence the sacrifices are offered to Goddess Kali who is worshipped as Bhubaneshvari in front of the temple. She is four-armed, dancing in intoxication on a corpse. She is holding a sword in the upper right hand, noose in the upper left hand, and severed head in her left hand. There are two sets of attendant divinities attached to the front entrance of Lankeshvari temple of which Ganga and Yamuna are meant for the deity Lankeshvari. Whereas Chhanda and Prachanda representing the sword and skull of human in hands and garlands of human skulls on body are meant for the terrific Goddess Kali. The present temple was built during the rule of Rana Singh Deo II (AD 1627-AD 1658).

KANAKA DURGA TEMPLE OF JUNAGARH

The temple of Kanaka Durga is later than that of Lankeshvari. The bronze image of Durga of this temple is fashioned like that of Goddess Lankeshvari. She is four-armed with *Chakra* in her upper right hand and *Sankha* in upper left hand. In her other two hands she holds a spear which pierces the chest of Mahisasura. Her mount lion is depicted on the pedestal.[27]

MANIKESHVARI TEMPLE OF BHAWANIPATNA

Bhawanipatna is the district headquarter of Kalahandi. It contains important *Shakta* monuments like Manikeshvari, Kali Thakurani, etc. The Manikeshvari temple is *Panchayatana* on plan. He is identified as the family deity of 'Chhindaka Naga' dynasty of *Chakrakata Mandala* (Baster in M.P., Kalahandi and Koraput of Orissa) in 11th century AD.[28] After the disintegration of Chhindaka dynasty, this deity came under the possession of the Gangas. In subsequent period, Ramachandra Deo, the sixth king of the Naga dynasty of Kalahandi, brought the deity from the Ganga royal family of Gudapur. He installed the same at Bhawanipatna. The present temple was completed during the reign of Udit Narayana Deo and his son Bhanja Mohana Deo.

MANIKESHVARI TEMPLE OF KARLAPAT

We can find a temple of Manikeshvari at Karlapat in the district of Kalahandi. This temple is later than Manikeshvari temple of Bhawanipatna.

RAKTAMBARI TEMPLE OF KHARIAR

The Goddess Raktambari is the family deity of Khariar. The festival of *Dussehra* used to be celebrated before Raktambari by the ex-*zamindars* with great pomp accompanied by the sacrifice of a large number of animals.

TEMPLE OF TALGUDA

The place called Talguda was ruled by Naga rulers. The annual festival of *Dussehra* is also celebrated here before the shrine of Dokari Thakurani, the presiding deity of the temple. On *Mahashtami* day a buffalo is sacrificed before the deity at midnight.[29]

A number of Samaleshvari temples are found in different places of the district like Bhawanipatna, Dumarbahal, etc. It is known from the above discussion that *Shakti* cult was widely prevalent in the district of Kalahandi and to facilitate the cult, a number of *Shakta* monuments were established from early times to the present day.

NOTES AND REFERENCES

1. Senapati, N. (ed.), *Orissa District Gazetteers,* Kalahandi, Cuttack, 1980, p. 1.
2. *Ibid.,* Bolangir, 1971, pp. 490-92.
3. *New Aspect of History of Orissa,* Vol. I, S.U., 1981, p. 24.
4. 'Kosalesu Kusam Viram Uttaresu Tatha Lovam', *Rāmāyaṇa,* VII, CL. 107, p. 1002.
5. Bajpai, K.D. and S.K. Pandey, *Malhar,* Sagar University, 1987, pp. 21-22.
6. Das, M.N. (ed.), *Sidelights on History and Culture of Orissa,* Cuttack, 1977, p. 40.
7. Senapati, N. (ed.), *op. cit.,* p. 50.
8. *Ibid.,* p. 538.
9. *Ibid.,* p. 2.
10. *Ibid.*
11. *Ibid.,* p. 1.
12. *Ibid.,* p. 2.
13. Mohapatra, R.P., *Archaeology in Orissa (Sites and Monuments),* Vol. 11, Delhi, p. 232.
14. *Ibid.*
15. Bhatt, S.C. (ed.), *Encyclopaedia, District Gazetteers of India,* Vol. 9, New Delhi, 1997, p. 709.
16. Mohapatra, R.P., *op. cit.,* Vol. IV, Delhi, 1986, p. 233.
17. *OHRJ,* Vol. XIV, Nos. 3-4, p. 26.
18. Behera, S.C. (ed.), *Interim Excavation Reports,* Sambalpur, pp. 1-2; *JKHRS,* Vol. IV, p. 244.
19. *JKHRS,* Vol. 1, pp. 107-110; *Ibid.,* Vol. IV, p. 249; *EI,* Vol. XXX, pp. 274-278; S.C. Behera (ed.), *op. cit.,* pp. 4-5. J.P. Singh Deo, *Cultural Profile of South Kosala,* Delhi, 1987, p. 329.

20. *JKHRS*, Vols. III and IV, Nos. 1, 2, 3, p. 249; S.C. Behera (ed.), *op. cit.*, p. 8; *New Dimension of Tourism in Orissa*, Bhubaneswar.
21. Fabri, C., *History of the Art of Orissa*, 1976, Calcutta, 1974, p. 40; N. Senapati (ed.), *op. cit.*, p. 37.
22. *Ibid.*
23. Senapati, N. (ed.), *op. cit.*, p. 119.
24. *Ibid.*, *JKHRS*, Vol. IV, p. 250; Rajasri Devi (ed.), *Kharial Raj Itihasa* (Oriya), Khariar, p. 81.
25. Mohapatra, R.N., *op. cit.*, p. 335.
26. Senapati, N. (ed.), *op. cit.*, p. 37.
27. *JKHRS*, Vol. IV, p. 250; N. Senapati (ed.), *op. cit.*, p. 446; R.P. Mahapatra, *op. cit.*, p. 236.
28. Senapati, N. (ed.), *op. cit.*, pp. 450-451.
29. *Ibid.*

25

Suvarnapurpattana

A Venue of Medieval Riverine Trade

Kedarnath Mishra

Suvarnapur is well known as one of the distinguished capital headquarters of South Kosala under the Somavamsis during the Medieval period. Located on the confluence of the Mahanadi and Tel, it fulfilled all the characteristics of a strategic place. The Somavamsis, after leaving Sirpur,[1] treated Sonepur as a shock absorber against the impending invasions of the Kalachuris and Teluguchodas. In course of time they enriched this land of legends by extending royal patronage to its growing riverine trade and earned for the tract the eulogized designation 'Suvarnapurpattana'.[2]

Prior to the Somavamsi occupation of Khinjali *Mandala,*[3] the overall prosperity of Suvarnapur appears to have been fostered by a powerful merchant association known by the name 'Kamalavana Vanika Samgha'.[4] It is unfortunate for the posterity to bring them to the limelight of Orissan history due to paucity of source materials. The only alternative, therefore, is to develop hypotheses over and above the available sources and cross-flourishing between Suvarnapurpattana and the neighbouring kingdoms.

At the outset, reference may be made to the *Sonepur Plates*[5] of Janamejaya issued from Arama-Kataka[6] during his 17th regnal year. Interestingly enough, this epigraphic record exclusively highlights the reputation of the merchant association 'Kamalavana Vanika Samgha' as the receiver of royal donation in the form of a village Gottaikela located in the Luputtarakhanda in Kosala from Janamejaya Mahābhavagupta. This proceeds to record that the merchant association bestowed the same village, after having registered it as a deed, to two temples – one dedicated to Lord Kesava and the other to Lord Aditya. In some form or the other, this epigraphic evidence establishes the reputation of the merchant association as an outstanding agency for sponsoring even non-commercial projects of public importance. It is indeed a matter of utter surprise that the contributes of such a commercial organization were not communicated either to history or literature by the successors of Janamejaya. One cannot deny that medieval despotism might have prevented the princes to let the leading traders supersede the so-called unsurpassable royal authority in the socio-economic fields and if it is a fact then Janamejaya appears to be an exception in at least giving us the clue about 'Kamalvana Vanika Samgha' and allied subjects.

Moreover, *Sonepur Plate* does not specify the area of operation opted by the concerned association and simply identifies the merchants of this association as 'Immigrants from Khadirapadar and residents of Suvarnapur'.[7] This induces historians to represent them as mere local merchants roaming in the streets of Sonepur. But latest researches in the field of medieval trade and commerce of Orissa supplement logistic support to the much wider range of riverine trade of Suvarnapur piloted by the 'Kamalavana Vanika Samgha'.

During 5th century the terms *Mahavana* and *Mahakantara* denoted the undivided Kalahandi district as revealed by the *Allahabad Pillar Inscription* of Samudragupta. Later on, a new nomenclature entitled this tract as *Kamalavana* which remained in vogue throughout the medieval period as is amply testified by the *Narla Shiva temple Inscription*.[8] This inscription speaks about Kamala *Mandala* ruled by Madana Mahadev in *Rama*[9] *Vana*[10] *Rudra*[11] *Samvatsara*. The chronogram mentioned above corresponds to 1153 *Saka* era or AD 1231. N.K. Sahu believes that the name Kalahandi might have been derived from the term *Kamala Mandala*.[12] On the basis of these epigraphic evidences, it appears reasonable to identify the merchants of 'Kamalavana Vanika Samgha' as immigrants from Kalahandi who subsequently preferred to settle down at Sonepur as it was a unique venue of riverine trade. Thus, what the author of *Sonepur Charter* speaks about these merchants as 'Immigrants from Khadirapadar' may be safely identified as immigrants from Rajpadar or Belkhandi situated on the confluence of Tel and Utei. J.D. Beglar who visited Belkhandi in 1874-75 addressed the place as an abode 'of ruins of great interest and undoubted high antiquity'.[13]

The formation of a merchant association, comprising the traders of undivided Kalahandi and Bolangir districts with Sonepur as their commercial headquarters, was probably a topographical necessity as far as riverine trade was concerned. In the *Maranjamura Charter*[14] of the Somavamsi king Mahāśivagupta Yayāti II dated 11th century AD the 'Pattana'

Suvarnapur figures. The word 'Pattana' added to Suvarnapur obviously implies that the present town of Sonepur was nothing short of a port-town during the Medieval period.[15] As a matter of fact, riverine trading centres supplemented maritime trade and no wonder, acquired parallel importance with that of a sea port. The river system of the upper Mahanadi Valley places Sonepur at the centre. The major rivers of the valley such as Tel, Sukhtel and Ang join the mainstream, the Mahanadi, in and near Sonepur. While the Mahanadi emerging from the Amarkantaka constituted the life-line of South Kosala, its tail-end did the same job for Utkala and Kaliṅga throughout the Medieval period. The tail as such merging in the Bay of Bengal appears to have added additional splendour to Che-li-ta-lo,[16] the famous seaport of international fame. Moreover, the Kalingan traders who were specialists in maritime contact with South-East Asia via Bay of Bengal appears to have been professionally backed by the riverine traders of South Kosala. But historians, while assessing the prospect of maritime commerce of ancient and medieval Orissa, pin-point their attention to the Kalingan maritime traders of South Kosala sponsored by the 'Kamalvana Vanika Samgha', which possibly extended consistent logistic support to the Kalingan traders in connection with the export of pearls, precious stones and diamond. Ptolemy refers categorically to the 'territory of Sabarai' which is reasonably identified with the region of Sambalpur as an important place containing diamonds.[17] Of late, the discovery of *Gopalpur Grants*[18] dating back to the Somavanmsi king Mahābhavagupta Janamejaya reveal that 'Suvarnapur shines with shops full of conch-shells, sea-shells, pearls, gems, corals and gold'.[19] It is worth noting that this grant uplifts the status of Suvarnapur as *Mahakantakavara*. In contrast, we find no authentic reference to Kalingan territory as a source of gems and diamonds. Then wherefrom did the Kalingan traders get the same and export them to distant South-East Asia? B.C. Majumdar, on this score, rightly remarks that diamond as an article had no source in Kaliṅga but it was another valuable commodity of sale in Kaliṅga.[20] Thus, a correlation between South Kosala as a territory rich in diamond deposit and Kaliṅga as a diamond exporting zone makes it clear that the former supplied the article through the Mahanadi and the latter exported the same to South-East Asia. Moreover, the description of Che-li-ta-lo given by Hiuen Tsang appears incomprehensive as it misses the one and the only mainstream *chitrotpala* while shaping the topography of the great sea port. It is on account of this lacuna that Mr. Waddel tends to transliterate Che-li-ta-lo as Chitratole identified with the Mahanadi River.[21] Nevertheless, the Chinese pilgrim locates Che-li-ta-lo near the sea-shore in the south-east of the Odra country and refers to it as 'a resting place for sea-going traders and strangers from distant lands'.[22] Alexander Cunningham, on the other hand, identifies it with Charitrapura and locates the same somewhere near Puri.[23] But from the view-point of topographical accuracy, it must be located at the point where the river Mahanadi mingles with the Bay of Bengal as per the commercial coordination between Suvarnapurpattana and Che-li-ta-lo. It is a matter of regret that neither the *Periplus* nor the *Geographike huphegesis* of Ptolemy[24] highlight the transparent river system of the upper Mahanadi Valley for which the riverine trade of the tract has been cast into oblivion.

During the Medieval period, diamond was found in abundance from the river-bed of the Mahanadi covering a wider area from Sambalpur to Boudh. Of all these places Suvarnapur commanded a unique place in procuring this article from the river-bed due to the role of a specialized professional called 'Jhara' who still constitute a major community in Sonepur.[25] They appear to have been employed by the Kamalavana Vanika Samgha to extract raw diamond from the river-bed and process them to finished product. Apparently, therefore, they did possess as they do now, sufficient skill and knowledge about navigation. As the Mahanadi was not suitable for navigation during the summer, the Jharas desperately remained engaged during this period in looking for diamonds from the river-bed and sailed for Che-li-ta-lo only during the winter for selling them there.[26]

The river Tel, rising from Navarangpur district and joining the Mahanadi at Sonepur, played a major role to accelerate the riverine trade of Suvarnapur. In fact, it rendered the same service to Suvarnapurpattana as the Mahanadi did for Che-li-ta-lo. The Tel, otherwise known as Telvaha[27] in Buddhist literature and Tailavahi in the epigraphic records of the Somavamsis, tells us the tales of riverine trade during the early times. The *Sera Vanija Jataka* speaks about the merchants sailing in the Telavaha with their merchandise.[28] Further, Panini in his *Astadhyayi* refers to Taitilaka *Janapada*, a territory to the west of Kaliṅga, as famous for brisk trade in rhinoceros hide.[29] Doubtlessly, the *Janapada* mentioned above cannot be other than the territory centring round Titilagarh. Supplementing these evidences we may cite the archaeological finding from the excavation of Asurgarh in the district of Kalahandi in 1973 to understand the economic stability of the Tel Valley. The first layer of the excavated site belonging to 5th century AD brought as many as 539 punch-marked silver coins to limelight.[30] Such coins were in circulation in India in the 4th-5th century AD as known from the works of Buddhaghosa.[31] The excavation also disclosed terracotta figures of animals, terracotta ornaments and pieces of bluish glass bangles.[32] It goes without saying that such a prosperous civilization could not have been possible without the leading role of trading community. The Tel is by far the longest and most important river in the district of Kalahandi. Fed by perennial hill streams like Sagada, Ret, Raul and Utei, the Tel carried a large flow of water in the winter. It seems that the merchants of Kamalavana found it feasible to carry articles, most of which were precious stones and rhinoceros hide, through this river up to Suvarnapurpattana. After availing transit, they seem to have made joint ventures with the merchants of Sonepur down the course of Mahanadi up to Che-li-ta-lo.

It is desirable from the above analysis to deduce that the breeding grounds of 'Kamalavana Vanika Samgha' were the Tel Valley, Maraguda Valley of Kalahandi and the river-bed of the Mahanadi bordering Sonepur. All these areas were extremely rich with precious stones of unique standard which provided stimulus for centuries to the riverine trade from Suvarnapur-*pattana* to Che-li-ta-lo.

In course of the prolonged commercial intercourse the riverine traders of Suvernapurpattana appears to have prepared the ground for the commercial unification of South with Kaliṅga Kosala and Utkala in the same way as the Zollverein[33] did for the German states. No wonder, it became sheer logic of history for the Somavamsis to accomplish their political unification without, however, acknowledging the contribution of the real architects who remotely remained behind the screen. The painful silence of history on such crucial issue is, in fact, disappointing and it can be mitigated only by further research.

It is equally difficult to comment on the decline of the glorious riverine trade between the upper and lower valleys of the Mahanadi due to absence of reliable materials. What appears probable on this score is that the 'Kamalavana Vanika Samgha' might have lost royal patronage with the fall of the Somavamsis towards the first decade of the 12th century AD and accordingly they could have opted for a limited area of operation instead of sailing for Che-li-ta-lo from the security view-point. One cannot miss the point noted by Chales Fabri that these merchants played a vital role in patronizing the Buddhist monasteries located at Ganiapali on the bank of Ang, Vaidyanath on the bank of Tel and Sonepur and Boudh on the bank of Mahanadi.[34]

NOTES AND REFERENCES

1. Sirpur located on the bank of the Mahanadi in Chhattisgarh State was the oldest capital of the Somavamsis.
2. *Journal of Bihar and Orissa Research Society*, 11, p. 52.
3. Khinjali *Mandala* denoted Sonepur-Baud-Phulbani region during the Bhauma-Kara rule.

4. Dehejia, Vidya, *Early Stone Temples of Orissa*, p. 17.
5. *Ibid.*
6. Arama Kataka is identified with Rampur in the District of Suvernapur.
7. Dehejia, *op. cit.*, p. 17.
8. Sahu, N.K., *Utkal University History of Orissa*, Vol. I, p. 129.
9. In chronogram, the term *Rama* denotes 3.
10. *Vana* denotes 5.
11. *Rudra* denotes 11. The year 3511 is reversed to get the *Saka* era 1153, which is equal to AD 1231.
12. Sahu, *op. cit.*, p. 129.
13. *Kalahandi District Gazetteer*, p. 37.
14. *JBORS*, 11, p. 52.
15. Sah, A.P., *Life in Medieval Orissa*, p. 110.
16. Das, D., *The Early History of Kaliṅga*, p. 251.
17. *Ibid.*, p. 253.
18. *Orissa Historical Research Journal*, Vol. XXXIX, pp. 92 ff.
19. *Ibid.*
20. Majumdar, B.C., *Orissa in the Making*, p. 78.
21. Das, *op. cit.*, p. 251.
22. *Ibid.*
23. Sah, *op. cit.*, p. 109.
24. Das, *op. cit.*, pp. 251 ff.
25. Field study undertaken in Sonepur during the month of August 1996. The Jharas worship Goddess Manikeshwari as their presiding deity for procuring plenty of *manikyas* (gold) from the river-bed.
26. *Ibid.*
27. *Kalahandi District Gazetteer*, p. 42.
28. *Ibid.*
29. *Ibid.*, p. 36.
30. *Ibid.*
31. *Ibid.*
32. All the findings are preserved in the N.K. Sahu Museum of Sambalpur University.
33. *Zollverein* is a German term which implies economic union of the German States before the political unification of Germany.
34. Fabri, Charles Louis, *History of the Art of Orissa*, p. 78.